W9-BQY-167

Da Capo Press Music Reprint Series

GENERAL EDITOR

FREDERICK FREEDMAN

VASSAR COLLEGE

JOHANN SEBASTIAN BACH

JOHANN SEBASTIAN BACH
HIS LIFE, ART, AND WORK

BY

JOHANN NIKOLAUS FORKEL

NOTES AND APPENDICES BY

CHARLES SANFORD TERRY

𝄢 DA CAPO PRESS • NEW YORK • 1970

A Da Capo Press Reprint Edition

This Da Capo Press edition of
Johann Sebastian Bach
is an unabridged republication of the
first edition published in London in 1920

Library of Congress Catalog Card Number 75-125044

SBN 306-70010-7

Published by Da Capo Press
A Division of Plenum Publishing Corporation
227 West 17th Street, New York, N. Y. 10011

All Rights Reserved

Manufactured in the United States of America

For Distribution and Sale only in the United States of America

JOHANN SEBASTIAN BACH

45066

JOHANN SEBASTIAN BACH.
circ. 1720.
(*From the picture by Johann Jakob Ihle, in the Bach Museum, Eisenach.*)

JOHANN SEBASTIAN BACH

HIS LIFE, ART, AND WORK

TRANSLATED FROM THE GERMAN OF

JOHANN NIKOLAUS FORKEL

WITH NOTES AND APPENDICES BY

CHARLES SANFORD TERRY
LITT. D. CANTAB.

LONDON
CONSTABLE AND COMPANY LTD.
1920

CONTENTS

[1] It should be stated that the original has no chapter headings.

ILLUSTRATIONS

INTRODUCTION

JOHANN NIKOLAUS FORKEL, author of the monograph of which the following pages afford a translation, was born at Meeder, a small village in Saxe-
Coburg, on February 22, 1749, seventeen months
before the death of Johann Sebastian Bach, whose
first biographer he became. Presumably he would
have followed the craft of his father, the village
shoemaker, had not an insatiable love of music
seized him in early years. He obtained books,
and studied them with the village schoolmaster.
In particular he profited by the ' Vollkommener
Kapellmeister' of Johann Mattheson, of Hamburg, the sometime friend of Handel. Like Handel,
he found a derelict Clavier in the attic of his home
and acquired proficiency upon it.

Forkel's professional career, like Bach's half a
century earlier, began at Lüneburg, where, at the
age of thirteen (1762), he was admitted to the choir
of the parish church. Thence, at the age of
seventeen (1766), he proceeded to Schwerin as
' Chorpräfect,' and enjoyed the favour of the
Grand Duke. Three years later he betook himself (1769), at the age of twenty, to the University

of Göttingen, which he entered as a law student, though a slender purse compelled him to give music lessons for a livelihood. He used his opportunity to acquire a knowledge of modern languages, which stood him in good stead later, when his researches required him to explore foreign literatures. Concurrently he pursued his musical activities, and in 1774 published at Göttingen his first work, 'Ueber die Theorie der Musik,' advocating the foundation of a music lectureship in the University. Four years later (1778) he was appointed its Director of Music, and from 1779 to 1815 conducted the weekly concerts of the Sing-Akademie. In 1780 he received from the University the doctorate of philosophy. The rest of his life was spent at Göttingen, where he died on March 17, 1818, having just completed his sixty-ninth year.

That Forkel is remembered at all is due solely to his monograph on Bach. Written at a time when Bach's greatness was realised in hardly any quarter, the book claimed for him pre-eminence which a tardily enlightened world since has conceded him. By his generation Forkel was esteemed chiefly for his literary activity, critical ability, and merit as a composer. His principal work, 'Allgemeine Geschichte der Musik,' was published in two volumes at Leipzig in 1788 and 1801. Carl Friedrich Zelter, Goethe's friend and correspondent, dismissed the book contemptuously as that of

an author who had ' set out to write a history of
music, but came to an end just where the history
of music begins.' Forkel's work, in fact, breaks
off at the sixteenth century. But the curtailed
' History ' cleared the way for the monograph on
Bach, a more valuable contribution to the literature of music. Forkel already had published, in
three volumes, at Gotha in 1778, his ' Musikalisch-
kritische Bibliothek,' and in 1792 completed his
critical studies by publishing at Leipzig his ' Allgemeine Literatur der Musik.'

Forkel was also a student of the music of the
polyphonic school. He prepared for the press the
scores of a number of sixteenth century Masses,
Motets, etc., and fortunately received proofs of
them from the engraver. For, in 1806, after the
Battle of Jena, the French impounded the plates
and melted them down. Forkel's proofs are still
preserved in the Berlin Royal Library. He was
diligent in quest of Bach's scattered MSS., and his
friendship with Bach's elder sons, Carl Philipp
Emmanuel and Wilhelm Friedemann, enabled him
to secure precious relics which otherwise might
have shared the fate of too many of Bach's manu-
scripts. He took an active interest in the proposal
of Messrs. Hoffmeister and Kühnel, predecessors of
C. F. Peters at Leipzig, to print a ' kritisch-
korrecte ' edition of Bach's Organ and Clavier
works. Through his friend, Johann Gottfried
Schicht, afterwards Cantor at St. Thomas's,

Leipzig, he was also associated with Breitkopf and Haertel's publication of five of Bach's six extant Motets in 1802-3.

As a composer Forkel has long ceased to be remembered. His works include two Oratorios, ' Hiskias ' (1789) and ' Die Hirten bey der Krippe ' ; four Cantatas for chorus and orchestra ; Clavier Concertos, and many Sonatas and Variations for the Harpsichord.

In 1802, for reasons which he explains in his Preface, Forkel published from Hoffmeister and Kühnel's ' Bureau de Musique ' his ' Ueber Johann Sebastian Bachs Leben, Kunst und Kunstwerke. Für patriotische Verehrer echter musikalischer Kunst,' of which a new edition was issued by Peters in 1855. The original edition bears a dedication to Gottfried Baron van Swieten [1] (1734-1803), Prefect of the Royal Library, Vienna, and sometime Austrian Ambassador in Berlin, a friend of Haydn and Mozart, patron of Beethoven, a man whose age allowed him to have seen Bach, and whose career makes the association with Bach that Forkel's dedication gives him not undeserved. It was he, an ardent Bach enthusiast, who introduced the youthful Mozart to the music of the Leipzig Cantor. ' I go every Sunday at twelve o'clock to the Baron van Swieten,' Mozart writes in 1782, ' where nothing is played but Handel and

---

[1] ' Seiner Excellenz dem Freyheren van Swieten ehrerbietigst gewidmet von dem Verfasser.'

Bach, and I am now making a collection of the
Fugues of Bach.' The merit and limitations of
Forkel's book will be considered later. For the
moment the fact deserves emphasis that, inadequate as it is, it presented a fuller picture of Bach
than so far had been drawn, and was the first to
render the homage due to his genius.

In an illuminating chapter (xii.), ' Death and
Resurrection,' Schweitzer has told the story of
the neglect th' t obscured Bach's memory after
his death in 1750. Isolated voices, raised here
and there, acclaimed his genius. With Bach's
treatise on ' The Art of Fugue ' before him, Johann
Mattheson (1681-1664), the foremost critic of the
day, claimed that Germany was 'the true home
of Organ music and Fugue.' Friedrich Wilhelm
Marpurg (1718-95), the famous Berlin theorist,
expressed the same opinion in his preface to the
edition of that work published shortly after Bach's
death. But such appreciations were rare. Little
of Bach's music was in print and available for
performance or critical judgment. Even at St.
Thomas's, Leipzig, it suffered almost complete
neglect until a generation after Forkel's death.
The bulk of Bach's MSS. was divided among his
family, and Forkel himself, with unrivalled opportunity to acquaint himself with the dimensions of Bach's industry, knew little of his
music except the Organ and Clavier compositions.

In these circumstances it is not strange that
Bach's memory waited for more than half a
century for a biographer. Forkel, however, was
not the first to assemble the known facts of
Bach's career or to assert his place in the music of
Germany.

Putting aside Johann Gottfried Walther's brief
epitome in his ' Lexikon ' (1732), the first and most
important of the early notices of Bach was the
obituary article, or ' Nekrolog,' contributed by his
son, Carl Philipp Emmanuel, and Johann Friedrich
Agricola, one of Bach's most distinguished pupils,
to the fourth volume of Mizler's ' Musikalische
Bibliothek,' published at Leipzig in 1754. The
authors of this appreciation give it an intimacy
which renders it precious. But Mizler's periodical
was the organ of a small Society, of which Bach
had been a member, and outside its associates
can have done little to extend a knowledge of the
subject of the memoir.

Johann Friedrich Agricola contributed notes
on Bach to Jakob Adlung's ' Musica mechanica
Organoedi,' published in two volumes at Berlin in
1768. The article is valuable chiefly for Agricola's
exposition of Bach's opinions upon Organ and
Clavier building.

With the intention to represent him as ' the
coryphaeus of all organists,' Johann Adam Hiller,
who a few years later became Cantor at St.
Thomas's, Leipzig, published there in 1784 a

brief account of Bach in his 'Lebensbeschrei-
bungen berühmter Musikgelehrten und Tonkünstler neuerer Zeit.'

Four years after Hiller's notice, Ernst Ludwig
Gerber published at Leipzig, in two volumes,
1790-92, his 'Historisch-biographische Lexikon
der Tonkünstler.' As in Hiller's case, Gerber,
whose father had been Bach's pupil, was chiefly
interested in Bach as an organist.

Coincidently with Gerber, another of Bach's
pupils, Johann Martin Schubart, who succeeded
him at Weimar in 1717, sketched his characteristics
as a performer in the 'Aesthetik der Tonkunst,'
published at Berlin by his son in the 'Deutschen
Monatsschrift' in 1793.

In 1794 appeared at Leipzig the first volume of a
work which Spitta characterises as fantastic and
unreliable, so far as it deals with Bach, Friedrich
Carl Gottlieb Hirsching's 'Historisch-literarisches
Handbuch' of notable persons deceased in the
eighteenth century.

Last of Forkel's forerunners, A. E. L. Siebigke
published at Breslau in 1801 his 'Museum
deutscher Tonkünstler,' a work which adds
nothing to our knowledge of Bach's life, but
offers some remarks on his style.

Little, if any, information of value, therefore,
had been added to the 'Nekrolog' of 1754 when
Forkel, in 1802, produced his monograph on Bach
and his music. Nor, viewed as a biography, does

Forkel much enlarge our knowledge of the conditions of Bach's life. He had the advantage of
knowing Bach's elder sons, but appears to have
lacked curiosity regarding the circumstances of
Bach's career, and to have made no endeavour to
add to his imperfect information, even regarding
his hero's life at Leipzig, upon which it should have
been easy for him to obtain details of utmost
interest. His monograph, in fact, is not a ' Life '
in the biographic sense, but a critical appreciation
of Bach as player, teacher, and composer, based
upon the Organ and Clavier works, with which
alone Forkel was familiar.

It would be little profitable to weigh the value
of Forkel's criticism. We are tempted to the conclusion that Bach appealed to him chiefly as a
supreme master of technique, and our hearts would
open to him more widely did not his appreciation of Bach march with a narrow depreciation
of Haydn, Mozart, and Beethoven, the last of
whom, he declared *ex cathedra*, had not produced
' a single work which can be called a masterpiece.' Gluck he frankly detested.

But Forkel's monograph is notable on other
grounds. It was the first to claim for Bach a
place among the divinities. It used him to
stimulate a national sense in his own people.
Bach's is the first great voice from out of Germany
since Luther. Of Germany's own Risorgimento,
patently initiated by Goethe a generation after

Johann Sebastian's death, Bach himself is the harbinger. In his assertion of a distinctive German musical art he set an example followed in turn by Mozart, Weber, and Wagner. 'With Bach,' wrote Wagner, ' the German Spirit was born anew.' It is Forkel's perpetual distinction that he grasped a fact hidden from almost all but himself. In his Preface, and more emphatically in the closing paragraph of his last Chapter, he presents Bach as the herald of a German nation yet unformed.

It is a farther distinction of Forkel's monograph that it made converts. With its publication the clouds of neglect that too long had obscured Bach's grandeur began to melt away, until the dizzy altitude of his genius stood revealed. The publication of the five Motets (1803) was followed by that of the Magnificat in 1811, and of the Mass in A in 1818. A beginning was made with the Cantatas in 1821, when Breitkopf and Haertel published ' Ein' feste Burg' (No. 80), commended in an article written (1822) by Johann Friedrich Rochlitz (1769-1842), the champion of Beethoven, as now of Bach. Another enthusiastic pioneer was Carl Friedrich Zelter (1758-1832), conductor of the Berlin Sing-Akademie, who called Bach ' a sign of God, clear, yet inexplicable.' To him in large measure was due the memorable revival of the ' St. Matthew Passion ' at Berlin, which the youthful Mendelssohn, Zelter's pupil,

conducted in March 1829, exactly one hundred
years after the first production of the mighty work
at Leipzig.   In the following years it was given
at Dresden and many other German towns.
Leipzig heard it again after a barren interval in
1841, and did tardy homage to its incomparable
composer by erecting (1843) the statue that
stands in the shadow of St. Thomas's Church,
hard by the Cantor's home for a quarter of a
century.

Meanwhile, in 1830 and 1831 the ' St. Matthew
Passion ' and ' St. John Passion ' had been engraved, and by 1845 the B minor Mass was in
print.   The credit of having revived it belongs to
Johann Nepomuk Schelble (1789-1837), conductor
of the Frankfort Caecilienverein, though the Berlin
Sing-Akademie was the first to give a performance,
considerably curtailed, of the whole work in 1835.
A little later, in the middle of the forties, Peters
began to issue his ' kritisch-korrecte ' edition of
the Organ works, which at length made Bach
widely known among organists.   But the publication of the Cantatas proceeded slowly.   Only
fourteen of them were in print in 1850, when the
foundation of the Bachgesellschaft, on the centenary of Bach's death, focused a world-wide homage.
When it dissolved in 1900 its mission was accomplished, the entire works [1] of Bach were published,

---

[1] So far the New Bachgesellschaft has published only a single
Cantata overlooked by the old Society.   See *infra*, p. 280.

and the vast range of his genius was patent to the world.

It remains to discuss the first English version of Forkel's monograph, published in 1820, with the following title-page :

LIFE OF JOHN SEBASTIAN BACH; with a Critical View of his Compositions. By J. N. Forkel, Author of The Complete History of Music, etc., etc. Translated from the German. London : Printed for T. Boosey and Co., Holles-Street, Cavendish-Square. 1820.

The book was published in February 1820 ; it was announced, with a slightly differently worded title-page, in the ' New Monthly Magazine and Universal Register ' for March 1820 (p. 341), and the ' Scots Magazine ' for the same month (vol. lxxxv. p. 263). The 'New Monthly' states the price as 5s., the ' Quarterly Review ' (vol. xxiii. p. 281) as 6s. The book contains xi+116+3 pages of Music Figures, crown octavo, bound in dark unlettered cloth. It has neither Introduction, notes (other than Forkel's), nor indication of the translator's identity. Much of the translation is so bad as to suggest grave doubts of the translator's comprehension of the German original ; while his rendering of Forkel's critical chapters rouses a strong suspicion that he also lacked technical equipment adequate to his task. It is, in fact, difficult to understand how such an unsatisfactory piece of work found its way into print.

The character of the 1820 translation has a close bearing upon its authorship. In the article on Bach in the new ' Grove ' it is attributed to Samuel Wesley (1766-1837), an attractive suggestion, since Wesley was as enthusiastic a Bach pioneer in this country as Forkel himself was in Germany. But the statement is not correct. In Samuel Wesley's ' Letters to Mr. Jacobs relating to the Introduction into this Country of the Works of J. S. Bach ' (London, 1875) we find the clue. On October 17, 1808, Wesley writes : ' We are (in the first place) preparing for the Press an authentic and accurate Life of Sebastian, which Mr. Stephenson the Banker (a most zealous and scientific member of our Fraternity) has translated into English from the German of Forkel.'

Unfortunately, it is impossible to identify Stephenson precisely, or to detect his activities in the musical circle in which Wesley includes him. In 1820 there was in Lombard Street a firm of bankers under the style of ' Remington, Stephenson, Remington, and Toulmin,' the active partner being Mr. Rowland Stephenson, a man of about forty in that year. The firm was wound up in bankruptcy in 1829, Stephenson having absconded to America the previous year. He appears to have been the only banker of that name holding such a recognised position as Wesley attributes to him, though it remains no more than a conjecture that he was the author of the translation issued in

1820.[1] But whoever 'Stephenson the Banker' may have been, the poverty of his work fails to support Wesley's commendation of his 'scientific' equipment, and suggests that his purse rather than his talents were serviceable to Wesley's missionary campaign.

For the facts of Bach's life, and as a record of his artistic activities, Forkel admittedly is inadequate and often misleading. Stephenson necessarily was without information to enable him to correct or supplement his author. Recent research, and particularly the classic volumes of Spitta and Schweitzer, have placed the present generation in a more instructed and therefore responsible position. The following pages, accordingly, have been annotated copiously in order to bring Forkel into line with modern scholarship. His own infrequent notes are invariably indicated by a prefixed asterisk. It has been thought advisable to write an addendum to Chapter II. in order to supplement Forkel at the weakest point of his narrative.

Readers of Spitta's first volume probably will remember the effort to follow the ramifications of the Bach pedigree unaided by a genealogical Table. It is unfortunate that Spitta did not

[1] In 'The News' of January 4, 1829, he is described as the second son of the late John Stephenson of Great Ormonde Street, Queen Square, whom he had succeeded in the partnership of the firm. His wife was dead, and of his eight children the eldest was also in the Bank.

set out in that form the wealth of biographical material his pages contain. To supply the deficiency, and to illustrate Forkel's first Chapter, a complete Genealogical Table is provided in Appendix VI., based mainly upon the biographical details scattered over Spitta's pages.

In Chapter IX. Forkel gives a list of Bach's compositions known to him. It is, necessarily, incomplete. For that reason Appendices I. and II. provide a full catalogue of Bach's works arranged under the periods of his career. In the case of the Oratorios, Cantatas, Motets, and ' Passions,' it is not difficult to distribute them upon a chronological basis. The Clavier works also can be dated with some approximation to closeness. The effort is more speculative in the case of the Organ music.

In his Preface Forkel suggests the institution of a Society for the publication and study of Bach's works. The proposal was adopted after half a century's interval, and in Appendix III. will be found a complete and detailed catalogue of the publications of the Old and New Bachgesellschaft from 1850 to 1918 inclusive. The Society's issues for 1915-18 have not yet reached this country. The present writer had an opportunity to examine them in the Library of the Cologne Conservatorium of Music in the spring of this year.

In this Introduction will be found a list of works bearing on Bach, which preceded Forkel's monograph.   Appendix IV. provides a bibliography of Bach literature published subsequently to it.

Grateful acknowledgment is made to Mr. Ivor Atkins, of Worcester Cathedral, and to Mr. W. G. Whittaker, of Newcastle-upon-Tyne, who have read these pages in proof, and improved them by their criticism.   C. S. T.

October 1, 1919.

FORKEL'S PREFACE

MANY years ago I determined to give the public an account of the life of Johann Sebastian Bach, with some reflections upon his genius and his works. The brief article by Carl Philipp Emmanuel Bach [1] and Herr Agricola, [2] formerly composer to the Court of Prussia, contributed to the fourth volume of Mizler's ' Musical Library,' [3] can hardly be deemed adequate by Bach's admirers and, but for the desire to complete my ' General

[1] Carl Philipp Emmanuel Bach, third son of Johann Sebastian Bach, b. 1714; Kammermusikus to Frederick the Great of Prussia (1746), Kapellmeister at Hamburg (1768); d. 1788.

[2] Johann Friedrich Agricola, of Dobitsch, b. 1720; studied composition with Bach at Leipzig; Court Composer (1751) and, after Carl Heinrich Graun's death (1759), Kapellmeister to Frederick the Great of Prussia; d. 1774. See Spitta, ' Johann Sebastian Bach,' iii. 243 ff.

[3] Lorenz Christoph Mizler (1711-78), a pupil of Bach, founded at Leipzig in 1738 the ' Sozietät der musikalischen Wissenschaften,' of which Bach and Handel were members. Mizler's journal, the ' Neu-eröffneter Musikalischer Bibliothek,' was its organ. It appeared from 1736 to 1754. In Part I. of vol. iv. (1754) C. P. E. Bach and Agricola collaborated in the obituary notice, or ' Nekrolog,' which is almost the earliest literary authority for Bach's life. It covered less than twenty pages. (See Schweitzer, ' J. S. Bach ' (trans. Ernest Newman), i. 189 ff. and Spitta, i. Pref.) Agricola's association with Bach's son in the preparation of the obituary notice is explained by the fact that for the last ten years of Sebastian's life Agricola was in closer relations with him than Carl Philipp Emmanuel, who no longer was resident in Leipzig.

History of Music,'[1] I should have fulfilled my purpose long ago. As Bach, more than any other artist, represents an era in the history of music, it was my intention to devote to the concluding volume of that work the materials I had collected for a history of his career. But the announcement that Messrs. Hoffmeister and Kühnel, the Leipzig music-sellers and publishers, propose to issue a complete and critical edition of Bach's works has induced me to change my original plan.[2]

Messrs. Hoffmeister and Kühnel's project promises at once to advance the art of music and enhance the honour of the German name. For Bach's works are a priceless national patrimony ; no other nation possesses a treasure comparable to it. Their publication in an authoritative text will be a national service and raise an imperishable monument to the composer himself. All who hold Germany dear are bound in honour to promote the undertaking to the utmost of their power. I deem it a duty to remind the public of this obligation and to kindle interest in it in every true German heart. To that end these pages

[1] Forkel's ' Allgemeine Geschichte der Musik ' (2 vols. 1788-1801) had only come down to the sixteenth century when its author diverted his pen to a biography of Bach.

[2] The firm of Hoffmeister and Kühnel was founded at Leipzig in 1800 by Franz Anton Hoffmeister, who started, in 1801, a subscription for the publication of Bach's works, to which Forkel alludes. The scheme failed to mature, and its accomplishment was reserved to C. F. Peters, who purchased Hoffmeister's ' Bureau de Musique ' in 1814. See articles on Hoffmeister and Peters in Grove's ' Dictionary.'

appear earlier than my original plan proposed ;
for they will enable me to reach a larger number
of my fellow countrymen.   The section on Bach
in my ' History of Music ' probably would have
been read by a handful of experts or musical
artists.   Here I hope to speak to a larger audience.
For, let me repeat, not merely the interests of
music but our national honour are concerned to
rescue from oblivion the memory of one of
Germany's greatest sons.

One of the best and most effective means of
popularising musical masterpieces is to perform
them in public.   In that way works of merit
secure a widening audience.   People listen to
them with pleasure in the concert room, church,
or theatre, remember the agreeable impression
they created, and purchase them when published,
even though they cannot always play them.   But
Bach's works unfortunately are rarely heard
nowadays ;   for the number of persons capable
of playing them adequately is at best inconsiderable.   It would have been otherwise had
Bach given touring performances of his music,[1]
a labour for which he had neither time nor liking.
Many of his pupils did so, and though their skill
was inferior to their master's, the admiration

---

[1] Though Bach never ventured upon such tours as Mozart or
Berlioz, for instance, undertook, he loved travelling, and his artistic
journeys made him famous throughout Germany, at least as an
organist.   Forkel himself describes (*infra*, pp. 19, 23) his notable
visits to the Courts of Berlin and Dresden.

and astonishment they excited revealed the grandeur of his compositions. Here and there, too, were found persons who desired to hear on their own instrument pieces which the performer had played best or gave them most pleasure. They could do so more easily for having heard how the piece ought to sound.

But, to awaken a wide appreciation of musical masterpieces depends upon the existence of good teachers. The want of them is our chief difficulty. In order to safeguard their credit, the ignorant and incompetent of their number are disposed to decry good music, lest they should be asked to play it. Consequently, their pupils, condemned to spend time, labour, and money on second-rate material, will not after half a dozen years, perhaps, show themselves farther advanced in sound musical appreciation than they were at the outset. Whereas, under a good teacher, half the time, labour, and money produces progressive improvement. Time will show whether this obstacle can be surmounted by making Bach's works accessible in the music shops and by forming a Society among the admirers of his genius to make them known and promote their study.[1]

[1] In 1802, it must be remembered, not a note of Bach's concerted Church music was in print except the tunes he wrote for Schemelli's Hymn-book (1736) and the vocal parts of an early Cantata (No. 71). Of his instrumental works engraved by 1802 Forkel gives a list *infra*, p. 137. It was hardly until the foundation of the Bachgesellschaft in

At any rate, if music is really an art, and not a mere pastime, its masterpieces must be more widely known and performed than in fact they are.   And here Bach, prince of classic composers, can render yeoman service.[1]   For his music is so well calculated to educate the student to distinguish what is trivial from what is good, and to comport himself as an artist in whatever branch of the art he makes his own.   Moreover, Bach, whose influence pervades every musical form, can be relied on more than any other composer to correct the superficiality which is the bane of modern taste.   Neglect of the classics is as prejudicial to the art of music as it would be fatal to the interests of general culture to banish Greek and Latin writers from our schools.   Modern taste exhibits no shame in its preference for agreeable trifles, in its neglect of everything that makes a demand, however slight, upon its attention.   To-day we are menaced by a proposal

1850, to celebrate the centenary of Bach's death, that the systematic publication of his concerted Church music began.   Before that date, however, Peters of Leipzig had taken in hand the abandoned scheme of Hoffmeister and Kühnel, to which Forkel alludes, and in which he participated.

[1] It is notable that Forkel makes no mention of Haydn, Mozart, or Handel, whose English domicile had divorced him from Germany's service.   Forkel's pessimism is the more curious, seeing that Beethoven was already thirty years old, and that Mozart in 1786, after giving him a subject to extemporise upon, had remarked, ' Listen to that young man ; he will some day make a noise in the world ' (Holmes, ' Life of Mozart,' Dent's ed., p. 223).   Forkel, in fact, appreciated neither Mozart nor Beethoven and thoroughly detested Gluck.

to banish the classics from our schoolrooms. Equally short-sighted vision threatens to extinguish our musical classics as well. And is it surprising ? Modern art displays such poverty and frivolity that it well may shrink from putting itself in context with great literature, particularly with Bach's mighty and creative genius, and seek rather to proscribe it.

I fain would do justice to the sublime genius of this prince of musicians, German and foreign ! Short of being such a man as he was, dwarfing all other musicians from the height of his superiority, I can conceive no greater distinction than the power to comprehend and interpret him to others.[1] The ability to do so must at least connote a temperament not wholly alien from his own. It may even hint the flattering prospect that, if circumstances had opened up the same career, similar results might have been forthcoming. I am not presumptuous to suggest such a result in my own case. On the contrary I am convinced that there are no words adequate to express the thoughts Bach's transcendent genius stirs one to utter. The more intimately we are acquainted with it the greater must be our admiration. Our utmost eulogy, our deepest expressions of homage,

---

[1] As has been pointed out in the Introduction, Forkel stood almost alone in 1802 in his opinion of Bach's pre-eminence. Even Beethoven placed Bach after Handel and Mozart, but knew little of his music on which to found a decision.

must seem little more than well-meant prattle. No one who is familiar with the work of other centuries will contradict or hold my statement exaggerated, that Bach cannot be named except in tones of rapture, and even of devout awe, by those who have learnt to know him. We may discover and lay bare the secrets of his technique. But his power to inspire into it the breath of genius, the perfection of life and charm that moves us so powerfully, even in his slightest works, must always remain extraordinary and insoluble.

I do not choose to compare Bach with other artists. Whoever is interested to measure him with Handel will find a just and balanced estimate of their relative merits, written by one fully informed for the task, in the first number of the eighty-first volume of the ' Universal German Library,' pages 295-303.[1]

So far as it is not derived from the short article in Mizler's ' Library ' already mentioned,[2] I am indebted for my information to the two eldest

---

[1] The anonymous article in the ' Allgemeine deutsche Bibliothek,' to which Forkel alludes, deals with Bach's Clavier and Organ works and upon them asserts Bach's superiority over Handel. The judgment was unusual. Bach's fame was gravely prejudiced by German Handel-worship, which the first performance of the ' Messiah ' at Leipzig in 1786 stimulated. Johann Adam Hiller, Bach's third successor in the Cantorate of St. Thomas', was largely responsible. He neglected, and even belittled, the treasures of Bach's art which the library of St. Thomas' contained. See Schweitzer, i. 231.

[2] The ' Nekrolog.' See *supra*, p. xxiv.

sons of Bach himself.[1] Not only was I personally acquainted with them, but I corresponded
regularly for many years with both,[2] particularly
Carl Philipp Emmanuel. The world knows them
as great artists. But probably it is not aware
that to the last moment of their lives they spoke
of their father's genius with enthusiastic admiration.[3] From my early youth I have been inspired by an appreciation no less deep than theirs.
It was a frequent theme of conversation and
correspondence between us.

Thus, having been in a position to inform myself
on all matters relating to Bach's life, genius, and
work, I may fairly hold myself competent to communicate to the public what I have learnt and to
offer useful reflections upon it. I take advantage

[1] Carl Philipp Emmanuel and Wilhelm Friedemann. The latter
was born in 1710, and after holding Organistships at Halle and Dresden,
died at Berlin in 1784, leaving his widow and daughter in great poverty.
The former received a grant from the receipts of the 'Messiah'
performance alluded to in note 1, *supra*. A man of brilliant musical
attainments, Wilhelm Friedemann's character was dissolute and unsteady. See Schweitzer, i. 146 ff.

[2] Two letters written by C. P. E. Bach to Forkel in 1775, conveying a good deal of information reproduced by Forkel in this monograph, are printed in facsimile by Dr. Max Schneider in his 'Bach-
Urkunden' (N.B.G., xvii. (3)).

[3] Forkel's statement is entitled to respect. On the other hand
there is nothing in the recorded careers of either of Bach's sons that
bears him out on this point. Schweitzer (i. 229) endorses Eitner's
judgment : 'Bach's sons were the children of their epoch, and never
understood their father ; it was only from piety that they looked at
him with childlike admiration.' Dr. Charles Burney spent several days
with Carl Philipp Emmanuel at Hamburg in 1772, but during the
whole time the son never played to him a note of his father's music.

of my opportunity the more readily because it permits me to draw attention to an enterprise [1] that promises to provide a worthy monument to German art, a gallery of most instructive models to the sincere artist, and to afford music lovers an inexhaustible source of sublimest pleasure.

[1] *i.e.* Hoffmeister and Kühnel's project.

CHAPTER I

THE FAMILY OF BACH

IF there is such a thing as inherited aptitude for art it certainly showed itself in the family of Bach. For six successive generations scarcely two or three of its members are found whom nature had not endowed with remarkable musical talent, and who did not make music their profession.[1]

Veit Bach,[2] ancestor of this famous family,

---

[1] The accuracy of this statement is apparent from the Genealogy appended to this volume. Bach's sons represented the sixth generation from Veit Bach, the sixteenth century ancestor of the family. Veit himself was not a professional musician ; one of his sons was a Spielmann ; thereafter for the next 150 years all but seven of his descendants, whose professions are known, were Organists or Cantors or Town Musicians. Many of them, moreover, were men of the highest attainments in their profession.

[2] He took his name from St. Vitus (Guy), patron saint of the church of Wechmar, a fact which sufficiently disproves Forkel's statement that his original domicile was in Hungary. The Bachs were settled in Wechmar as early as *circ.* 1520. Veit migrated thence to Hungary, though there is no adequate foundation for the statement that he settled at Pressburg. He returned to Wechmar during the beginning of the Counter-Reformation under the Emperor Rudolph II. (1576-1612), and died at Wechmar, March 8, 1619. See Spitta, i. 4.

Apart from church and town registers, laboriously consulted by Spitta in tracing the Bach genealogy, we owe our knowledge of it to an MS. drawn up by Bach in 1735 which is now in the Berlin Royal Library after being successively in the possession of Carl Philipp Emmanuel, Forkel, and G. Pölchau, the Hamburg teacher of music.

gained a livelihood as a baker at Pressburg in
Hungary.   When the religious troubles of the
sixteenth century broke out he was driven to seek
another place of abode, and having got together
as much of his small property as he could, retired
with it to Thuringia, hoping to find peace and
security there.   He settled at Wechmar, a village
near Gotha,[1] where he continued to ply his trade
as a baker and miller.[2]   In his leisure hours he
was wont to amuse himself with the lute,[3] playing
it amid the noise and clatter of the mill.   His
taste for music descended to his two sons [4] and
their children, and in time the Bachs grew to be
a very numerous family of professional musicians,

The original entries in it are stated by Carl P. Emmanuel to be by
his father.   Forkel also owned a Bach genealogical tree, given him by
Carl Philipp Emmanuel : it has disappeared.   Traces of it exist in
a work published at Pressburg by Johann Matthias Korabinsky in
1784, its insertion being due to the assumption that the Bachs were
a Hungarian family.   Forkel shared that error.   See Spitta's Preface
on the whole question.   The MS. genealogy of 1735 is published by
the New Bachgesellschaft (xvii. 3) in facsimile.

[1] Veit, in fact, returned to his native village.   His name, as has
been pointed out, implies a connection with Wechmar that must have
dated from infancy.   Moreover, there was living there in 1561 one
Hans Bach, an official of the municipality, who may be regarded
confidently as Veit's father.

[2] It has been suggested that the name Bach is the sole authority
for the statement that Veit was a baker.   But Spitta points out that
the vowel in the name is pronounced long and was frequently written
BAACH in the seventeenth century, a fact which makes it difficult to
associate the word with ' Bäcker ' (Baker).

[3] In the Genealogy Johann Sebastian calls the instrument a Cyth-
ringen.

[4] Hans Bach (d. Dec. 26, 1626) and (?) Lips Bach (d. Oct. 10, 1620).
See *infra*, Genealogical Tables i. and ii. and note to the latter.

Cantors, Organists, and Town Musicians,[1] throughout Thuringia.

Not all the Bachs, however, were great musicians.
But every generation boasted some of them who
were more than usually distinguished. In the
first quarter of the seventeenth century three
of Veit Bach's grandchildren showed such exceptional talent that the Count of Schwarzburg-
Arnstadt thought it worth while to send them at
his expense to Italy, then the chief school of
music, to perfect themselves in the art.[2] We do
not know whether they rewarded the expectations
of their patron, for none of their works has survived. The fourth generation[3] of the family
produced musicians of exceptional distinction,

[1] The 'Stadt Pfeiferei,' or official town musical establishment,
descended from the musicians' guilds of the Middle Ages and was presided over by the Stadt Musiker, who enjoyed certain ancient privi-
leges and the monopoly of providing the music at open-air festivities.
Johann Jakob Brahms, the father of Johannes, was a member of such
a corporation at Hamburg, after having served his apprenticeship for
five years elsewhere. See Florence May, 'Johannes Brahms,' vol. i.
pp. 48 ff.

[2] See Genealogical Table II. The three young Bachs were the sons
of Lips Bach and, presumably, nephews of Hans the 'Spielmann.'
The youngest of them was named Jonas; the name of another was
certainly Wendel. It is remarkable, in a period in which Italy was
regarded as the Mecca of musicians, that exceedingly few of the Bach
family found their way thither. Besides the three sons of Lips Bach,
only Johann Nikolaus, 1669-1753 (see Table VI.), Johann Sebastian
Bach's son Johann Christian, 1735-82 (see Table VIII.), and Carl P. E.
Bach's son Sebastian (see Table VII.) seem to have visited Italy.

[3] i.e. from Veit Bach. Of the three names Forkel mentions the
first two were a generation before Johann Sebastian; the third, Johann
Bernhard, was of the same generation as Johann Sebastian; none of
the three belonged to Johann Sebastian's branch.

and several of their compositions, thanks to
Johann Sebastian Bach's regard for them, have
come down to us. The most notable of these
Bachs are :

1. Johann Christoph Bach, Court and Town
Organist at Eisenach.[1]   He was particularly happy
in his beautiful melodies and in setting words to
music.   In the ' Archives of the Bachs,' [2] which
was in Carl Philipp Emmanuel's possession at
Hamburg, there is a Motet by Johann Christoph
in which he boldly uses the augmented sixth, a
proceeding considered extremely daring in his day.[3]
He was also an uncommon master of harmony,
as may be inferred from a Cantata composed by
him for Michaelmas, to the words ' Es erhub sich
ein Streit,' etc., which has twenty-two obbligato
parts in correct harmony.[4]   Yet another proof
of his rare skill is in the alleged fact that he never

[1] Eldest son of Heinrich Bach (see Table VI.).   Whether he was
Court as well as Town Organist at Eisenach cannot be stated positively.

[2] The ' Alt-Bachische Archive' is a collection of the compositions of
various members of the family, before and after Johann Sebastian,
formed largely by the latter.   From C. P. E. Bach it passed to G.
Pölchau and from him to the Berlin Royal Library.

[3] Johann Christoph composed several Motets (see them discussed
in Spitta, i. 75 ff.).   The daring work to which Forkel alludes was
written about 1680 and is lost.   Though the augmented sixth was
then and remained unusual, Johann Christoph's is not the earliest use
of it.   Spitta finds it in Giacomo Carissimi (1604-74).

[4] The Cantata (' And there was war in heaven ') is analysed by
Spitta (i. 44).   The score is unusually full : two five-part choirs ;
Vn. 1 and 2, 4 Violas, Contrabasso, Fagotto, 4 Trombe, Timpani,
Organ.   In 1726 Johann Sebastian Bach wrote a Cantata for Michael-
mas on the same text (Rev. xii. 7).

played the Organ or Clavier in less than five parts.[1] Carl Philipp Emmanuel had a particularly warm regard for him.[2] I remember the old man playing some of his compositions to me on the Clavier at Hamburg, and how quizzically he looked at me when one of these daring passages occurred.[3]

2. Johann Michael Bach, Organist and Town Clerk at Gehren.[4] He was the younger brother of Johann Christoph, and like him, a particularly good composer. The Archives already mentioned [5] contain several of his Motets, including one for eight voices in double chorus,[6] and many compositions for Church use.

3. Johann Bernhard Bach, Musician in the

---

[1] Spitta (i. 101 n.) characterises the statement as 'a mythical exaggeration.' In a chapter devoted to the instrumental works of Johann Christoph and his brother he instances a collection of forty-four Organ Chorals by the former, not one of which is in five parts.

[2] In the Bach genealogy already referred to C. P. E. Bach designates Johann Christoph a 'great and impressive composer.'

[3] A 'Lamento' published under Johann Christoph's name seems actually to have been composed by his father Heinrich (see Pirro, 'J.-S. Bach,' 9 n.). Johann Christoph, however, is the composer of the Motet 'Ich lasse dich nicht,' so often attributed to Johann Sebastian.

[4] See Table VI. He was the father of Johann Sebastian's first wife.

[5] See note, p. 4 *supra*.

[6] Spitta (i. 59 ff.) mentions twelve Motets by Michael Bach. Several of them are for eight voices. Forkel probably refers to the most remarkable of Michael's Motets, in which he detects the romantic spirit of Johann Sebastian. It is set to the words 'Unser Leben ist ein Schatten' ('Life on earth is but a shadow'). The first choir consists of 2 S., A., 2 T., B., and the second choir of A.T.B. only. Spitta analyses the work closely (i. 70-72). Novello publishes his five-part Motet 'Christ is risen' with an English text.

Prince's Kapelle and Organist at Eisenach.[1]   He
is said to have composed remarkably fine Suites,
or Overtures, in the French style.[2]

Besides these three men, the Bachs boasted
several able composers in the generations preceding Johann Sebastian,[3] men who undoubtedly
would have obtained higher positions, wider
reputation, and more brilliant fortune if they
could have torn themselves from their native
Thuringia to display their gifts elsewhere in
Germany or abroad.   But none of the Bachs
seems to have felt an inclination to migrate.
Modest in their needs, frugal by nature and training, they were content with little, engrossed in
and satisfied by their art, and wholly indifferent

---

[1] He succeeded his cousin Johann Christoph at Eisenach in 1703.
See Table III.

[2] Spitta (i. 24 ff.) mentions four Suites, or Overtures, Clavier pieces,
and Organ Chorals as being by him.   That Johann Sebastian Bach
highly esteemed the Suites is proved by the fact that he copied the
parts of three of them with his own hand at Leipzig.

[3] It is a curious fact that, prior to the career of Johann Sebastian
Bach, the composers of the Bach family occur invariably in other
branches than his.   With two exceptions, the gift of composition
appears to have been possessed, or exercised, solely by Heinrich Bach
(see Table VI.), his two sons Johann Christoph and Johann Michael,
already discussed, and his grandson, Johann Nikolaus (son of Johann
Christoph).   Heinrich Bach was a very productive composer in all
forms of musical art employed at that time in church (Sp. i. 36).
His grandson, Johann Nikolaus, composed a Mass and a comic operetta
(ib., 132 ff.).   The only other Bach composer known to Spitta is
Georg Christoph, founder of the Franconian Bachs (see Table IV.)
and Cantor at Themar and Schweinfurt (ib. 155).   The other Bach
composer outside Heinrich Bach's branch is Johann Bernhard, already
mentioned by Forkel.

to the decorations which great men of that time
were wont to bestow on artists as special marks of
honour. The fact that others who appreciated
them were thus distinguished did not rouse the
slightest envy in the Bachs.

The Bachs not only displayed a happy content-
edness, indispensable for the cheery enjoyment of
life, but exhibited a clannish attachment to each
other. They could not all live in the same
locality. But it was their habit to meet once a
year at a time and place arranged beforehand.
These gatherings generally took place at Erfurt,
Eisenach, and sometimes at Arnstadt. Even
after the family had grown very large, and many
of its members had left Thuringia to settle in
Upper and Lower Saxony and Franconia, the
Bachs continued their annual meetings. On these
occasions music was their sole recreation. As
those present were either Cantors, Organists, or
Town Musicians, employed in the service of the
Church and accustomed to preface the day's work
with prayer, their first act was to sing a Hymn.
Having fulfilled their religious duty, they spent
the rest of the time in frivolous recreations. Best
of all they liked to extemporise a chorus out of
popular songs, comic or jocular, weaving them
into a harmonious whole while declaiming the
words of each. They called this hotch-potch a
'Quodlibet,' laughed uproariously at it, and
roused equally hearty and irrepressible laughter

in their audience.[1] It is suggested that German
Comic Opera has its origin in these trifles. But
the 'Quodlibet' was a familiar institution in
Germany at a much earlier period. I possess a
collection of them printed and published at
Vienna in 1542.[2]

But these light-hearted Thuringians, and even
those of their family who treated their art more
seriously and worthily, would not have escaped
oblivion had there not emerged in the fulness of
time one whose genius and renown reflected their
splendour and brilliancy on his forbears. This
man, the glory of his family, pride of his countrymen, most gifted favourite of the Muse of Music,
was Johann Sebastian Bach.

[1] In the Quodlibet different voices sang different well-known
melodies, sacred and profane, and sought to combine them to form
a harmonious whole. For an example see Variation 30 of the 'Aria
mit 30 Veränderungen' (Peters' ed., bk. 209 p. 83). In it Bach
combines two popular songs of his period.

[2] See article ' Quodlibet ' in Grove.

BACH'S HOME AT EISENACH.

CHAPTER II

THE CAREER OF BACH

JOHANN SEBASTIAN BACH was born on March 21, 1685,[1] at Eisenach, where his father, Johann Ambrosius Bach, was Court and Town Musician.[2] Johann Ambrosius had a twin brother, Johann Christoph, Musician to the Court and Town of Arnstadt,[3] who so exactly resembled him that even their wives could distinguish them only by their dress. The twins appear to have been quite remarkable. They were deeply attached, alike in disposition, in voice, and in the style of their music. If one was ill, so was the other. They died within a short time of each other, and were objects of wondering interest to all who knew them.[4]

In 1695, when Johann Sebastian was not quite ten years old, his father died. He lost his mother at an earlier period.[5] So, being left an orphan,

[1] The date is conjectural, and is deduced from the fact that the infant was baptized on March 23. The Gregorian Calendar was not adopted in Germany until 1701. Had it been in use in 1685 Bach's birthday would be March 31.

[2] Johann Ambrosius' Court appointment is to be inferred from the fact that in 1684 the Duke refused him permission to return to Erfurt.

[3] See Table IV.

[4] Johann Ambrosius survived his brother by nearly eighteen months.

[5] His mother died in May 1694, and his father in January 1695. At the latter date Johann Sebastian was three months short of his tenth year.

he became dependent on his eldest brother, Johann Christoph, Organist at Ohrdruf,[1] from whom he received his earliest lessons on the Clavier.[2] His inclination and talent for music must already have been pronounced. For his brother no sooner had given him one piece to learn than the boy was demanding another more difficult. The most renowned Clavier composers of that day were Froberger,[3] Fischer,[4] Johann Caspar Kerl,[5] Pachelbel,[6] Buxtehude,[7] Bruhns,[8]

[1] Excepting Johann Jakob, a lad of thirteen years, Johann Christoph was Bach's only surviving brother, and the only one of the family in a position to look after him. Johann Jakob accompanied Sebastian to Ohrdruf (Pirro, p. 13) and afterwards apprenticed himself to his father's successor as Town Musician at Eisenach. One of the daughters was already married. What became of the other is not stated. See Table v.

[2] It is difficult to believe this statement. That the boy was destined for a musical career by his father hardly can be doubted. That he was of unusual precocity, the story told by Forkel in the text proves. His father's asserted neglect to instruct him is therefore hardly credible.

[3] Johann Jakob Froberger, born at Halle (date unknown); Court Organist at Vienna, 1637-57; d. 1667.

[4] Johann Caspar Ferdinand Fischer, c. 1660-1738 (actual dates of his birth and death unknown); Kapellmeister to Markgraf Ludwig of Baden at Schloss Schlackenwerth in Bohemia. His 'Ariadne Musica Neo-Organoedum' (1702) was the precursor of Bach's 'Das wohl-temperirte Clavier.'

[5] Johann Caspar Kerl, b. 1628; Kapellmeister in Munich, 1656-74; Court Organist at Vienna, 1677-92; d. 1693.

[6] Johann Pachelbel, b. 1653, d. 1706. In 1695 he was Organist of St. Sebald's Church, Nürnberg. His influence upon the organ playing of his generation was enormous. Bach's brother, Johann Christoph, was his pupil.

[7] Dietrich Buxtehude, b. 1637, d. 1707; Organist (1668) of the Marien-kirche, Lübeck, and the chief musical influence in North Germany.

[8] Nikolaus Bruhns, b. circ. 1665, d. 1697; a pupil of Buxtehude; Organist at Husum; the greatest organist of his time after Buxtehude.

and Böhm.[1] Johann Christoph possessed a book
containing several pieces by these masters, and
Bach begged earnestly for it, but without effect.
Refusal increasing his determination, he laid
his plans to get the book without his brother's
knowledge. It was kept on a book-shelf which
had a latticed front. Bach's hands were small.
Inserting them, he got hold of the book, rolled it
up, and drew it out. As he was not allowed a candle,
he could only copy it on moonlight nights, and it
was six months before he finished his heavy
task. As soon as it was completed he looked
forward to using in secret a treasure won by so
much labour. But his brother found the copy
and took it from him without pity, nor did Bach
recover it until his brother's death soon after.[2]

Being once more left destitute,[3] Johann
Sebastian set out for Lüneburg with one of his
Ohrdruf schoolfellows, named Erdmann [4] (after-

[1] Georg Böhm, b. 1661 ; date of death uncertain (c. 1739); from
1698 Organist of the Johanniskirche, Lüneburg.

[2] In fact, Johann Christoph did not die until 1721, more than twenty
years after Sebastian ceased to be under his roof.

[3] The fact that Johann Christoph survived till 1721 disproves
Forkel's statement. The youthful Bach, aged fifteen in 1700, no doubt
seized the earliest opportunity to relieve his brother of the charge
of him. Moreover, Johann Christoph's family was increasing (see
Table v.). In spite of the story of Bach's midnight copying, it cannot
be questioned that he owed a good deal to his brother, who not only
taught him but, presumably, maintained him at the Ohrdruf Lyceum,
where Bach acquired a sound education and a considerable knowledge
of Latin. See Pirro, pp. 14-16, on Bach's education at Ohrdruf. He
left the Lyceum in March 1700.

[4] Georg Erdmann, Bach's fellow-pupil at the Lyceum.

wards Russian Resident at Danzig), and entered the choir of St. Michael's Convent. His fine treble voice procured him a fair livelihood. But unfortunately he soon lost it and did not at once develop another.[1]

Meanwhile his ambition to play the Organ and Clavier remained as keen as ever, and impelled him to hear and practise everything that promised him improvement. For that purpose, while he was at Lüneburg, he several times travelled to Hamburg to hear the famous organist,[2] Johann

---

[1] Bach's entry into the choir of St. Michael's Convent, Lüneburg, took place about Easter 1700. The step was taken upon the advice of Elias Herda, Cantor at the Ohrdruf Lyceum, himself a former member of St. Michael's. Bach remained at St. Michael's for three years, till 1703. The choir library was particularly rich in the best church music of the period, both German and Italian. Spitta is of opinion that Bach's talents as a violinist and Clavier player were also laid under contribution. His voice, as Forkel states, soon ceased to be serviceable. His maximum pay was one thaler (three shillings) a month and free commons.

[2] Probably Georg Böhm, who had relations with the Convent choir, inspired Bach to make the pilgrimage. Böhm, then at St. John's, Lüneburg, was a pupil of Reinken of Hamburg. Spitta (i. 196) suggests that Bach's cousin, Johann Ernst (see Table IV.), was at this time completing his musical education at Hamburg, a fact which may have contributed to draw Bach thither. He made more than one visit, on foot, to Hamburg. F. W. Marpurg published, in 1786, the story, which he received from Bach himself, that on one of his journeys from Hamburg, Bach sat down outside an inn and hungrily sniffed the savours from its kitchen. His pockets were empty and there seemed little prospect of a meal, when a window was opened and two herring heads were thrown out. Bach picked them up eagerly, and found in each of them a Danish ducat. Who was his benefactor he never discovered ; the gift enabled him to satisfy his hunger and pay another visit to Hamburg.

Adam Reinken.[1] Often, too, he walked to Celle to hear the Duke's French band play French music, which was a novelty in those parts.[2]

The date and circumstances of his removal from Lüneburg to Weimar are not precisely known.[3] He certainly became Court Musician there in 1703, when he was just over eighteen years of age.[4] But in the following year he gave up the post on his appointment as Organist to the new Church at Arnstadt, probably desiring to develop his taste for the Organ and realising that he would have better opportunities to do so at Arnstadt than at Weimar, where he was engaged simply to play the Violin.[5] At Arnstadt he set himself assiduously to study the works of the celebrated organists of the period, so far as his modest means permitted him, and in order to improve himself

[1] Johann Adam Reinken, b. 1623, became Organist of St. Catherine's Church, Hamburg, in 1654, and held the post until his death in 1722.

[2] His introduction to French music marked another step in Bach's progressive education. The reigning Duke of Celle (father-in-law of George I. of Great Britain and Ireland) had married a Frenchwoman. The Court Organist was a Frenchman. See Pirro, ' J. S. Bach,' pp. 24-27.

[3] He entered the Weimar service on April 8, 1703 (Pirro, p. 29).

[4] Bach's engagement was in the private band of the younger brother of the Duke. He remained in his new post only a few months. He was engaged as a Violin player, and since his interests were towards the Organ and Clavier, it is clear that he accepted the engagement as a temporary means of livelihood.

[5] He is, however, described in July 1703 as Court Organist (Pirro, p. 30). Bach was drawn to Arnstadt chiefly by the fact that the New Church recently had been equipped with a particularly fine Organ (specification in Spitta, i. 224), which existed until 1863. Bach inaugurated it on July 13, 1703, and entered on his duties as Organist of the church in the following month (Pirro, p. 30).

in composition [1] and Organ playing,[2] walked the
whole way to Lübeck to hear Dietrich Buxtehude,
Organist of St. Mary's Church in that city, with
whose compositions he was acquainted already.
He remained there about three months,[3] listening

[1] His earliest Church Cantata (No. 15) was composed here in 1704.
To the Arnstadt period (1703-7) also must be attributed the Capriccio
written on the departure of his brother, Johann Jakob (Peters bk. 208
p. 62), the Capriccio in honour of his Ohrdruf brother, Johann Christoph
(Peters bk. 215, p. 34), the Sonata in D major (Peters bk. 215, p. 44),
the Organ Prelude and Fugue in C minor (Novello bk. 2 p. 48), and
the Organ Fugue in C minor (Novello bk. 12 p. 95).

[2] In the 'Nekrolog' C. P. E. Bach and Agricola remark of the
Arnstadt period, that Bach then 'really showed the first-fruits of his
industry in the art of Organ-playing and composition, which he had
in great measure learnt only from the study of the works of the most
famous composers of the time, and from his own reflections on them '
(quoted in Spitta, i. 235).

[3] Bach's stipend at Arnstadt was not inconsiderable, and his duties
engaged him only at stated hours on Sundays, Mondays, and Thursdays.
He, therefore, had leisure and the means to employ it. In October
1705 he obtained four weeks' leave of absence and set off on foot to
Lübeck, after leaving an efficient deputy behind him. He stayed
away until February 1706. On his return the Consistory demanded
an explanation of his absence, and took the opportunity to remonstrate
with him on other matters. They charged him 'with having been
hitherto in the habit of making surprising *variationes* in the Chorals,
and intermixing divers strange sounds, so that thereby the congregation were confounded.' They charged him with playing too long
preludes, and after this was notified to him, of making them too short.
They reproached him ' with having gone to a wineshop last Sunday
during sermon,' and cautioned him that, ' for the future he must
behave quite differently and much better than he has done hitherto'
(see the whole charge in Spitta, i. 315 ff.). Bach also was on bad
terms with the choir, whose members had got out of hand and discipline. Before his Lübeck visit he engaged in a street brawl with
one of the scholars. Then, as later, he was a choleric gentleman.
In November 1706 he got into further trouble for having ' made music '
in the church with a ' stranger maiden,' presumably his cousin Maria
Barbara Bach, then on a visit to Arnstadt ; he married her a year
later. Clearly the relations between the Consistory and the brilliant

to the celebrated Organist, but without making himself known to him, and returned to Arnstadt with his experience much increased.

Bach's zeal and persevering diligence had already drawn attention to him, as is evident from the fact that he received in succession several offers of vacant organistships, one of which, at the Church of St. Blasius, Mühlhausen, he accepted in 1707.[1] Barely a year after he entered upon his duties there [2] he again visited Weimar and played to the Duke, who was so pleased with his performance that he offered him the post of Court Organist, which he accepted.[3] Weimar promised

young Organist were becoming difficult, and Bach's migration to Mühlhausen no doubt was grateful to both. His resignation was made formally on June 29, 1707.

[1] Bach was appointed on June 15, 1707, to succeed Johann Georg Ahle. Mühlhausen prided itself upon its musical traditions. Bach's Cantata, No. 71, written in February 1708 for the inauguration of the Mühlhausen Town Council, was engraved (the parts only), the only one of the 206 Cantatas which have come down to us which was printed during Bach's lifetime. He also composed Cantatas 131 and 196 at Mühlhausen, and perhaps three others. See *infra*, p. 188.

[2] Bach's petition to the Mühlhausen Consistory for permission to resign his post is dated June 25, 1708, and is printed in full by Spitta, i. 373. Bach mentions the Weimar post as having been offered to him, but bases his desire to resign the organ of St. Blasius, partly on the ground that his income was inadequate, partly because, though he had succeeded in improving the organ and the conditions of music generally, he saw 'not the slightest appearance that things will be altered' for the better. Mühlhausen, in fact, was a stronghold of Pietism and unsympathetic to Bach's musical ideals.

[3] He was Court Organist and Kammermusikus. In the latter post Bach was of use as a Violinist and Clavier player. The Court band, or Kapelle, on special occasions appeared in Hungarian costume, which Bach presumably donned. His income began at a sum nearly double that he had received at Arnstadt and Mühlhausen.

him a particularly agreeable atmosphere in which to cultivate his genius.[1] He applied himself closely to his work, and probably at this period achieved the mastery of the Organ that he ever afterwards possessed. At Weimar also he wrote his great compositions for that instrument.[2] In 1717[3] the Duke appointed him Concertmeister, a post which gave him further opportunity to develop his art, since it required him to compose and direct Church music.

It was about this time that Zachau, Handel's master, died at Halle, where he was Organist.[4] Bach, who by now had acquired a great reputation, was invited to succeed him.[5] He visited Halle

[1] The character of his employer, Duke Wilhelm Ernst of Saxe-Weimar, must be reckoned a factor in the development of the youthful Bach. The Duke was not only a cultured artist, but was also a man of genuine piety.

[2] Though Bach retouched them in later years and wrote others, it may be stated in general terms that his Organ works were the fruit of the Weimar period, which lasted from 1708 till 1717.

[3] Bach's promotion to the position of Concertmeister had taken place certainly before March 19, 1714, on which date Spitta (i. 517) prints a letter in which Bach gives himself the title. The increase in his income early in 1714 also supports the conclusion, while a letter of January 14, 1714, written by Bach, is not signed by him as Concertmeister. It would seem that his promotion took place in the interval between the two letters. As Concertmeister it was part of his duty to provide Cantatas for the church services. Twenty-two were written by him at Weimar. See *infra*, p. 188, for a list of them.

[4] Friedrich Wilhelm Zachau died on August 7 or 14, 1712.

[5] Spitta (i. 513) infers that, in the later years of the Weimar period, Bach spent part of the autumn of every year in visits to the Courts and larger towns of Germany in order to give Organ recitals and to conduct performances of his Cantatas. Besides the visit to Halle, in 1713, to which Forkel alludes, Bach performed at Cassel in 1713 or

and composed a work as a specimen of his skill. But for some reason unknown he did not obtain the post. It was given to a clever pupil of Zachau, named Kirchhoff.[1]

Johann Sebastian was now thirty-two years old. He had made good use of his opportunities, had studied hard as a player and composer, and by tireless enthusiasm had so completely mastered every branch of his art, that he towered like a giant above his contemporaries. Both amateurs and professional musicians already regarded him with admiration when, in 1717, Marchand, the French virtuoso, a celebrated Clavier and

1714 before the future Frederick I. of Sweden, who presented him with a ring which he drew from his finger. Bach's feet, an admirer recorded, ' flew over the pedal-board as if they had wings.' In December 1714 he visited Leipzig and performed Cantata No. 61, ' Nun komm, der Heiden Heiland.' In 1716 he was again invited to Halle, and at about the same time performed at Meiningen. Forkel records the famous contest with Marchand, the French Organist, at Dresden in 1717.

[1] Forkel's brief account follows the ' Nekrolog.' Bach was in Halle in the autumn of 1713, a year after Zachau's death. The latter's post was still vacant and a new and particularly large Organ (sixty-three speaking stops) was being erected. The authorities pressed Bach to submit himself to the prescribed tests, and he complied so far as to compose a Cantata and to conduct a performance of it. On his return to Weimar he received a formal invitation to accept the post. After some correspondence Bach refused it, partly, perhaps chiefly, on the ground that the income was inadequate. The refusal was answered by the groundless accusation that he had merely entertained the Halle proposal in order to bring pressure upon Weimar for a rise of salary. The misunderstanding was cleared away by 1716, when Bach visited Halle again. In the interval Zachau's post had been given to his pupil, Gottfried Kirchhoff. The whole matter is discussed at length in Spitta, i. 515 ff.

Organ player, visited Dresden. He played before
the King-Elector [1] and won such approbation that
he was offered a large salary to enter His Majesty's
service. [2] Marchand's chief merit was his finished
technique. Like Couperin, [3] his musical ideas
were weak to the point of banality, as we may
judge from his compositions. [4] Bach was an
equally finished player, and so rich in ideas that
Marchand's head would have swollen had he
been equally gifted. Volumier, Concertmeister
at Dresden, [5] was aware of these circumstances,
and knowing that the young German had his instrument and his imagination under the fullest
control, determined to arrange a contest between
the two men in order to give his sovereign the
satisfaction of judging their merits. With the
King's approbation, a message was dispatched

[1] Frederick Augustus I. of Saxony was elected, as Augustus II., to
the throne of Poland in 1697. He died in 1733.

[2] Louis Marchand, b. 1669, d. 1732; Organist to the French Court
and later of the Church of St. Honoré, Paris. His arrival in Dresden
was due to his being in disgrace at Versailles. Whether or not he was
offered a permanent engagement at the Saxon Court, he was regarded
as the champion of the French style, and as such the challenge was
issued to him by Bach.

[3] François Couperin, b. 1668, d. 1733; Organist of St. Gervais,
Paris. Forkel's judgment upon his art is not supported by modern
criticism.

[4] Bach, however, admired Marchand's compositions sufficiently to
give them to his pupils. See Pirro, p. 52.

[5] Jean-Baptiste Volumier, an acquaintance of Bach, according to
Spitta (i. 583). Eitner, 'Quellen Lexikon,' says that he was born in
Spain and educated in France. Grove's 'Dictionary' declares him a
Belgian. In 1709 he was appointed Concertmeister to the Saxon
Court. He died at Dresden in 1728.

to Bach at Weimar [1] inviting him to a contest
with Marchand. Bach accepted the invitation
and set out at once on his journey. Upon his
arrival at Dresden Volumier procured him an
opportunity to hear Marchand secretly. Far
from being discouraged by what he heard, Bach
wrote a polite note to the French artist challeng-
ing him to a trial of skill, and offering to play
at sight anything Marchand put before him,
provided the Frenchman submitted himself to
a similar test. Marchand accepted the challenge,
a time and place for the contest were fixed, and
the King gave his approval. At the appointed
hour a large and distinguished company assembled
in the house of Marshal Count Flemming.[2]
Bach arrived punctually ; Marchand did not
appear. After considerable delay he was sought
at his lodging, when it was discovered, to the
astonishment of all, that he had left Dresden
that morning without taking leave of anybody.
Bach therefore performed alone, and excited the
admiration of all who heard him, though Volumier
was cheated of his intention to exhibit the inferiority of French to German art. Bach was
overwhelmed with congratulations ; but the dis-
honesty of a Court official is said to have inter-

[1] It is more probable that Bach was at Dresden either expressly to
hear Marchand or upon one of his autumn tours.

[2] Some years earlier Flemming had witnessed Handel's triumphant
descent on the Saxon Court, but had failed to establish friendly relations with him. See Streatfield's 'Handel,' p. 87.

cepted a present of one hundred louis d'or sent to him by the King.[1]

Bach had not long returned to Weimar when Prince Leopold of Anhalt-Cöthen, a good judge of music and a first-rate amateur,[2] offered him the post of Kapellmeister. He entered at once upon his new office [3] and held it for about six years.[4] At this period, about 1722,[5] he visited

[1] The article on Marchand in Grove gives a different version of the affair, based upon Joseph Fétis (1784-1871). According to this story of the event, Bach, summoned from Weimar, attended Marchand's concert incognito, and after hearing Marchand perform, was invited by Volumier to take his seat at the Clavier. Bach thereupon repeated from memory Marchand's theme and variations, and added others of his own. Having ended, he handed Marchand a theme for treatment on the Organ and challenged him to a contest. Marchand accepted it, but left Dresden before the appointed hour.

[2] The Prince was brother-in-law of Duke Ernst August of Saxe-Weimar. Bach was, therefore, already known to him and showed the greatest regard for him both at Cöthen and after he had left his service.

[3] The reason for Bach's migration from Weimar to Cöthen was his failure to obtain the post of Kapellmeister at the former Court upon the death of Johann Samuel Drese in 1716. The post was given to Drese's son. On August 1, 1717, just before or after his Marchand triumph, Bach was appointed Kapellmeister to the Court of Cöthen. Duke Wilhelm Ernst refused to release him from his engagement, and Bach endured imprisonment from November 6 to December 2, 1717, for demanding instant permission to take up his new post. Probably his last work at Weimar was to put the 'Orgelbüchlein' into the form in which it has come down to us (see articles by the present writer in 'The Musical Times' for January–March 1917). With his departure from Weimar in 1718 Bach left behind him the distinctively Organ period of his musical fertility. Though his compositions were still by no means generally known, as a player he held an unchallenged pre-eminence.

[4] He was appointed to Cöthen on August 1, 1717, and was inducted at Leipzig on May 31, 1723.

[5] The date actually was November 1720. At Cöthen Bach had an inferior Organ and little scope for his attainments : his chief duties

Hamburg, played the Organ there, and excited general admiration. The veteran Reinken—he was nearly one hundred years old—was particularly impressed by Bach's performance. After he had treated the Choral ' An Wasserflüssen Babylon ' for half an hour in variation after variation in the true Organ style,[1] Reinken paid him the compliment of saying, ' I thought this art was dead, but I see that it survives in you.' Reinken had treated the same Choral in a similar manner some years before and had had his work engraved, showing that he thought highly of it. His praise therefore was particularly flattering to Bach.[2]

On the death of Kuhnau in 1723 [3] Bach was appointed Director of Music and Cantor to St. Thomas' School, Leipzig,[4] a position which he

were in connection with the Prince's band. The yearning to get back to the Organ, which eventually took him to Leipzig in 1723, shows itself in his readiness to entertain an invitation to Hamburg in 1720.

[1] Three Organ movements by Bach upon Wolfgang Dachstein's melody, ' An Wasserflüssen Babylon,' are extant. See notes upon them and their relation to the Hamburg extemporisation in Terry, ' Bach's Chorals,' Part III.

[2] As at Halle in 1713, Bach does not appear to have gone to Hamburg specially to compete for the post of Organist to the Church of St. James, vacant by the death of Heinrich Friese in September 1720. He was not able to stay to take part in the final tests, nor was he asked to submit to them, since his visit to Hamburg had given him an opportunity to display his gifts. In the result the post was given to Johann Joachim Heitmann, who acknowledged his appointment by forthwith paying 4000 marks to the treasury of the Church. See Spitta, ii. 17 ff.

[3] Johann Kuhnau died on June 25, 1722.

[4] On the title-pages of his published works Bach describes himself as ' Capellm. und Direct. Chor. Mus. Lips.'

occupied until his death. Prince Leopold of Anhalt-Cöthen had great regard for him and Bach left his service with regret.[1] But he saw the finger of Providence in the event; for the Prince died shortly afterwards.[2] The loss of his patron affected him deeply, and moved him to compose a funeral Cantata containing remarkably fine double choruses which he himself conducted at Cöthen.[3] While he was at St. Thomas' he was appointed honorary Kapellmeister to the Duke of Weissenfels [4] and, in the following year

[1] Forkel has practically nothing to say regarding the Leipzig period of Bach's musical life. That a professed historian of music, setting before the public for the first time the life of one whom he so greatly extolled, and with every inducement to present as complete a picture of him as was possible, should have taken no trouble to carry his investigations beyond the point C. P. E. Bach and Agricola had reached in the 'Nekrolog' of 1754 is almost incredible. The only reason that can be adduced, apart from the lack of a really scientific impulse, is that Forkel was almost entirely ignorant of the flood of concerted church music which poured from Leipzig from 1723 to 1744. His criticism of Bach as a composer is restricted practically to Bach's Organ and Clavier works.

[2] On November 19, '1728. Latterly his interest in music had waned. The fact, along with Bach's concern for the education of his sons and his desire to return to the Organ, explains his abandonment of the more dignified Cöthen appointment.

[3] The score of this work was in Forkel's possession, but was missing from his library in 1818 and was assumed to be lost until, in 1873, Rust was able to show that Bach used for the occasion certain choruses and Arias from the 'St. Matthew Passion,' which he was then writing, with the first chorus of the 'Trauer-Ode' as an opening of the extemporised work. See Spitta, ii. 618; Schweitzer, ii. 208.

[4] In 1723 he received the title 'Hochfürstlich Weissenfelsische wirkliche Kapellmeister' and retained it till his death. He retained also his Cöthen appointment.

(1736), received the title of Court Composer to the King-Elector of Poland-Saxony.[1]   The two compliments are not of great consequence, and the second was to some degree corollary to Bach's position as Cantor of St. Thomas' School.[2]

Carl Philipp Emmanuel, Bach's second son, entered the service of Frederick the Great of Prussia in 1740.   So widely was Bach's skill recognised by this time that the King, who often heard him praised, was curious to meet so great an artist.   More than once he hinted to Carl Philipp Emmanuel that it would be agreeable to welcome his father to Potsdam, and as Bach did not appear, desired to know the reason. Carl Philipp did not fail to acquaint his father with the King's interest.   But for some time Bach was too occupied with his duties to accede to the invitation.   However, as Carl Philipp continued to urge him, he set out for Potsdam towards the end of 1747, in company with his eldest son, Wilhelm Friedemann.[3]   It was the King's custom to hold a private concert every

---

[1] Augustus III. Bach had petitioned for the appointment in a letter dated July 27, 1733 (Spitta, iii. 38), forwarding a copy of the newly-written Kyrie and Gloria of the B minor Mass.

[2] There does not appear to be any ground for the suggestion that the post of Hofcomponist to the Dresden Court was attached *ex officio* to the St. Thomas' Cantorate. Bach applied for it in 1733, taking advantage of the recent accession of the new sovereign, Augustus III., in February 1733.

[3] Friedemann was then at Halle.

evening, and to take part on the flute in a Concerto
or two. One evening,[1] when he had got out his
flute and the musicians were at their desks, an
official brought him a list of the strangers newly
arrived at Potsdam. Flute in hand the King
ran through the names, and suddenly turning to
the waiting musicians, said with considerable
excitement, ' Gentlemen, Old Bach has arrived.'
The flute was put away for the evening, and
Bach, who had alighted at his son's lodging, was
summoned immediately to the Palace. Wilhelm
Friedemann, who accompanied his father, often
told me the story. Nor am I likely to forget the
racy manner in which he related it. The courtesy
of those days demanded rather prolix compliments,
and the first introduction of Bach to so illustrious
a monarch, into whose presence he had hurried
without being allowed time to change his travelling dress for a Cantor's black gown, obviously
invited ceremonial speeches on both sides. I will
not dwell on them ; Wilhelm Friedemann related

[1] May 7, 1747, according to Spitta, quoting Friedrich Wilhelm
Marpurg's 'Historisch-kritische Beyträge zur Aufnahme der Musik,'
which appeared in 5 vols. between 1754-1778. On the other hand,
Spener, who first records the event, states briefly : ' May 11, 1747. His
Majesty was informed that Kapellmeister Bach had arrived in Potsdam,
and that he was in the King's ante-chamber, waiting His Majesty's
gracious permission to enter, and hear the music. His Majesty at once
commanded that he should be admitted ' (Spitta, iii. 231 n.). If the
Marpurg and Spener dates are reliable, it looks as though Friedemann's story of his father, travel-stained and weary, being hurried
incontinent into the presence of the King is a piece of picturesque
embroidery.

a lengthy and formal conversation between the King and the Cantor.[1]

More worthy of record is the fact that the King gave up his concert for that evening and invited Bach, already known as ' Old Bach,' to try the Silbermann pianofortes [2] which stood in various parts of the Palace.[*] Accompanied from room to room by the King and the musicians, Bach tried the instruments and improvised upon them before his illustrious companion. After some time he asked the King to give him a subject for a Fugue, that he might treat it extempore. The King did so, and expressed his astonishment at Bach's profound skill in developing it. Anxious to see to what lengths the art could be carried, the King desired Bach to improvise a six-part Fugue. But as every subject is not suitable for polyphonic

[1] Clearly this was a story that Wilhelm Friedemann prided himself on the telling, and Forkel's remark suggests the need for caution in accepting all its details. Frederick's courtesy to Bach, however, tends to discredit the story that ten years earlier (1737) Handel deliberately refused to meet the King at Aix-la-Chapelle owing to the peremptoriness of his summons. Mr. Streatfield (p. 145) also shows that Frederick was not at Aix until 1741, when Handel was writing the 'Messiah' in London.

[2] Gottfried Silbermann, a pioneer of the modern pianoforte. Bach was already familiar with his Claviers with hammer action, and indeed had offered useful criticism of which Silbermann had taken advantage. See Spitta, ii. 46.

[*] The pianofortes manufactured by Silbermann, of Freiberg, pleased the King so much, that he resolved to buy them all. He collected fifteen. I hear that they all now stand, unfit for use, in various corners of the Royal Palace. [Robert Eitner, in 1873, found one of the pianos in Frederick the Great's room at Potsdam.]

treatment, Bach himself chose a theme and, to the astonishment of all who were present, developed it with the skill and distinction he had shown in treating the King's subject. His Majesty expressed a wish to hear him on the Organ also. Accordingly, next day, Bach inspected all the Organs in Potsdam,[1] as the evening before he had tried the Silbermann pianofortes. On his return to Leipzig he developed the King's theme in three and six parts, added *Canones diversi* upon it, engraved the whole under the title ' Musikalisches Opfer ' and dedicated it to the royal author of the theme.[2]

His visit to Potsdam was Bach's last journey. The indefatigable diligence he had shown all his life, and particularly in his younger years, when successive days and nights were given to study, seriously affected his eye-sight. The weakness grew with age and became very distressing in character. On the advice of friends who placed great confidence in the skill of a London oculist lately come to Leipzig,[3] Bach submitted to an

---

[1] According to another account, which Spitta (iii. 232) follows, Bach played before a large congregation in the Church of the Holy Spirit, Potsdam. The King does not appear to have been present. The extemporisation of the six-part Fugue took place in Frederick's presence on the evening of that day.

[2] Bach's letter to Frederick accompanying the gift is dated 7th July 1747. He calls it ' a musical offering, of which the noblest portion is the work of Your Majesty's illustrious hand.' In addition to Forkel's analysis it contains a Sonata for Flute, Violin, and Clavier, and a canon perpetuus for the same three instruments.

[3] John Taylor (1703-72), oculist to George II. The operation took place in the winter of 1749-50. Taylor is said to have operated on

operation, which twice failed. He lost his sight completely in consequence, and his hitherto vigorous constitution was undermined by the drugs administered to him. He sank gradually for full half a year, and expired on the evening of July 30, 1750, in the sixty-sixth year of his age.[1] Ten days before his death [2] he was suddenly able to see again and to bear the light. A few hours later he was seized by an apoplexy and inflammatory fever, and notwithstanding all possible medical aid, his weakened frame succumbed to the attack.

Such was the career of this remarkable man. I will only add that he was twice married, and that he had by his first wife seven, and by his second wife thirteen children; in all, eleven sons and nine daughters.[3] All of his sons had an

---

Handel in 1751 (see the article on him in the 'Dict. Nat. Biography.'). Streatfield ('Handel,' p. 212), however, does not mention Taylor, and his account suggests that Samuel Sharp, of Guy's Hospital, was the operator in Handel's case.

[1] The actual date was July 28, at 8.45 P.M. Bach was working to the very moment of his collapse on July 18. Probably his last work was the Choral Prelude (Novello bk. xvii. 85) on the melody 'Wenn wir in höchsten Nöthen sein.' Facing eternity, he bade his son-in-law, Altnikol, inscribe the movement with the title of the Hymn, 'Vor deinen Thron tret ich hiemit,' whose first stanza filled his mind:

> Before Thy throne, my God, I stand,
> Myself, my all, are in Thy hand.

An addendum to the Genealogy, in C. P. E. Bach's hand, gives July 30 as the date of his father's death.

[2] July 18.

[3] See Genealogical Tables VII. and VIII.

admirable talent for music, but only the elder
ones fully developed it.[1]

[1] The statement is misleading.   Of the five sons of the first marriage,
two were famous, two died in infancy, and the fifth abandoned a pro-
mising musical career for the law.   Of the six sons of the second
marriage, one was imbecile, three died in infancy, two were famous.

THE CHURCH AND SCHOOL OF ST. THOMAS, LEIPZIG, IN 1723.

CHAPTER IIA[1]

BACH was inducted into his office as Cantor of St. Thomas' School at nine o'clock on the morning of Monday, May 31, 1723. He died in his official residence there at a quarter to nine on the evening of Tuesday, July 28, 1750. He was buried early on the morning of Friday, July 31, in the churchyard of St. John's, Leipzig.

The announcement of his death, made from the pulpit of St. Thomas' on the day of his funeral, described him as 'Court Composer to His Majesty the King of Poland and Electoral and Serene Highness of Saxony, Kapellmeister to His Highness the Prince of Anhalt-Cöthen, and Cantor to St. Thomas' School of this town.' Bach usually designated himself 'Director Chori Musici Lipsiensis,' or shortly, 'Director Musices.' Circumstances led him to emphasise a title which asserted a musical prerogative not confined to the School and the churches it served.

The Cantor of St. Thomas' was charged formerly with the musical direction of four Leipzig

---

[1] See Introduction, p. xxi, *supra*.

churches : St. Thomas', St. Nicolas', St. Peter's, and the New Church. He was also responsible for the music in the University Church of St. Paul, the so-called 'old service,' held originally on the Festivals of Easter, Whit, Christmas, and the Reformation, and once during each University quarter. On high days music also had to be provided at St. John's Church.

Bach, as Cantor, succeeded to a more restricted responsibility, which dated from the early years of the eighteenth century. The New Church, originally the Church of the Franciscans, had been restored to use in 1699. In 1704 Georg Philipp Telemann, who came to Leipzig as a law student three years before, was appointed Organist there. He also founded the Collegium Musicum, or University Musical Society, a farther slight upon the Cantor's position. Not until 1729 did the Society pass under Bach's direction and its members become available as auxiliaries in the church choirs under his charge. Notwithstanding that Bach's predecessor Kuhnau had protested against Telemann's independence, the direction of the New Church's music passed out of the Cantor's control, though the School continued to provide the choristers. Six years later the University Church of St. Paul also began an independent course. In 1710 the authorities resolved to hold a University service in the church every Sunday. Kuhnau asserted his prerogative as Cantor. But he was only able to maintain it by offering to provide the music for the ' new service ' as well as for the ' old service ' at the fee of twelve thalers which the University so far had paid for the latter. After his death the University appointed (April 3, 1723) Johann Gottlieb Görner, already Organist of St. Nicolas' since 1721, to control the music both of the ' old ' and ' new ' services, for which the University provided the choir. Not until after a direct appeal to the King did Bach succeed, in 1726, in compelling the University to restore to the Cantor his emoluments in regard to the ' old service,' the conduct of which had been restored to him on his appointment as Cantor. The ' new service ' remained under Görner's direction. As to St. Peter's, its services, which had entirely ceased, were revived in 1711. The music, however, was simple, and consisted only of hymns.

Thus Bach, as Cantor, was responsible for the music in the two principal churches, St. Thomas' and St. Nicolas'. The School also provided the choir for St. Peter's and the New Church. The junior and least competent singers sang at St. Peter's. The rest were pretty equally distributed between the other three churches. At the New Church the music was performed under the direction of a Chorpräfect. At St. Thomas' and St. Nicolas' Bach personally directed the concerted music. On ordinary Sundays a Cantata or Motet was performed in each church alternately. At the great Festivals, New Year, Epiphany, Ascension Day, Trinity Sunday, and the Annunciation, Cantatas were sung at both churches, the two choirs singing at Vespers in the second church the Cantata performed by them in the morning at the other church. On these occasions the second choir was conducted by a Chorpräfect.

The principal Sunday service in both churches began at seven in the morning, ended at eleven, and observed the following order :

1. Organ Prelude.
2. Motet, related to the Gospel for the Day ; (omitted in Lent and replaced by the Benedictus).
3. Introit.
4. Kyrie, sung alternately, in German and Latin.
5. The Lord's Prayer, intoned at the altar.
6. Gloria, intoned at the altar and answered either by the Choir's 'Et in terra pax hominibus,' or by the congregation with the Hymn, 'Allein Gott in der Höh' sei Ehr,' the German version of the Gloria.
7. Collect, intoned in Latin ; preceded by the preces 'Dominus vobiscum' and 'Et cum spiritu tuo.'
8. Epistle.
9. Litany, in Advent and Lent only ; intoned by four boys, the Choir responding.

10. Hymn, appropriate to the Gospel.
11. Gospel.
12. Credo, intoned ; (in Lent, last three Sundays of Advent, and Festivals of Apostles, the Nicene Creed, sung in Latin).
13. Prelude, followed by a Cantata, lasting about twenty minutes ; on alternate Sundays in each church.
14. The Creed in German, ' Wir glauben all' an einen Gott,' sung by the congregation.
15. Sermon, lasting one hour (8-9 A.M.).
16. Hymn, ' Herr Jesu Christ, dich zu uns wend',' followed by the reading of the Gospel, on which the Sermon had been based.
17. General Confession, prayers, and Lord's Prayer.
18. Blessing.
19. Hymn.
20. Communion Service ; Hymns and Organ extemporisation.
21. Benediction.

Vespers began at a quarter past one and was a comparatively simple service ; the music consisted of Hymns, a Motet, and the Magnificat.

On the last three Sundays in Advent and throughout Lent neither Cantatas nor Motets were sung. The Organ was silent.

On the three great Festivals the appointed Hymn for the season was sung at the beginning of the principal service, before the Organ Prelude : at Christmas, ' Puer natus in Bethlehem ' ; at Easter, ' Heut' triumphiret Gottes Sohn ' ; at Whitsuntide, ' Spiritus Sancti gratia.' During the Communion service the Sanctus and concerted music were sung. A festal hymn followed the Benediction. The three great Festivals were each observed for three consecutive days, on the first and second of which Cantatas were sung at both churches. On the third day concerted music was sung at only one of the two churches.

The other week-day Festivals for which Cantatas were provided were the Feast of the Circumcision (New Year's Day), Epiphany, Ascension Day, Purification of the B.V.M., Annunciation of the B.V.M., Visitation of the B.V.M., Feast of St. John Baptist (Midsummer Day), Feast of St. Michael the Archangel. The Reformation Festival was kept on October 31, or if that date was a Saturday or Monday, on the previous or following Sunday.

On Good Friday the Passion was performed in the two principal churches alternately.

Leipzig adopted no official Hymn-book. The compilation from which the Hymns were chosen by Bach was the eight-volumed ' Gesangbuch ' of Paul Wagner, published at Leipzig for Dresden use in 1697. It contained over five thousand Hymns but no music, merely the name of the tune being stated above the Hymn. For the

most part the Hymns for special, and even for
ordinary, occasions were prescribed by custom.
Otherwise the power of selection was in the hands
of the Cantor, and Bach's exercise of it caused
some friction with the clergy in 1728.

The provision and direction of the music at
weddings and funerals was in the Cantor's hands.
He arranged the choirs and the music sung at the
scholars' annual processions and perambulations
of the town, which took place at Michaelmas,
New Year, and on St. Martin's and St. Gregory's
Days.

Augmenting the School's choristers, the Town
Musicians took part in the Church services and
were under the Cantor's direction.   Their numbers
and efficiency were inadequate.

Upon the staff of the School the Cantor ranked
third after the Rector and Sub-Rector, and took
a share in the general instruction of the scholars.
Class III. went to Bach for Latin lessons, a duty
which the Council eventually permitted him to
fulfil by deputy.   Singing classes were held by
the Cantor on three days of the week, Mondays,
Tuesdays, and Wednesdays, at nine and noon, and
on Fridays at noon.   His instruction in singing
was given to the four upper classes only.   On
Saturday afternoons the Cantata was rehearsed.
Once in four weeks the Cantor took his turn to
inspect the scholars.   Like the other masters,
he was required to conform to the regulations

of the School House, in which he lived. He rose
at five in summer, at six in winter, dined at ten
and supped at five in the afternoon.

Holidays were numerous. A week's vacation
was given at the Easter, Michaelmas, and New
Year Fairs. At Midsummer the School had a
month of half-holidays. Whole holidays were
given on the birthdays of the four upper masters.
There were no morning lessons on Saints' Days,
on the occasion of funeral orations in the University
Church, and on the quarterly Speech Days.
Hence, though Bach's office carried large responsibility, it left him considerable leisure for composition.

As Cantor Bach had an official residence in the
left wing of the School House. In 1723, the
Cantor's wing was of two storeys only, dwarfed
by the greater elevation of the main edifice and
under the shadow of the church. Bach brought
to Leipzig four children of his first marriage,
and his second wife, Anna Magdalena, presented
him with a son or daughter annually from 1723
to 1729. The accommodation of the Cantor's
lodging therefore rapidly became inadequate. In
the spring of 1731 Bach found a house elsewhere
while an additional storey was added to it, which
provided a new music-room, a good-sized apart-
ment whence a passage led to the big schoolroom
in the main building. The new wing was formally
opened and dedicated on June 5, 1732, when

Bach's secular Cantata 'Froher Tag, verlangte Stunden' was performed ; the libretto being by his colleague Winkler. From thenceforward till his death eighteen years later Bach's occupancy was not disturbed. The wing continued to be the official residence of the Cantor until the School moved to the suburbs of the city in 1877.

In addition to his residence, which he occupied rent free, the Cantor enjoyed a revenue from various and fluctuating sources, amounting in gross to 700 thalers (=£106 per annum). His fixed stipend was only 100 thalers (=£15). About 12 thalers came to him from endowments. In kind he was entitled to 16 bushels of corn and 2 cords of firelogs, together with 2 measures of wine at each of the three great Festivals. From the University, after his successful protest, he received 12 thalers for directing the 'old service.' By far the larger part of Bach's income was derived from fluctuating sources. They were of three kinds : (1) School monies, (2) funeral fees, (3) wedding fees. The School monies represented perquisites derived from funds obtained by the scholars, partly by their weekly collections from the public, partly from the four annual processions or perambulations of the city. From the weekly collections a sum of six pfennigs multiplied by the number of the scholars was put aside for the four upper masters, among whom the Cantor ranked third. From the money collected at the

New Year, Michaelmas, and St. Martin's Day processions the Rector took a thaler, the Cantor and the Sub-Rector each took one-eleventh of the balance, sixteen thirty-thirds went to the singers, and one-quarter of what remained fell to the Cantor. Out of the money collected on St. Gregory's Day (March 12) the Rector took one-tenth for the entertainment of the four upper masters, and the Cantor took one-third of the residue. For funerals one thaler 15 groschen was paid when the whole school accompanied the procession and a Motet was sung at the house of the deceased. When no Motet was sung the Cantor's fee was 15 groschen. For weddings he received two thalers.

Reckoned in modern currency, and judged by the standard of the period, the Cantor's income was not inadequate and served to maintain Bach's large family in comfort. When he died in 1750, in addition to a mining share valued at 60 thalers, he possessed in cash or bonds about 360 thalers, silver plate valued at 251 thalers, instruments valued at 371 thalers, house furniture valued at 29 thalers, and books valued at 38 thalers. His whole estate was declared at 1158 thalers, or somewhat less than the savings of two years' income. But for the inequitable distribution of his property, owing to his intestacy, which left Anna Magdalena only about 400 thalers and the mining share, Bach's widow and unmarried daughters ought not to have been afflicted with excessive poverty, as in fact they were.

At the beginning of his Cantorate Bach worked amid discouraging and unsatisfactory conditions. The Rector, Johann Heinrich Ernesti, was over seventy years of age in 1723. The School was badly managed, its discipline was relaxed, the better-to-do citizens withheld their sons from it, and its numbers were seriously diminished. In 1717 the junior classes contained only 53 as against 120 in Ernesti's earlier years. The proximity and operatic traditions of Dresden and Weissenfels also had a bad effect; the St. Thomas' boys, after attaining musical proficiency, were apt to become restless, demanding release from their indentures, and even running away to more attractive and lucrative occupations. Moreover, the governors of the School were the Town Council, a body which had little sympathy with or appreciation of Bach's artistic aims and temperament. To these difficulties must be added another. The Town Musicians, on whom Bach relied for the nucleus of his orchestra, were few in number and inefficient.

So long as Ernesti lived, there was little prospect of reform. But, after his death, in October 1729, Bach made vigorous representations to the Town Council. Already he had remonstrated with the Council for presenting to foundation scholarships boys who lacked musical aptitude. The Council retaliated by accusing Bach of neglecting his singing classes, absenting himself without leave, and of other irregularities. He was declared to be ' incorrigible ' and it was resolved (August 2, 1730) to sequestrate the Cantor's income, in other words, to withhold from him the perquisites to which he was entitled for the conduct of the Church services.[1]

Bach was not deterred from offering, three weeks later (August 23, 1730), a ' sketch of what constitutes well-appointed Church music, with a few impartial reflections on its present state of decay ' in Leipzig. The document reveals the conditions amid which Bach worked. Its representations may be summarised :

The foundation scholars of St. Thomas' are of four classes : Trebles, Altos, Tenors, Basses.

A choir needs from four to eight ' concertists ' (solo singers) and at least two ' ripienists ' to each chorus part, i.e. a minimum of twelve voices.

The foundation scholars number fifty-five, by whom the choirs of the four Churches, St. Thomas', St. Nicolas', St. Peter's, and the New Church are provided.

For the instrumental accompaniments at least twenty players are required : viz., 2 or 3 first Violins, 2 or 3 second Violins, 4 Violas, 2 Violoncelli, 1 Contrabasso, 2 or more Flutes, 2 or 3 Oboi,

---

[1] In view of Bach's memorial of August 23, 1730 (infra), this seems to be the meaning of the resolution.

1 or 2 Fagotti, 3 Trombe, 1 Timpani. To fill
these places there are eight Town Musicians, and
at the moment there are no players available for
third Tromba, Timpani, Viola, Violoncello, Contrabasso, third Oboe (or Taille).

To augment the Town Musicians the Cantor has
been ⌈wont⌋ in the past to employ University
students and instrumental players in the School.
Upon the former ' at all times ' he relies for Viola,
Violoncello, and Contrabasso, and ' generally ' for
the second Violins. But the Council, by its recent
resolution, no longer affords the Cantor the means
to employ them. To place the scholars in the
orchestra weakens the choir, to which they naturally belong.

By presenting to foundation scholarships boys
unskilled and ignorant of music, the resources at
the Cantor's disposal are still farther lessened.

Hence, Bach concludes, ' in ceasing to receive
my perquisites I am deprived of the power of
putting the music into a better condition.'

No answer was made to Bach's memorial, and
he contemplated resigning his position. But with
the advent of Johann Matthias Gesner as Rector
in September 1730 a happier period dawned upon
the ' incorrigible ' Cantor. In 1732 Gesner procured the withdrawal of the Council's ban on
Bach's perquisites. The fallen fortunes of the
School revived, and Bach did not again make an
effort to leave Leipzig. In 1736 the grant of the

post of Hof-Componist to the Saxon Court gave
him at length a title which compelled the defer-
ence of his civic masters.

Bach's early misunderstanding with the University cut him off from association with the most
dignified, if not the most important, institution
in Leipzig, and deprived him of opportunity to
display his genius beyond the radius of his Church
duties. The situation changed in 1729, when he
became director of the University Society, and he
held the post for about ten years. The Society
gave weekly concerts on Fridays, from 8 to 10,
and an extra concert, during the Fair season, on
Thursdays at the same hour. It performed vocal
and instrumental music and was the medium
through which Bach presented his secular Cantatas, Clavier and Violin Concertos, and Orchestral
Suites to the public. The proficiency of his elder
sons and pupils, and his wife's talent as a singer,
were a farther source of strength to the Society,
whose direction undoubtedly made these years the
happiest in Bach's life. He took his rightful place
in the musical life of the city, and relegated to a
position of inferiority the smaller fry, such as
Görner, who had presumed on Bach's aloofness
from the University and Municipality to insinuate
themselves. His increasing reputation as an
organist, gained in his annual autumn tours, also
enlightened his fellow-townsmen regarding the
superlative worth of one whom at the outset

they were disposed to treat as a subordinate official.

The Leipzig of Bach's day offered various opportunities for musical celebration ; official events in the University, 'gratulations' or 'ovations' of favourite professors by their students, as well as patriotic occasions in which town and gown participated. The recognised fee for *pièces d'occasion* of a public character was fifty thalers. Bach's conductorship of the University Society enabled him to perform festival works with the resources they required, and to augment the band and chorus needed for their adequate performance.

Even before he undertook the direction of the University Society, Bach more than once provided the music for University celebrations. On August 3, 1725, his secular Cantata, 'Der zufriedengestellte Aeolus,' was performed at the students' celebration of Doctor August Friedrich Müller's name-day. In 1726 he revived an old Cantata [1] to celebrate the birthday of another of the Leipzig teachers. In the same year the appointment of Dr. Gottlieb Kortte as Professor of Roman Law was celebrated by Bach's Cantata 'Vereinigte Zwietracht der wechselnden Saiten.' In 1733 the birthday of another Professor was marked by the performance of the Cöthen Cantata to yet another text ('Die Freude reget sich'). On November 21,

---

[1] 'Steigt freudig in die Luft,' first performed at Cöthen, set to a new text, 'Schwingt freudig euch empor.'

1734, the lost Cantata 'Thomana sass annoch betrübt' was sung at the induction of Gesner's successor, Johann August Ernesti, as Rector of St. Thomas' School.

But Bach's activity as a secular composer at Leipzig was chiefly expended on patriotic celebrations. His compositions of this character are particularly numerous during the years 1733-36, while he was seeking from the Dresden Court the post of Hof-Componist. The first of these celebrations took place on May 12, 1727, the birthday of Augustus II. of Poland-Saxony, when Bach's Cantata, 'Entfernet euch, ihr heitern Sterne,' was performed in the Market Place by the University Society. The King was present and listened to the performance from a convenient window. The music is lost. Six years elapsed before Bach was invited to collaborate in another celebration of the royal House. On September 5, 1733, less than two months after his application for the post of Hof-Componist, the University Society celebrated the eleventh birthday of the Electoral Prince by performing Bach's *dramma per musica*, 'Die Wahl des Herkules,' or 'Herkules auf dem Scheidewege.' Barely three months later, on December 8, 1733, Bach produced another Cantata in honour of the royal family, 'Tönet, ihr Pauken, erschallet Trompeten,' of which he was both author and composer. On no less than three occasions in 1734 Bach did

homage to his unheeding sovereign. In January
the University Society, under Bach's direction,
performed his Cantata ' Blast Lärmen, ihr Feinde '
to celebrate the coronation of Augustus III. The
music had already done duty in Dr. Müller's
honour in 1725. On the following October 5,
1734, when the King visited Leipzig, Bach's
hurriedly written Cantata, ' Preise dein Glücke,
gesegnetes Sachsen,' whose first chorus became the
' Osanna' of the B minor Mass, was performed in
the Market Place. Two days later, on October 7,
1734, the King's birthday was celebrated by
another Bach Cantata, ' Schleicht spielende
Wellen,' performed by the Collegium Musicum.
In 1738, having received the coveted title of Hof-
Componist in the interval (1736), Bach performed
a work—' Willkommen, ihr herrschenden Götter
der Erden '—now lost, in honour of the marriage
of the Princess Maria Amalia of Saxony to Charles
of Sicily, afterwards Charles III. of Spain.

Apart from his musical activities and the house
in which he lived there is little that permits us
to picture Bach's life at Leipzig. Association
with his friends Johann Christian Hoffmann,
Musical Instrument Maker to the Court, Marianne
von Ziegler, J. C. Gottsched and his musical wife,
Johann Abraham Birnbaum, among the Pro-
fessoriate, Picander and Christian Weiss, Bach's
regular librettists, suggests the amenities of an
academic and literary circle. But the claims of

his art and the care of his large family had the
first call upon Bach's interest.   And few men had
a happier home life.   While his elder sons were
at home the family concerts were among his most
agreeable experiences.   As his fame increased,
his house became the resort of many seeking to
know and hear the famous organist.   Late in the
thirties he resigned his directorship of the University Society.   His sons were already off his
hands and out of his house, and he turned again
to the Organ works of his Weimar period.   Their
revision occupied the last decade of his life, and the
hitherto constant flow of Church Cantatas ceased.
Pupils resorted to him and filled his empty house,
to one of whom, Altnikol, he gave a daughter in
marriage.

A man of rigid uprightness, sincerely religious ;
steeped in his art, earnest and grave, yet not
lacking naïve humour ;   ever hospitable and
generous, and yet shrewd and cautious ;   pug-
nacious when his art was slighted or his rights
were infringed ;   generous in the extreme to his
wife and children, and eager to give the latter
advantages which he had never known himself ;
a lover of sound theology, and of a piety as deep
as it was unpretentious—such were the qualities
of one who towers above all other masters of music
in moral grandeur.

Four, perhaps only three, contemporary
portraits of Bach are known.   One is in the

possession of the firm of Peters at Leipzig and
once belonged to Carl Philipp Emmanuel's
daughter, who with inherited impiety sold it to
a Leipzig flute player. The second hung in
St. Thomas' School and is reproduced at p. 48
of this volume. It was painted in 1746 and
restored in 1913. Both portraits are by Elias
Gottlieb Haussmann, Court Painter at Dresden.
The third portrait belonged to Bach's last pupil,
Kittel, and used to hang on the Organ at Erfurt,
whence it disappeared after 1809, during the
Napoleonic wars. Recently Professor Fritz
Volbach of Mainz has discovered a fourth portrait,
which is printed at p. 92 of the present volume.
He supposes it to be none other than the Erfurt
portrait, as indeed it well may be, since it represents a man of some sixty years, austere in
countenance, but of a dignity that is not so
apparent in Haussmann's portraiture.[1]

Bach left no will. In consequence his widow,
Anna Magdalena, burdened with the charge of
a step-daughter and two daughters, was entitled
to only one-third of her husband's estate. Neither

[1] The well-known portrait by C. F. Rr. Liszewski in the Joachimsthal
Gymnasium, Berlin, was painted in 1772, twenty-two years after
Bach's death. It represents him at a table with music-paper before
him and an adjacent Clavier. Pirro uses for his frontispiece a portrait
by Geber, which bears no resemblance whatever to the Haussmann or
Volbach pictures. Mention must also be made of a singularly engaging
picture of Bach at the age of thirty-five. It hangs in the Eisenach
Bach Museum and is by Johann Jak. Ihle. It is reproduced as the
frontispiece of this volume.

Carl Philipp Emmanuel nor Wilhelm Friedemann was her own child. But the fact cannot
excuse gross neglect of their father's widow.
Her own sons were in a position to make such a
contribution to her income as would at least have
kept want from her door. In fact she was permitted to become dependent on public charity,
and died, an alms-woman, on February 27, 1760,
nearly ten years after her great husband. The
three daughters survived her. One died in 1774,
the second in 1781. The third, Regine Susanna,
survived them, her want relieved by gifts from
a public that at last was awakening to the
grandeur of her father. Beethoven contributed
generously. Regine Susanna died in December
1809, the last of Bach's children. In 1845 her
nephew, Johann Christoph Friedrich's son, also
died. With him the line of Johann Sebastian
Bach expired.

JOHANN SEBASTIAN BACH.
circ. 1746.
From the picture by Haussmann.)

CHAPTER III

As a Clavier player Bach was admired by all who
had the good fortune to hear him and was the
envy of the virtuosi of his day. His method
greatly differed from that of his contemporaries
and predecessors, but so far no one has attempted
to explain in what the difference consisted.

The same piece of music played by ten different performers equally intelligent and competent will produce a different effect in each
case. Each player will emphasise this or that
detail. This or that note will stand out with
differing emphasis, and the general effect will
vary consequently. And yet, if all the players
are equally competent, ought not their performances to be uniform ? The fact that they
are not so is due to difference of touch, a quality
which to the Clavier stands as enunciation to
human speech. Distinctness is essential for the
enunciation of vowels and consonants, and not less
so for the articulation of a musical phrase. But
there are gradations of distinctness. If a sound
is emitted indistinctly it is comprehensible only

with effort, which occasions us to lose much of the pleasure we should otherwise experience. On the other hand, over-emphasis of words or notes is to be avoided. Otherwise the hearer's attention will be diverted from the *tout ensemble*. To permit the general effect to be appreciated every note and every vowel must be sounded with balanced distinctness.

I have often wondered why Carl Philipp Emmanuel Bach's 'Essay on the Right Manner of playing the Clavier' [1] does not elucidate the qualities that constitute a good touch. For he possessed in high degree the technique that made his father pre-eminent as a player. True, in his chapter on 'Style in Performance,' he writes, 'Some persons play as if their fingers were glued together; their touch is so deliberate, and they keep the keys down too long; while others, attempting to avoid this defect, play too crisply, as if the keys burnt their fingers. The right method lies between the two extremes.' But it would have been more useful had he told us how to reach this middle path. As he has not done so, I must try to make the matter as clear as is possible in words.

Bach placed his hand on the finger-board so that his fingers were bent and their extremities poised perpendicularly over the keys in a plane

[1] His 'Versuch über die wahre Art das Klavier zu spielen' was published (Part I.) in 1753.

parallel to them.[1] Consequently none of his fingers was remote from the note it was intended to strike, and was ready instantly to execute every command. Observe the consequences of this position. First of all, the fingers cannot *fall* or (as so often happens) be *thrown* upon the notes, but are *placed* upon them in full control of the force they may be called on to exert. In the second place, since the force communicated to the note needs to be maintained with uniform pressure, the finger should not be released perpendicularly from the key, but can be withdrawn gently and gradually towards the palm of the hand. In the third place, when passing from one note to another, a sliding action instinctively instructs the next finger regarding the amount of force exerted by its predecessor, so that the tone is equally regulated and the notes are equally distinct. In other words, the touch is neither too long nor too short, as Carl Philipp Emmanuel complains, but is just what it ought to be.[2]

Many advantages arise from holding the hand in Bach's position and from adopting his touch,

[1] Forkel's meaning can be made clear in the following manner: place the thumb and fingers of either hand upon the notes C D E F G of the pianoforte so that the three middle fingers lie more or less flat upon the keys; then draw back the three middle fingers until they form an arch having their tips approximately in a straight line with the tips of the thumb and little finger upon the keys.

[2] It must be remembered that Forkel is speaking of the Clavier and not of the Pianoforte.

on the Clavichord and Harpsichord,[1] and on the Organ as well. I point out merely the most important of them. To begin with, if the fingers are bent, their movements are free. The notes are struck without effort and with less risk of missing or hitting too hard, a frequent fault with people who play with their fingers elongated or insufficiently bent. In the second place, the sliding finger-tip, and the consequently rapid transmission of regulated force from one finger to another, tend to bring out each note clearly and to make every passage sound uniformly brilliant and distinct to the hearer without exertion. In the third place, stroking the note with uniform pressure permits the string to vibrate freely, improves and prolongs the tone, and though the Clavichord is poor in quality, allows the player to sustain long notes upon it. And the method has this advantage : it prevents over-expenditure of strength and excessive movement of the hand. We gather that the action of Bach's fingers was so slight as to be barely perceptible. Only the top joint seemed to move. His hand preserved its rounded shape even in the most intricate passages. His fingers rested closely upon the keys, very much in the position required for a ' shake.' An unemployed finger remained in a

---

[1] The Harpsichord, as its name implies, was an instrument whose strings were plucked by a plectrum. Bach preferred the older Clavier, or Clavichord, which could be regulated, as the other could not, by nicety of touch. See note, p. 58, *infra*.

position of repose. It is hardly necessary to say that other limbs of his body took no part in his performance, as is the case with many whose hands lack the requisite agility.[1]

A man may possess all these qualities, however, and remain an indifferent performer on the Clavier, just as clear and agreeable enunciation does not necessarily make a good speaker. To be a first-rate performer many other qualities are needed, and Bach possessed them all in a notable degree.

Some fingers are longer and stronger than others. Hence players are frequently seduced to use the stronger whenever they can readily do so. Consequently successive notes become unequal in tone, and passages which leave no choice as to the finger to be used may become impossible to play. Bach recognised this fact very early in his career. To get over the difficulty he invented exercises for his own use in which the fingers of both hands were made to practise passages in every conceivable position. By this means every finger on both hands equally became strong and service-

---

[1] Schweitzer (i. 208) points out that Bach's touch was modern, in that he realised that ' singing tone ' depends not only upon the manner in which the keys are struck, but, to a great extent, on the regulation of their ascent.

Of Handel's touch, Burney writes (quoted by Rockstro, p. 349): ' His touch was so smooth, and the tone of the instrument so much cherished, that his fingers seemed to grow to the keys. They were so curved and compact when he played, that no motion, and scarcely the fingers themselves, could be discovered.'

able, so that he could play a rapid succession of chords, single and double ' shakes,' and running passages with the utmost finish and delicacy, and was equally fluent in passages where some fingers play a ' shake ' while the others on the same hand continue the melody.

Besides these improvements, Bach invented a new system of fingering.[1] Before his time, and even in his early years, it was usual for the player to pay attention to harmony rather than counterpoint. Even so it was not customary to use every one of the twenty-four major and minor keys. The Clavichord was still what we term ' gebunden '; that is, several keys struck the same string, which, therefore, could not be accurately tuned.[2] Consequently it was usual to employ only those keys whose notes were tuned with some approximation to accuracy. Again,

---

[1] At the beginning of the seventeenth century, as Spitta points out (ii. 34), the art of fingering had not developed. Speaking generally, neither thumb nor little finger was employed. It was not until the beginning of the eighteenth century that a scientific method emerged, a development rendered necessary by the advance in the modes of musical expression. C. P. E. Bach, quoted by Schweitzer (i. 206), puts this concisely : ' My late father told me that in his youth he had heard great men who never used the thumb except when it was necessary to make big stretches. But he lived in an epoch when there came about gradually a most remarkable change in musical taste, and therefore found it necessary to work out for himself a much more thorough use of the fingers, and especially of the thumb, which, besides performing other good services, is quite indispensable in the difficult keys, where it must be used as nature intends.'

[2] According to Mr. Arnold Dolmetsch, Clavichords with special strings for each note (*bundfrei*) were known in Bach's time.

good players in those days hardly ever used the thumb, except when a large interval had to be stretched. But when Bach began to melodise harmony so that his middle parts not merely filled in but had a tune of their own, when, too, he began to deviate from the Church modes then in general vogue in secular music, using the diatonic and chromatic scales indifferently, and tuning the Clavier in all the twenty-four keys, he found himself compelled to introduce a system of fingering better adapted to his innovations than that in use, and in particular, to challenge the convention which condemned the thumb to in-activity. It is held by some writers that Couperin forestalled Bach's method of fingering, in his 'L'Art de toucher le Clavecin,' published in 1716. But that is not the case. In the first place, Bach was above thirty years old in 1716, and had already developed a distinctive method of his own. And in the second place, Couperin's system differs materially from Bach's, though both made more frequent use of the thumb than was so far customary. When I say 'more frequent use' I do so advisedly ; for whereas in Bach's system the thumb is the principal finger—for the difficult keys, as they are called, are unplayable without it—it is not equally indispensable with Couperin, whose thematic material was not so intricate as Bach's, nor did he compose or play in such difficult keys. Consequently Couperin had not an equally urgent need to use the thumb. We need only compare Couperin's with Bach's system of fingering, as Carl Philipp Emmanuel explains it,[1] to discover that Bach's permits every passage, however intricate and polyphonic, to be played with ease, whereas Couperin's is hardly effective even for his own compositions. Bach was acquainted with Couperin's works and highly esteemed them,[2] as he did those of other French Clavier composers, for their finish and brilliance. But he considered them affected in their excessive use of ornaments, scarcely a single note being free from them. He held them, also, superficial in matter.

Bach's easy, unconstrained use of the fingers, his musical touch, the clearness and precision of every note he struck, the resourcefulness of his fingering, his thorough training of every finger of both hands, the luxuriance of his thematic material and his original method of stating it, all contributed to give him almost unlimited power over his instrument, so easily did he surmount the difficulties of its keyboard. Whether he improvised or played his compositions from notes, he systematically employed every finger of each hand, and his fingering was as uncommon as the compositions themselves, yet so accurate that he

[1] In the ' Essay ' already referred to. For a discussion of Couperin's method see Spitta, ii. 37 ff.

[2] For instance, the Rondeau in B flat in Anna Magdalena's ' Notenbuch ' (No. 6) (1725) is by Couperin.

never missed a note.   Moreover, he read at sight other people's compositions (which, to be sure, were much easier than his own) with the utmost facility.   Indeed, he once boasted to a friend at Weimar that he could play at sight and without a mistake anything put before him.   But he was mistaken, as his friend convinced him before the week was out.   Having invited Bach to breakfast one morning, he placed on the Clavier, among other music, a piece which, at a first glance, seemed perfectly easy.   On his arrival, Bach, as was his custom, sat down at the Clavier to play or look through the music.   Meanwhile his friend was in the next room preparing breakfast.   In a short time Bach took up the piece of music destined to change his opinion and began to play it.   He had not proceeded far before he came to a passage at which he stopped.   After a look at it he began again, only to stop at the same place.   ' No,' he called out to his friend, who was laughing heartily in the next room, ' the man does not exist who can play everything at sight.   It can't be done.' With that he got up from the Clavier in some annoyance.[1]

Bach also could read scores with remarkable facility and play them on the Clavier.   He found no more difficulty in piecing together the

[1] No doubt the friend who prepared this trap for Bach was Johann Gottfried Walther.   His compositions frequently were characterised by intricacy.

separate parts when laid side by side before him.[1]
He often did so when a friend brought him a new
Trio or Quartet for Strings and wished to hear
how it sounded. If a Continuo part, however
badly figured, was put before him he could improvise a Trio or Quartet upon it. Nay, when
he was in the mood and at the height of his
powers, he would convert a Trio into a Quartet
by extemporising a fourth part. On such occasions
he used a Harpsichord with two manuals and
pedal attachment.

Bach preferred the Clavichord to the Harpsichord, which, though susceptible of great variety
of tone, seemed to him lacking in soul. The
Pianoforte was still in its infancy and too coarse.[2]

[1] Mozart had the same gift. When visiting St. Thomas' School
in 1789, he heard with astonishment a performance of Bach's Motet,
'Singet dem Herrn ein neues Lied.' 'At the conclusion he expressed
his delight, and said, "Now that is something from which a man may
learn." On being informed that Bach was Cantor to this school, and
that his Motets were venerated there as reliques, he was eager to see
them. No score being to be obtained, they handed him the separate
parts, and it was interesting to observe his manner of reading them,
holding some in his hands, some on his knees, placing some on chairs
around him; seeming thoroughly lost to everything, and not rising till
he had thoroughly satisfied his curiosity' (Holmes, 'Life of Mozart,'
ed. Dent, p. 251).

[2] There were in Bach's time three 'Clavier' instruments in use.
The oldest, the Clavichord, as a rule, had two strings to every
note, set in motion by a 'tangent' striking them from below. Its
advantage was that it permitted the tone to be regulated by the
touch. For that reason, though its tone was weak, Bach preferred
it. The Clavicembalo, or Harpsichord, as it is called in the text, was
in general known as the 'Flügel,' the strings being plucked, or flipped
by a quill or metal pin, after the manner of the modern mandoline.
The third instrument was the 'piano e forte,' or Hammerclavier.

Both for practice and intimate use he regarded the Clavichord as the best instrument and preferred to express on it his finest thoughts. He held the Harpsichord, or Clavicembalo, incapable of the gradations of tone obtainable on the Clavichord, an instrument which, though feeble in quality, is extremely flexible.

No one could adjust the quill plectrums of his Harpsichord to Bach's satisfaction ; he always did it himself. He tuned his Harpsichord and Clavichord, and was so skilful in the operation that it never took him more than a quarter of an hour. It enabled him to play in any key he preferred, and placed the whole twenty-four of them at his disposal, so that he could modulate into the remoter as easily and naturally as into the more nearly related keys. Those who heard him frequently could hardly detect the fact that he had modulated into a distant key, so smooth were his transitions. In chromatic movements his modulation was as easy and sequent as in diatonic. His ' Chromatic Fantasia,' which is now published,[1] bears out my statement. In his extemporisation he was even freer, more brilliant and expressive.

The Clavicembalo was also built with two keyboards, like an Organ, and a pedal-board provided with strings. It was for this instrument that the so-called Organ Sonatas of Bach were written. He possessed five Clavicembali, but not a single Clavichord at the time of his death. For that reason it has been questioned whether Forkel is accurate in stating that Bach preferred the latter instrument. See Schweitzer, i. 200 ff.   [1] Peters bk. 207 p. 4.

When he played his own music Bach usually adopted a brisk pace.   He contrived to introduce so much variety that every piece became a sort of conversation between its parts.   If he wished to express deep emotion he did not strike the notes with great force, as many do, but expressed his feeling in simple melodic and harmonic figures,[1] relying rather on the internal resources of his art than external dynamics.   Therein he was right. True emotion is not suggested by hammering the Clavier.   All that results is that the notes cannot be heard distinctly, much less be connected coherently.

[1] The truth of this remark is very evident in the ' Orgelbüchlein.'

CHAPTER IV

WHAT has been said regarding Bach's admirable
Clavier playing applies generally to his skill as
an organist. The Clavier and Organ have points
in common, but in style and touch are as different
as their respective uses. What sounds well on
the Clavier is ineffective on the Organ, and *vice
versa.* The most accomplished Clavier player
may be, and usually is, a bad organist unless he
realises the differing natures of the two instruments
and the uses they serve. I have come across
only two men who can be regarded as exceptions
to this general rule—Bach and his eldest son,
Wilhelm Friedemann. Both were finished Clavier
performers, but no trace of the Clavier style was
apparent when they played the Organ. Melody,
harmony, and pace were carefully selected with
due regard to the nature and distinctive use of
each instrument. When Wilhelm Friedemann
played the Clavier his touch was elegant, delicate,
agreeable. When he played the Organ he inspired
a feeling of reverent awe. On the one he was

charming. On the other he was solemn, impressive. So also was his father, and to an even greater degree. Wilhelm Friedemann was a mere child to him as an organist, and frankly admitted the fact.[1] The music that extraordinary man wrote for the Organ is full of dignity, awe-inspiring, saturated with the atmosphere of devotion. His improvisation was even more inspired, dignified, and impressive : for then his imagination was untrammelled by the irksomeness of expressing himself on paper. What is the essence of this art ? Let me, though imperfectly, attempt an answer.

When we compare Bach's Clavier compositions with those written for the Organ it is at once apparent that they differ essentially in melodic and harmonic structure. Hence we conclude that a good organist must select fitting themes for his instrument, and let himself be guided by its character and that of the place in which it stands and by the objects of its use. Its great body of tone renders the Organ ill-adapted to light and jaunty music. Its echoes must have liberty to rise and fall in the dim spaces of the church, otherwise the sound becomes confused, blurred, and unintelligible. What is played upon it

---

[1] Forkel writes as though he were in a position by personal knowledge to compare the gifts of Bach and his son. In fact he was born in 1749 and was less than two years old when Bach died.

must be suited to the place and the instrument, in other words, must be congruous to a solemn and majestic fabric. Occasionally and exceptionally a solo stop may be used in a Trio, etc. But the proper function of the Organ is to support church singing and to stimulate devotional feeling. The composer therefore must not write music for it which is congruous to secular surroundings. What is commonplace and trite can neither impress the hearer nor excite devotional feeling. It must therefore be banished from the Organ-loft. How clearly Bach grasped that fact ! Even his secular music disdained trivialities. Much more so his Organ music, in which he seems to soar as a spirit above this mortal planet.

Of the means by which Bach attained to such an altitude as a composer for the Organ we may notice his harmonic treatment of the old Church modes, his use of the obbligato pedal, and his original registration. The remoteness of the ecclesiastical modes from our twenty-four major and minor keys renders them particularly appropriate to the service of religion. Any one who looks at Bach's simple four-part Hymn tunes (*Choralgesänge*) will at once convince himself of the fact. But no one can realise how the Organ sounds under a similar system of harmonic treatment unless he has heard it. It becomes a choir of four or five parts, each in its natural

compass.   Compare   the   following   chords   in
divided harmony :

with these :

which is the more usual form organists employ.
We realise instantly the effect when music in four
or more parts is played in the same manner.
Bach always played the Organ so, adding the
obbligato pedal, which few organists know how
to use properly.   He employed it not only to
sound the low notes which organists usually play
with the left hand, but he gave it a regular
part of its own, often so complicated that many
organists would find it difficult to play with their
five fingers.

To these qualities must be added the exquisite
art Bach displayed in combining the stops of the
Organ.   His registration frequently astonished
organists and Organ builders, who ridiculed it at
first, but were obliged in the end to admit its

admirable results and to confess that the Organ gained in richness and sonority.[1]

Bach's peculiar registration was based on his intimate knowledge of Organ building and of the properties of each individual stop. Very early in his career he made a point of giving to each part of the Organ the utterance best suited to its qualities, and this led him to seek unusual combinations of stops which otherwise would not have occurred to him. Nothing escaped his notice which had the slightest bearing on his art or promised to advance it. For instance, he made a point of observing the effect of large musical compositions in different surroundings. The practised ear, which enabled him to detect the slightest error in music even of the fullest and richest texture, and the art and rapidity with which he tuned his instrument, alike attest his intuitive skill and many-sidedness. When he was at Berlin in 1747 he was shown the new Opera House. He took in its good and bad qualities at a glance, whereas others had done so only after experience. He was shown the large adjoining Saloon and went up into the gallery that runs round it. Merely glancing at the roof he remarked, 'The architect has secured a novel effect which, probably, neither himself nor any one else suspected.' The Saloon, in fact, is a parallelogram. If a

---

[1] On Bach's use of the stops see Spitta, i. 394 ff., and Pirro's 'L'Orgue de J.-S. Bach.'

person puts his face to the wall in one corner of it and whispers a few words, another person at the corner diagonally opposite can hear them distinctly, though to others between them the words are inaudible. The effect arises from the span of the arches in the roof, as Bach saw at a glance. These and similar observations suggested to him striking and unusual combinations of Organ stops.

Bach brought the methods I have indicated to bear upon Church music, and they help to explain his extraordinarily dignified and inspired playing, which was at once so appropriate and filled the listener with deep awe and admiration. His profound knowledge of harmony, unfailing originality, freedom from a secular style, his complete command of the instrument, both manuals and pedals, whence flowed a generous stream of the richest and most abundant fancy, the infallible and swift judgment which allowed him always to select from the treasury of his mind precisely the musical ideas best suited to the occasion immediately before him, his intuitive grasp of every detail, and his power to make it serve his artistic ends—in a word, his transcendent genius brought the art of Organ playing to a degree of perfection which, till then, it had never attained and hardly will attain again. Quantz [1] has expressed the

[1] Johann Joachim Quantz, b. 1697; flute player and composer; taught Frederick the Great the flute; settled at Berlin as Kammermusikus and Court Composer; d. 1773.

same opinion. ' The admirable Johann Sebastian Bach,' he writes, ' brought the art of Organ playing to its highest perfection. It is to be hoped that when he dies it will not be suffered to decline or be lost, as is to be feared from the small number of people who nowadays bestow pains upon it.' [1]

Strangers often asked Bach to play to them between the hours of divine service. On those occasions he was wont to select and treat a theme in various ways, making it the subject of each extemporisation even if he continued playing for two hours. As a beginning he played a Prelude and Fugue on the Great Organ. Then he developed it with solo stops in a Trio or Quartet. A Hymn-tune followed, whose melody he interrupted in the subtlest fashion with fragments of the theme in three or four parts. Last came a Fugue, with full Organ, in which he treated the subject alone or in association with one or more accessory themes. Here we have the art which old Reinken of Hamburg considered to be lost, but which, as he afterwards found, not only survived but attained its greatest perfection in Bach.

Bach's pre-eminent position and his high reputation often caused him to be invited to examine candidates for vacant organistships, and to report on new Organs. In both cases he acted so conscientiously and impartially that he generally made

---

[1] The ' Nekrolog ' sums up more briefly than Forkel, in a judgment which, without doubt, is the very truth : ' Bach was the greatest Organ player that has yet been known.'

enemies. Scheibe, late Director of Music at the Danish Court, who as a young man was examined by Bach on such an occasion, was so incensed by Bach's unfavourable verdict that he afterwards avenged himself in his ' Critical Musician ' by violently attacking his examiner.[1] In his examination of Organs Bach equally exposed himself to trouble. He could as little prevail on himself to praise a bad instrument as to recommend a bad organist. He was, therefore, severe, though always fair, in the tests he applied, and as he was thoroughly acquainted with the construction of the instrument it was hopeless to attempt to deceive him. First of all he drew out all the stops, to hear the Full Organ. He used to say jokingly, that he wanted to find out whether the instrument had good lungs ! Then he gave every part of it a most searching test. But his sense of fairness was so strong that, if he found the work really well done, and the builder's remuneration

---

[1] Johann Adolph Scheibe, a native of Leipzig, was an unsuccessful candidate for the Organistship of St. Thomas' Church in 1729. Bach was one of the judges. In 1737 Scheibe published in the ' Kritische Musikus ' a criticism of Bach which, while doing justice to his powers as an organist, characterised his compositions as ' turgid and confused in character.' Bach was incensed by the criticism and asked his friend, Professor Birnbaum of Leipzig, to answer it. Scheibe replied in 1739, with a wholly unjustified challenge of Bach's general education and culture. In his ' Phoebus and Pan,' performed in 1731, Bach had already had the satisfaction of representing Scheibe as ' Midas ' and calling him an ass. On the whole matter see Schweitzer, i. 178 ff. and Spitta, iii. 252. Scheibe conducted the Court orchestra at Copenhagen from 1742-49 and died there in 1776.

too small, so that he was likely to be a loser, Bach endeavoured, and often successfully, to procure for him an adequate addition to the purchase price.

When the examination was over, especially if the instrument pleased him, Bach liked to exhibit his splendid talent, both for his own pleasure and the gratification of those who were present. Such demonstrations of his powers invariably invited the verdict, that he was conclusively ' the prince of Clavier and Organ players,' a title which Sorge, the late highly-esteemed organist at Lobenstein,[1] once gave him in a dedicatory Preface.

[1] Georg Andreas Sorge, ' Court and Town Organist to the Count of Reuss and Plau at Lobenstein,' in his dedication thus commended Bach : ' The great musical virtue that Your Excellency possesses is embellished with the excellent virtue of affability and unfeigned love of your neighbour.' See Schweitzer, i. 155.

CHAPTER V

BACH'S first attempts at composition, like all early efforts, were unsatisfactory. Lacking special instruction to direct him towards his goal, he was compelled to do what he could in his own way, like others who have set out upon a career without a guide. Most youthful composers let their fingers run riot up and down the keyboard, snatching handfuls of notes, assaulting the instrument in wild frenzy, in hope that something may result from it. Such people are merely Finger Composers—in his riper years Bach used to call them Harpsichord Knights—that is to say, their fingers tell them what to write instead of being instructed by the brain what to play.[1] Bach abandoned that method of composition when he observed that

---

[1] The following passage from the Autobiography of Hector Berlioz (ed. Dent, p. 11) is relevant : ' My father would never let me learn the piano ; if he had, no doubt I should have joined the noble army of piano thumpers. . . . Sometimes I regret my ignorance, yet, when I think of the ghastly heap of platitudes for which that unfortunate piano is made the daily excuse—insipid, shameless productions, that would be impossible if their perpetrators had to rely, as they ought, on pencil and paper alone—then I thank the fates for having forced me to compose silently and freely by saving me from the tyranny of finger-work, that grave of original thought.'

The Bach Statue at Eisenach.

brilliant flourishes lead nowhere. He realised that musical ideas need to be subordinated to a plan and that the young composer's first need is a model to instruct his efforts. Opportunely Vivaldi's Concertos for the Violin,[1] then recently published, gave him the guidance he needed. He had often heard them praised as admirable works of art, and conceived the happy idea of arranging them for the Clavier.[2] Hence he was led to study their structure, the musical ideas on which they are built, the variety of their modulations, and other characteristics. Moreover, in adapting to the Clavier ideas and phrases originally written for the Violin Bach was compelled to put his brain to work, and so freed his inspiration from dependence on his fingers. Henceforth he was able to draw ideas out of his own storehouse, and having placed himself on the right road, needed only perseverance and hard work to succeed. And how persevering he was ! He even robbed

[1] Antonio Vivaldi, d. 1743 ; a master of form. That fact turned the attention of German composers to him ; while the popularity of his Violin Concertos also attracted musicians, like Bach, whose work at Cöthen was in close association with the Court Kapelle or band.

[2] Bach re-wrote sixteen Vivaldi Violin Concertos for the Clavier, four of them for the Organ, and developed one into a Concerto for four Claviers and a quartet of strings which Forkel enumerates (*infra*, p. 132) as a composition of Bach's (Peters bk. 260). Bach learnt from Vivaldi ' clearness and plasticity of musical structure.' See article ' Vivaldi ' in Grove; Spitta, i. 411 ff; Schweitzer, i. 192 ff. The Vivaldi Clavier Concertos are in Peters bk. 217; the Organ Concertos in Novello bk. 11. Not all these transcriptions are based on Vivaldi. See Schweitzer, i. 193.

himself of sleep to practise in the night what he had written during the day! But the diligence he bestowed upon his own compositions did not hinder him from studying the works of Frescobaldi,[1] Froberger, Kerl, Pachelbel, Fischer, Strungk,[2] Buxtehude, Reinken, Bruhns, Böhm, and certain French organists who were famed in those days as masters of harmony and fugue.[3]

The models he selected—Church musicians for the most part—and his own disposition inclined him to serious and exalted subjects. But in that kind of music little can be accomplished with inadequate technique. Bach's first object, therefore, was to develop his power of expressing himself before he attempted to realise the ideal that beckoned him. Music to him was a language, and the composer a poet who, whatever the idiom he affects, must first of all have at his disposal the means of making himself intelligible to others. But the technique of his period Bach found limited in variety and insufficiently pliable. Therefore he set himself at the outset to refashion the accepted harmonic system. He did so in a manner characteristically individual and bearing the impress of his personality.

---

[1] Girolamo Frescobaldi, b. 1583, d. 1644; Organist of St. Peter's, Rome.

[2] Delphin Strungk, b. 1601, d. 1694; Organist of St. Martin's, Brunswick; composed for the Organ.

[3] Purcell should be added to those whom Forkel mentions as Bach's models. See *infra*, p. 261.

If the language of music is merely the utterance of a melodic line, a simple sequence of musical notes, it can justly be accused of poverty. The addition of a Bass puts it upon a harmonic foundation and clarifies it, but defines rather than gives it added richness. A melody so accompanied—even though all the notes are not those of the true Bass—or treated with simple embellishments in the upper parts, or with simple chords, used to be called 'homophony.' But it is a very different thing when two melodies are so interwoven that they converse together like two persons upon a footing of pleasant equality. In the first case the accompaniment is subordinate, and serves merely to support the first or principal part. In the second case the two parts are not similarly related. New melodic combinations spring from their interweaving, out of which new forms of musical expression emerge. If more parts are interwoven in the same free and independent manner, the apparatus of language is correspondingly enlarged, and becomes practically inexhaustible if, in addition, varieties of form and rhythm are introduced. Hence harmony becomes no longer a mere accompaniment of melody, but rather a potent agency for augmenting the richness and expressiveness of musical conversation. To serve that end a simple accompaniment will not suffice. True harmony is the interweaving of several melodies, which emerge now in the upper, now in the middle, and now in the lower parts.

From about the year 1720, when he was thirty-five, until his death in 1750, Bach's harmony consists in this melodic interweaving of independent melodies, so perfect in their union that each part seems to constitute the true melody. Herein Bach excels all the composers in the world.* At least, I have found no one to equal him in music known to me. Even in his four-part writing we can, not infrequently, leave out the upper and lower parts and still find the middle parts melodious and agreeable.

But in harmony of this kind each part must be highly plastic ; otherwise it cannot play its rôle as an actual melody and at the same time combine with the other parts. To produce it Bach followed a course of his own, upon which the text-books of his day were silent, but which his genius suggested to him. Its originality consists in the freedom of his part writing, in which he transgresses, seemingly, at any rate, rules long established and to his contemporaries almost sacred. Bach, however, realised their object, which was simply to facilitate the flow of pure melody on a sound harmonic basis, in other words, successive and coexistent euphony, and he succeeded with singular success though by un-

---

* See Kirnberger's ' Kunst des reinen Satzes,' p. 157. [The work was published in two volumes at Berlin in 1771, 1776.]

familiar means. Let me explain my meaning more closely.

Between simple intervals there is little difficulty in deciding whether the second note must rise or fall. And in regard to phrases, or sections of a phrase, if we analyse their structure and follow out their harmonic tendency, their resolution is equally clear. But this sense of destination may be provoked in each part by different intervals. As we have observed already, every one of the four parts must flow melodically and freely. But to secure that result it will be necessary to introduce between the notes which begin a phrase and establish its general atmosphere other notes which often are not consonant with those employed in the other parts and whose incidence is governed by the accent. This is what we call a *transitus regularis et irregularis.*[1] Each part starts from a fixed point, and returns to it, but travels freely between them. No one has made more use of such progressions than Bach in order to colour his parts and give them a characteristic melodic line. Hence, unless his music is played with perfect fluency, occasional passages will sound harshly and we may be tempted to accuse him of exaggeration. But the charge is ill founded. Once we play them as Bach intended

---

[1] *Transitus regularis* = a passing note on the unaccented portions of the bar ; *transitus irregularis* = a passing note on the accented part of the bar.

them, such passages reveal their full beauty and their attractive though bizarre dissonance opens up new vistas in the realm of sound.

But, to speak in detail of Bach's transgression of recognised rules. To begin with, he admitted octaves and fifths provided they sounded well ; that is, when the cause of their being forbidden did not arise.[1] Everybody knows that there are positions in which they sound well, and others when they should be avoided, owing to the harsh effect or thin harmony they produce. Bach's octaves and fifths never produce bad or thin harmony, and he was very definite as to when they could and could not be used. In certain circumstances he would not permit hidden fifths and octaves even between the middle parts, though we exclude them only between the outer parts. Yet, on occasion he used them in such a barefaced manner as to puzzle the beginner in composition. But their use very soon commends itself. Even in the last revision of his early compositions we find him altering passages, which at first sight appear impeccable, with the object of enriching their harmony and without scrupling to use hidden octaves. A remarkable instance occurs

[1] Spitta (iii. 315 ff.) prints a treatise by Bach, 'Rules and Instructions for playing Thorough-bass or Accompaniment in Four Parts,' dated 1738. Rule 3 of chap. vi. states : ' Two fifths or two octaves must not occur next one another, for this is not only a fault, but it sounds wrong. To avoid this there is an old rule, that the hands must always go against one another, so that when the left goes up the right must go down, and when the right goes up the left must go down.'

in the first part of the ' Well-tempered Clavier,'
in the E major Fugue, between the fifth and fourth
bars from the end.[1] I regret to this hour that,
on looking over the later text, from which Hoffmeister and Kühnel's edition of that work is
printed,[2] I was so foolish as to reject Bach's
amended reading there, merely because the harmony is unorthodox though more pleasing. I
stupidly preferred the older, more correct, and
harsher reading, though in the later text the
three parts run easily and smoothly. And what
more can one demand ?

Again, there is a rule that every note raised
by an accidental cannot be doubled in the chord,
because the raised note must, from its nature,
resolve on the note above. If it is doubled, it
must rise doubled in both parts and, consequently, form consecutive octaves. Such is the
rule. But Bach frequently doubles not only notes
accidentally raised elsewhere in the scale but
actually the *semitonium modi* or leading - note
itself. Yet he avoids consecutive octaves. His
finest works yield examples of this.

Again, Bach's statement that ' over a pedal
point all intervals are permissible that occur in
the three scales '[3] should be regarded rather as

---

[1] Actually the third beat of the fourth bar from the end. P. bk. 1
p. 37 Fugue no. 9.

[2] Forkel edited the ' Wohltemperirte Clavier ' for Hoffmeister in
1801.

[3] The rule is not in the ' Rules and Instructions ' already referred to.

an expansion than a violation of the recognised rule. In general what is called an Organ point is merely a retarded close. Bach, however, did not hesitate to employ it in the middle of a piece ; a striking example occurs in the last Gigue of the ' English Suites.'[1] On a first hearing this Gigue, imperfectly rendered, may not sound well. But it grows more beautiful as it becomes more familiar, and what seemed harsh is found to be smooth and agreeable, until one never tires of playing and hearing it.

Bach's modulation was as original and characteristic as his harmony, and as closely related to it. But the two things, though closely associated, are not the same. By harmony we mean the concordance of several parts ; by modulation, their progression through keys. Modulation can take place in a single part. Harmony requires more than one. I will endeavour to make my meaning clearer.

Most composers stick closely to their tonic key and modulate out of it with deliberation. In music that requires a large number of performers, and in a building, for instance a church, where the large volume of sound dies away slowly, such a habit shows good sense in the composer who wishes his work to produce the best possible effect. But in chamber or instrumental music it is not always a proof of wisdom, but rather of mental poverty. Bach saw clearly that the two

[1] Suite No. 6, in D minor (P. bk. 204 p. 84).

styles demand different treatment. In his large choral compositions he bridles his exuberant fancy. In his instrumental works he lets himself go. As he never courted popularity, but always pursued his ideal, Bach had no reason to suppress the nobility of his inspirations, or to lower their standard for public consumption. Nor did he ever do so. Therefore every modulation in his instrumental work is a new thought, a constantly progressive creation in the plane of the chosen keys and those related to them. He holds fast to the essentials of harmony, but with every modulation introduces a new suggestion and glides so smoothly to the end of a piece that no creaking of machinery is perceptible ; yet no single bar—I might almost say no part of a bar— is like another. Every modulation bears a strict relationship to the key from which it proceeds, and springs naturally from it. Bach ignored, or rather despised, the sudden sallies by which many composers seek to surprise their hearers. Even in his chromatic passages his progressions are so smooth and easy that we are hardly conscious of them, however extreme they may be. He makes us feel that he has not stepped outside the diatonic scale, so quick is he to seize upon the consonances common to dissonant systems and combine them to his sure purpose.

CHAPTER VI

BACH'S treatment of harmony and modulation powerfully influenced his melody. The strands of his harmony are really concurrent melodies. They flow easily and expressively, never engross the hearer's attention, but divide his interest, as now one now the other becomes prominent. Even when they are noticeable they seem obscured by the melodic parts that accompany them—I say ' seem obscured,' for if the hearer is sufficiently instructed to distinguish the several melodies in the *ensemble* he will discover them to be more clearly defined by their accompaniment.

The combination of several melodic lines obliges the composer to use devices which are unnecessary in homophonic music. A single melody can develop as it pleases. But when two or more are combined each must be so delicately and cleverly fashioned that it can be interwoven with the others in this direction and in that. And here we detect one at least of the reasons why Bach's melodies are so strangely original, and his tunes so clearly distinguishable from those of other composers. Provided that novelty does not degenerate into eccentricity or extravagance, and that clearness and facility of expression march with agreeableness, a composer's meritoriousness is proclaimed in his originality.* The one drawback is that the ordinary hearer cannot appreciate melodic beauties which are patent only to the expert.

But Bach's melodies are not invariably so handicapped. They are always original, it is true. But in his free compositions the melodies are so natural and spontaneous that, while they sound differently from those of other composers, their naturalness, and the sincerity of feeling that inspires them, make them intelligible to every listener. Most of the Preludes in the ' Well-tempered Clavier ' as well as a number of movements in the Suites are of this character.

Bach's melody, then, bears the unmistakable stamp of originality. And so does his *passage* work, as it is called. Such novelty, originality, and brilliancy are not found in any other composer. Examples are to be found in all Bach's Clavier works. But the most striking and original are in

---

* Many people hold the opinion that the best melody is one which the largest number of persons can understand and sing. But this cannot be admitted, for if it were true, popular airs which are sung up and down the country by all classes, even the lowest, must be accounted the finest and best. I should be inclined to state the proposition conversely : a melody which attracts everybody is invariably of the most ordinary kind. In that form the statement might, perhaps, pass as a principle.

the 'Great Variations,' [1] in the first Part of the
'Clavierübung,' [2] in the 'English Suites,' [3] and
the 'Chromatic Fantasia.' [4] In the last particularly Bach's fertility impresses us. The greater
part of its *passage* work is in the form of harmonic
arpeggios whose richness and originality match
the chords they represent.

In order to realise the care and skill Bach
expended on his melody and harmony, and how
he put the very best of his genius into his work,
I need only instance his efforts to construct
a composition incapable of being harmonised
with another melodic part. In his day it was
regarded as imperative to perfect the harmonic
structure of part-writing. Consequently the composer was careful to complete his chords and
leave no door open for another part. So far
the rule had been followed more or less closely in
music for two, three, and four parts, and Bach
observed it in such cases. But he applied it also
to compositions consisting of a single part, and to
a deliberate experiment in this form we owe
the six Violin and the six Violoncello Solo Suites,[5]

[1] Forkel alludes to the 'Goldberg Variations' (P. bk. 209).
[2] P. bks. 205, 206.   [3] P. bks. 203, 204.
[4] P. bk. 207.
[5] Bach wrote three Suites (Partita) and three Sonatas for Solo
Violin. They date from about 1720 and are in the keys of G minor,
B minor, A minor, D minor, C major, and E major (P. bk. 228). The
six Violoncello Suites date from the same period and are in G major,
D minor, C major, E flat major, C minor, and D major (P. bks. 238a,
238b).

which have no accompaniment and do not require one. So remarkable is Bach's skill that the solo instrument actually produces all the notes required for complete harmony, rendering a second part unnecessary and even impossible.

Bach's melody never palls on us, because of the presence in it of those qualities to which I have referred. It remains ' ever fair and young,' like Nature herself. In his earlier works, in which we find him still in bondage to the prevailing mode, there is a good deal that to-day seems antiquated. But when, as in his later works, he draws his melody from the living wells of inspiration and cuts himself adrift from convention, all is as fresh and new as if it had been written yesterday. Of how many compositions of that period can the same be said ? Even the works of ingenious composers like Reinhard Keiser [1] and Handel have become old-fashioned sooner than we or their composers might have supposed. Like other caterers for the public, they were obliged to pander to its taste, and such music endures no longer than the standard which produced it. Nothing is more inconstant and fickle than popular caprice and, in general, what is called fashion. It must be admitted, however, that Handel's Fugues are not yet out of date,

[1] Reinhard Keiser, b. 1673, d. 1739 ; scholar of the Leipzig Thomas-schule ; settled at Hamburg, 1694 ; composed a number of Operas, and for a time had a great vogue.

though there are probably few of his Arias that we now find agreeable.[1]

Bach's melody and harmony are rendered still more distinctive by their inexhaustible rhythmic variety. Hitherto we have discussed his music merely subjectively as harmony and melody. But to display vivacity and variety music needs to be uttered with rhythmic point and vigour. More than those of any other period composers of Bach's time found no difficulty in this, for they acquired facility in the management of rhythm in the 'Suite,' which held the place of our 'Sonata.' Between the initial Prelude and closing Gigue the Suite includes a number of characteristic French dance measures, whose rhythm is their distinguishing characteristic. Composers of Bach's day, therefore, were familiar with measures and rhythms which are now obsolete. Moreover skilful treatment was necessary in order that each dance might exhibit its own distinctive character and swing. Herein Bach exceeded his predecessors and contemporaries. He experimented with every kind of key and rhythm in order to give variety and colour to each movement. Out of his experience he acquired such facility that, even in

---

[1] It was precisely his agreeable operatic Arias that expressed Handel's genius in the eyes of his generation. With rare exceptions that branch of his work is obsolete and his cult survives mainly in the 'Messiah,' which supports his quite posthumous reputation as 'musician in ordinary to the Protestant religion.' See Mr. R. A. Streatfield's 'Handel,' Introduction.

Fugue, with its complex interweaving of several parts, he was able to employ a rhythm as easy as it was striking, as characteristic as it was sustained from beginning to end, as natural as a simple Minuet.

The source of Bach's astonishing pre-eminence is to be sought in his facile and constant application of the methods we have discussed.   In whatever form he chose to express himself, easy or difficult, he was successful and seemingly effortless.[1]   There is not a note in his music that does not suggest consummate ease of workmanship. What he sets out to do he concludes triumphantly. The result is complete and perfect ; no one could wish for a single note to be other than it is.   Some illustrations will make my point clearer.

Carl Philipp Emmanuel, in the preface to his father's ' Vierstimmige Choralgesänge ' (' Fourpart Hymn-tunes '), which he edited,[2] says that

[1] Schweitzer advances the opinion, which may perhaps be challenged, that inevitable and natural as Bach's melodies are, they do not give the impression of ' effortless invention.'   Bach, he holds, worked like a mathematician, who sees the whole of a problem at once, and has only to realise it in definite values.   Hence, he agrees with Spitta, Bach's way of working was quite different from Beethoven's.   With Beethoven the work developed by means of episodes that are independent of the theme.   With Bach everything springs with mathematical certainty from the theme itself.   See Schweitzer (i. 211) on Bach's methods of working.

[2] Johann Sebastian Bach's ' Vierstimmige Choralgesänge ' were published in 1765 and 1769.   C. P. E. Bach was concerned only with the first volume.   Forkel perhaps refers to an edition of the ' Choralgesänge ' issued by Breitkopf in four parts at Leipzig in 1784, 1785, 1786, and 1787, and edited by C. P. E. Bach.

the world was accustomed to look for nothing but masterpieces from Bach. Some reviewers thought this praise exaggerated. But if the term ' master-piece ' is restricted to works written during the years of Bach's maturity [1] it is nothing less than the truth. Others have produced masterpieces in various forms which may be placed honourably by the side of his. For instance, certain Alle-mandes, Courantes, etc., by Handel and others are not less beautiful, though less richly wrought, than Bach's. But in Fugue, Counterpoint, and Canon he stands alone, in a grandeur so isolated that all around him seems desert and void. No one ever wrote Fugues to compare with his ; indeed, persons unacquainted with them cannot imagine what a Fugue is and ought to be. The ordinary Fugue follows a rule of thumb development. It takes a theme, puts another beside it, passes them into related keys, and writes other parts round them over a Continuo. Certainly this is Fugue : but of what merit ? Persons who know no other not unnaturally hold the whole species in little esteem, and the player who hopes to make such commonplace material convincing will need all his skill and imagination.

Bach's Fugue is of quite another kind. It pre-sents all the characteristics we are accustomed to

[1] Forkel indicates the period 1720-1750. But in 1720 Bach had already completed the ' Orgelbüchlein ' and the greater part of his Organ works.

in freer musical forms : a flowing and distinctive
melody, ease, clarity, and facility in the progression of the parts, inexhaustible variety of
modulation, purest harmony, the exclusion of
every jarring or unnecessary note, unity of form
and variety of style, rhythm, and measure, and
such superabundant animation that the hearer
may well ask himself whether every note is not
actually alive. Such are the properties of Bach's
Fugues, properties which excite the admiration
and astonishment of all who can appreciate the
intellectual calibre their composition demands.
How great a tribute of homage is due to work of
this kind, which exhibits all the qualities which
lend distinction to compositions in other musical
forms ! Moreover, while all Bach's Fugues of his
mature period have the foregoing properties in
common, each is endowed with peculiar excel-
lencies of its own, has its own distinctive indi-
viduality, and displays a melodic and harmonic
scheme in keeping with it. The man who can
play one of Bach's Fugues is familiar with, and can
play, one only ; whereas knowing one, we can
perform portfolios of Fugues by other performers
of Bach's period.

To what a height was the art of Counterpoint
carried by Bach's genius ! It enabled him to
develop out of a given subject a whole family of
related and contrasted themes, of every form and
design. It taught him to develop an idea logically

from the beginning to the end.   It gave him such a command of harmony and its infinite combinations that he could invert whole themes, note by note, in every part, without impairing in the least the flow of melody or purity of his harmony.   It taught him to write in canon at all intervals and in movements of all kinds so easily and naturally that the workmanship is not perceptible and the composition sounds as smoothly as though it were in the free style.   Lastly, it has given to posterity a legacy of works immensely various, which are, and will remain, models of contrapuntal form as long as music endures.*

I have written exclusively so far of Bach's Clavier and Organ work.   But in its expression music has two branches, instrumental and vocal, and as Bach excels in both of them, the reader will desire to hear somewhat respecting his vocal writings.

It was at Weimar that Bach first had occasion to write for the voice,[1] upon his appointment to

---

* There are people who conclude that Bach merely perfected harmony. But if we realise what harmony is, a means to extend and emphasise musical expression, we cannot imagine it apart from melody.   And when, as in Bach's case, harmony is actually an association of melodies, such a view becomes the more ridiculous.   It might perhaps be reasonable to say of a composer that his influence was restricted to the sphere of melody, because we may get melody without harmony.   But there cannot be real harmony without melody.   Hence the composer who has perfected harmony has influenced the whole, whereas the melodist has left his mark only on a fraction of his art.

[1] As has been pointed out already (*supra*, p. 14) Bach's earliest church Cantatas date from the Arnstadt period.

the Kapelle, which imposed on him the provision of music for the ducal chapel. His church music, like his Organ works, is devout and serious, and in every respect what church music ought to be. He makes a point also of not elaborating individual words, which leads to mere trifling, but interprets the text as a whole.[1] His choruses invariably are magnificent and impressive, and he frequently introduces Chorals into them,[2] making the other parts accompany their *Cantus* fugally, as was the practice in a Motet. As elsewhere in his works, the harmonic structure of his voice parts and instrumental accompaniment is rich. The declamation of the recitatives is expressive, and the latter have fine Continuo parts.[3] In his Arias, hardly one of which is not beautiful and expressive, Bach seems to have been handicapped by the inefficiency of his singers and instrumentalists, who constantly complained of the difficulty of his music. If he had been fortunate enough to have capable performers the merits of his church music

[1] The statement certainly needs a caveat. No composer of his period studied his text more closely or reverently than Bach. No one, on the other hand, was more readily fired by a particular word or image in his text to give it sometimes irrelevant expression.

[2] Of Bach's church Cantatas 206 have survived. In only 22 of them does Bach fail to introduce movements based upon the Lutheran Chorals.

[3] We must attribute to Forkel's general ignorance of Bach's concerted church music his failure to comment upon a much more remarkable feature of the recitatives, namely, their unique treatment of the human voice as a declamatory medium, a development as remarkable as Wagner's innovations in operatic form a century later.

would have been established and, like his other
works, they would still be sung and admired ; for
they contain treasures which deserve immortality.[1]

Among the works composed at Leipzig I single
out two Cantatas, one of which was performed at
Cöthen at the funeral of Bach's beloved Prince
Leopold, and the other in St. Paul's Church,
Leipzig, on the occasion of the funeral sermon in
honour of Christiana Eberhardine, Queen of
Poland and Electress of Saxony.[2] The first
contains double choruses of uncommon magnificence and most affecting sentiment.[3] The second
has only four-part choruses, but they are so de-
lightful and fresh that he who begins the work
will not pause till he has reached the end of it.
It was written in October 1727.

Bach also composed a great number of Cantatas,
chiefly for the choir of St. Thomas' School, Leipzig.[4]

[1] It was not the imperfections of the choir but the indifference of
Bach's successors at St. Thomas', Leipzig, that was chiefly responsible
for the neglect of his Cantatas in the latter half of the eighteenth
century.   Johann Friedrich Doles (1715-89) was the only Cantor who
realised the greatness of his predecessor's concerted church music.

[2] The 'Trauer-Ode' was performed on October 17, 1727.   Bach
finished the score two days before the performance !   A parallel case
is that of Mozart, who finished the overture of 'Don Giovanni' on the
morning of the first performance of the Opera, and actually played
it unrehearsed that evening.

[3] It has been pointed out already that Bach used the 'St. Matthew
Passion' music, set to other words, for the occasion.   No. 26 ('I would
beside my Lord be watching') was sung to the words 'Go, Leopold,
to thy rest' !

[4] Of the 206 surviving Cantatas, 172 were written for the Leipzig
choir.

The choir ordinarily numbered fifty singers, and sometimes more, over whose musical training Bach presided like a father. He practised them so hard in Cantatas for single and double chorus that they became excellent singers. Among these works are some which, in profundity of conception, magnificence, richness of harmony and melody, and animation, surpass everything of their kind. But, like all Bach's works, and in common with other masterpieces, they are difficult to perform and need a numerous orchestra to produce their full effect.

Such are Bach's most important vocal compositions.[1] In minor forms of the art, *morceaux* for social entertainments and the like, he wrote little,[2] though he was of a most sociable disposition. For instance, he is said never to have composed a song.[3] And why should he ? They produce themselves so spontaneously that there is little call for genius to aid their gestation.

[1] Forkel's knowledge is very incomplete.

[2] Elsewhere Forkel mentions only one of the secular Cantatas.

[3] There is a tradition that Bach wrote a comic song, ' Ihr Schönen, höret an,' which was widely current about the time of his death (Spitta, iii. 181 n.). The Aria, ' So oft ich meine Tabakspfeife,' in A. M. Bach's ' Notenbuch ' of 1725, should be mentioned. See B. G. xxxix. sec. 4.

CHAPTER VII

BACH AS A TEACHER

IT not infrequently happens that talented composers and players are incapable of imparting their
skill to others. Either they have never troubled
to probe the mechanism of their own facility, or,
through the excellence of their instructors, have
taken the short cut to proficiency and allowed
their teacher and not their own judgment to decide
how a thing should be done. Such people are
useless to instruct beginners. True, they may
succeed in teaching the rudiments of technique,
assuming that they have been properly taught
themselves. But they are certainly unqualified
to teach in the full sense of the word. There is,
in fact, only one way to become a good teacher,
and that is to have gone through the discipline
of self-instruction, a path along which the beginner may go astray a thousand times before
attaining to perfection. For it is just this stumb-
ling effort that reveals the dimensions of the art.
The man who has adventured it learns the obstacles
that obstruct his path, and how to surmount them.
To be sure, it is a lengthy method. But if a man

JOHANN SEBASTIAN BACH.
(From the picture discovered by Professor Fritz Volbach.)

has patience to persevere he will reap a sure reward after an alluring pilgrimage. No musician ever founded a school of his own who has not followed such a course, and to his experience his teaching has owed its distinctive character.

This is so with Bach, who, only gradually discovering his full stature, was thirty years old before unremitting application raised him above the difficulties of his art. But he reaped his reward. Self-discipline set him on the fairest and most alluring path that it has ever been given to a musician to tread.

To teach well a man needs to have a full mind. He must have discovered how to meet and have overcome the obstacles in his own path before he can be successful in teaching others how to avoid them. Bach united both qualities. Hence, as a teacher he was the most instructive, clear, and definite that has ever been. In every branch of his art he produced a band of pupils who followed in his footsteps, without, however, equalling his achievement.

First of all let me show how he taught the Clavier.[1] To begin with, his pupils were made to acquire the special touch of which I have already spoken.[2] To that end for months together he made them practise nothing but simple exercises

[1] Bach's method has come down to us in treatises by two of his pupils, C. P. E. Bach's 'Essay' and Kirnberger's 'Die Kunst des reinen Satzes in der Musik,' to which reference has been made already.

[2] *Supra*, p. 50.

for the fingers of both hands, at the same time emphasising the need for clearness and distinctness. He kept them at these exercises for from six to twelve months, unless he found his pupils losing heart, in which case he so far met them as to write short studies which incorporated a particular exercise. Of this kind are the 'Six Little Preludes for Beginners,' [1] and the 'Fifteen Two-part Inventions,' [2] both of which Bach wrote during the lesson for a particular pupil and afterwards improved into beautiful and expressive compositions. Besides this finger practice, either in regular exercises or in pieces composed for the purpose, Bach introduced his pupils to the use of the various ornaments in both hands.

Not until this stage was reached did Bach allow his pupils to practise his own larger works, so admirably calculated, as he knew, to develop their powers. In order to lessen their difficulty, it was his excellent habit to play over to them the pieces they were to study, with the remark, 'That's how it ought to sound.' [3] It would be difficult to exaggerate the helpfulness of this method. The pupil's interest was roused by hearing the piece properly played. But that was not

[1] Bach wrote eighteen Preludes for Beginners. They are all in P. bk. 200.

[2] Most of these movements, which Bach called indifferently 'Inventions' (ideas) and 'Praeambula' (Preludes), were written in 1723. They are in P. bk. 201.

[3] Heinrich Nikolaus Gerber, who was Bach's pupil from 1724 to 1727, particularly emphasises this feature of Bach's teaching.

the sole result. Without the help thus given the pupil could only hope to overcome the difficulties of the piece after considerable effort, and would find it much less easy to realise a proper rendering of it. As it was, he received at once an ideal to aim at and was taught how to surmount the difficulties the piece presented. Many a young performer, still imperfect after a year's practice, probably would master his music in a month if he once had it played over to him.

Bach's method of teaching composition was equally sure and effective.[1] He did not begin with the dry details of counterpoint, as was the custom of other teachers in his day. Still less did he burden his pupils with the physical properties of sound, which he held to be matter for the theorist and instrument-maker rather than the composer. He started them off at once on four-part harmony over a figured Bass, making his pupils write each part on a separate stave in order to impress on them the need for accurate harmonic progression. Then he passed to Hymn tunes, setting the Bass himself and making his pupils write the Tenor and Alto parts. In time he let them write the Bass also. He insisted on correct harmony and on each part having a real melodic line. Every musician knows what models

[1] See on the whole matter Spitta, iii. 117 ff. Bach's method is illustrated by his ' Rules and Instructions ' (1738) printed by Spitta, iii. 315 ff., and also by the ' Einige höchst nöthinge Regeln ' at the end of A. M. Bach's ' Notenbuch ' (1725).

Bach has left us in this form.   The inner parts of his four-part Hymn-tunes are so smooth and melodious that often they might be taken for the melody.   He made his pupils aim at similar tunefulness, and until they showed a high standard of merit did not permit them to write compositions of their own.   Meanwhile he aimed at cultivating their feeling for pure harmony and for the order and connection of ideas and parts by familiarising them with the compositions of others.   Until they had acquired facility in those qualities he neither permitted them nor held them competent to put pen to paper.

Bach required his pupils in composition to work out their musical ideas mentally.   If any of them lacked this faculty he admonished him not to compose and discountenanced even his sons from attempting to write until they had first given evidence of genuine musical gifts.   Having completed their elementary study of harmony, Bach took his pupils on to the theory of Fugue, beginning with two-part writing.   In these and other exercises he insisted on the pupil composing away from the Clavier.[1]   Those who did otherwise he

[1] Mozart wrote as follows to a correspondent who asked him what his method of composition was : ' I can really say no more on this subject than the following ; for I myself know no more about it, and cannot account for it.   When I am, as it were, completely myself, entirely alone, and of good cheer—say, travelling in a carriage, or walking after a good meal, or during the night when I cannot sleep ; it is on such occasions that my ideas flow best and most abundantly. *Whence* and *how* they come, I know not ; nor can I force them.   Those

ridiculed as ' Harpsichord Knights.' In the second place he required rigorous attention to each part and its relation to the concurrent parts, permitting none, not even an inner one, to break off before it had finished what it had to say. He insisted upon a correct relation between each note and its predecessor. If he came upon one whose derivation or destination was not perfectly clear he struck it out as faulty. It is, indeed, a meticulous exactitude in each individual part that makes

ideas that please me I retain in memory, and am accustomed, as I have been told, to hum them to myself. If I continue in this way, it soon occurs to me how I may turn this or that morsel to account, so as to make a good dish of it, that is to say, agreeably to the rules of counterpoint, to the peculiarities of the various instruments, etc. All this fires my soul, and, provided I am not disturbed, my subject enlarges itself, becomes methodised and defined, and the whole, though it be long, stands almost complete and finished in my mind, so that I can survey it, like a fine picture or a beautiful statue, at a glance. Nor do I hear in my imagination the parts *successively*, but I hear them, as it were, all together. What a delight this is I cannot tell ! . . . When I proceed to write down my ideas, I take out of the bag of my memory, if I may use that phrase, what has previously been collected into it in the way I have mentioned. For this reason the committing to paper is done quickly enough, for everything is, as I said before, already finished ; and it rarely differs on paper from what it was in my imagination ' (*Life*, ed. Dent, p. 255).

Wagner, writing in 1851 to Uhlig, who could not understand how the libretto of ' Young Siegfried ' could be set to music, expresses the same idea as Mozart : ' What you cannot possibly imagine is a-making of itself ! I tell you, the musical phrases build themselves on these verses and periods without my having to trouble at all ; everything springs as if wild from the ground ' (Life, trans. Ellis, iii. p. 243).

Schumann writes in 1839 : ' I used to rack my brains for a long time, but now I scarcely ever scratch out a note. It all comes from within, and I often feel as if I could go on playing without ever coming to an end ' (Grove, vol. iv. p. 353).

Bach's harmony really multiple melody. Confused part-writing, where a note that belongs to the Tenor is given to the Alto, or *vice versa*, or the haphazard addition of extraneous parts to a chord which suddenly shows an increase of notes as if fallen from the sky, to vanish as suddenly as they came, are faults found neither in his own nor his pupils' writing. He regarded his musical parts as so many persons engaged in conversation. If there are three, each of them on occasion may be silent and listen to the others until it finds something relevant to say itself. But if, at an interesting point of the conversation, an interloping voice intervened, Bach regarded it as an intruder and let his pupils understand that it could not be admitted.

Notwithstanding his strictness on this point, Bach allowed his pupils considerable licence in other respects. In their use of certain intervals, as in their treatment of harmony and melody, he let them experiment within the limits of their ability, taking care to discountenance ugliness and to insist on their giving appropriate expression to the character of the composition. Beauty of expression, he postulated, was only attainable on a foundation of pure and accurate harmony. Having experimented in every form himself, he liked to see his pupils equally adventurous. Earlier teachers of composition, for instance, Berardi,[1]

[1] Angelo Berardi's 'Documenti armonici. Nelli quali con varii

Buononcini,[1] and Fux,[2] did not allow such liberty. They were afraid to trust their pupils to encounter difficulties, and short-sightedly prevented them from learning how to overcome them. Bach's system was wiser, for it took his pupils farther, since he did not limit their attention, as his predecessors did, to the harmonic structure, but extended it to the qualities that constitute good writing, namely, consistency of expression, variety of style, rhythm, and melody. Those who would acquaint themselves with Bach's method of teaching composition will find it fully set forth in Kirnberger's ' Correct Art of Composition.' [3]

As long as his pupils were under his instruction Bach did not allow them to study any but his own works and the classics. The critical sense, which permits a man to distinguish good from bad, develops later than the æsthetic faculty and may be blunted and even destroyed by frequent contact with bad music. The best way to instruct youth is to accustom it early to consort with the best models. Time brings experience and an instructed judgment to confirm the pupil's early attraction to works of true art.

discorsi, regole, ed essempii si dimonstrano gli studii arteficiosi della musica ' was published at Bologna in 1687.

[1] Giovanni Maria Buononcini, b. c. 1640, d. 1678 ; Maestro di Capella at Modena ; published his ' Musico prattico ' at Bologna in 1673, 1688.

[2] Johann Joseph Fux, b. 1660, d. 1741 ; Kapellmeister at Vienna ; published his ' Gradus ad Parnassum ' at Vienna in 1725.

[3] See *supra*, p. 74.

Under this admirable method of teaching all Bach's pupils became distinguished musicians, some more so than others, according as they came early or late under his influence, and had opportunity and encouragement to perfect and apply the instruction they received from him. His two eldest sons, Wilhelm Friedemann and Carl Philipp Emmanuel, were his most distinguished pupils, not because he gave them better instruction than the rest, but because from their earliest youth they were brought up amid good music at home. Even before they began their lessons they knew what was good. On the other hand, others, before they became Bach's pupils, either had heard no good music or their taste had been already vitiated by contact with bad. It at least attests the excellence of Bach's method that even his pupils thus handicapped took high rank in their profession and distinguished themselves in one or other of its branches.*

Bach's first pupil was JOHANN CASPAR VOGLER, who received instruction from him in his early days at Arnstadt and Weimar and, on Bach's testimony, was an exceedingly able player. He became organist, and later burgomaster, at Weimar, retaining his professional position. Some Choral

* I speak here only of those pupils who made music their profession. But, besides these, Bach had a great many other pupils. Every dilettante in the neighbourhood desired to boast of the instruction of so great and celebrated a man. Many gave themselves out to have been his pupils who had never been taught by him.

4-5066

Preludes by him for a two-manualed Organ with pedals were engraved about 1737.[1]

Other pupils of Bach who became famous were :

1. HOMILIUS, of Dresden. He was not only an excellent organist but a distinguished composer of church music as well.[2]

2. TRANSCHEL, of Dresden. He was a fine musician and performer on the Clavier. There exist in MS. six Polonaises by him which perhaps are superior to those of any composer but Wilhelm Friedemann Bach.[3]

3. GOLDBERG, of Königsberg. He was a very finished player on the Clavier, but without any marked talent for composition.[4]

4. KREBS, Organist at Altenburg. He was not only a player of the first rank, but also a prolific composer for the Organ, Clavier, and of church music. He was fortunate in having Bach's instruction for nine years.[5]

---

[1] See Spitta, i. 522 ; Schweitzer, i. 214 for further details regarding Vogler, who died *circ.* 1765.

[2] Gottfried August Homilius, b. 1714, d. 1785 ; pupil of Bach, *circ.* 1735. Cantor of the Kreuzschule, Dresden.

[3] Christoph Transchel (1721-1800) taught music at Leipzig and Dresden ; Bach's pupil and friend, *circ.* 1742. See Spitta, iii. 245.

[4] Johann Gottlieb (or Theophilus) Goldberg, clavicenist to Count Kaiserling (*infra*, p. 119) for whom Bach wrote the so-called 'Goldberg Variations.' He was born *circ.* 1720 and was a pupil of Bach from 1733-46.

[5] Johann Ludwig Krebs, b. 1713, d. 1780 ; Bach's pupil, 1726-35. Bach said of him that he was ' the best crab (Krebs) in the brook (Bach).'

Lincoln Christian College

5. ALTNIKOL, Organist at Naumburg. He was Bach's son-in-law and is said to have been a very competent player and composer.[1]

6. AGRICOLA, Court Composer at Berlin.[2] He is less known as a composer than as a theorist. He translated Tosi's [3] 'Il canto figurato' from Italian into German and provided the work with an instructive commentary.

7. MÜTHEL, of Riga. He was a good Clavier player and wrote for that instrument. His Sonatas and a Duet for two Claviers attest his ability as a composer.[4]

8. KIRNBERGER,[5] Court Musician at Berlin to the Princess Amalia of Prussia.[6] He was one of the most distinguished of Bach's pupils, full of genuine enthusiasm for his art and eager to assure its interests. Besides his exposition of Bach's system of teaching composition, we are indebted to him for the first logical treatise on harmony, in which he sets forth his master's teaching and

[1] Johann Christoph Altnikol, d. 1759.

[2] Johann Friedrich Agricola, b. 1720, d. 1774; pupil of Bach circ. 1738-41; Director of the Royal Chapel, Berlin.

[3] Pier Francesco Tosi, b. circ. 1650; singing master in London. His 'Opinioni de' cantori antichi e moderni, o sieno osservazioni sopra il canto figurato' was published at Bologna in 1723.

[4] Johann Gottfried Müthel, b. circ. 1720, d. circ. 1790; pupil of Bach in 1750 and resident in his house at the time of his death; organist of the Lutheran Church, Riga.

[5] Johann Philipp Kirnberger, b. 1721, d. 1783; Bach's pupil, 1739-41.

[6] Louisa Amalia, of Brunswick-Wolfenbüttel, wife of Frederick the Great's brother, and mother of his successor, Frederick William II. (1786-97).

practice. The first work is entitled 'Kunst des reinen Satzes,' and the second, 'Wahre Grundsätze zum Gebrauch der Harmonie.'[1] He served the interests of his art also by other writings and compositions, and was an excellent teacher. The Princess Amalia was his pupil.

9. KITTEL, Organist at Erfurt. He is a sound, though not a finished, player, and is distinguished as a composer by several Organ Trios, so excellent that Bach himself might have written them. He is the sole survivor (1802) of Bach's pupils.[2]

10. VOIGT, of Anspach,[3] and an organist named SCHUBART[4] were mentioned to me by Carl Philipp Emmanuel as having been Bach's pupils. He knew nothing about them except that they entered his father's house after he left it.[5]

---

[1] The second work was published in 1773 at Berlin. For the first, see *supra*, p. 74.

[2] Johann Christian Kittel, b. 1732, d. 1809; one of Bach's latest pupils; Organist of the Predigerkirche, Erfurt. He is said to have possessed a portrait of his master and to have rewarded his pupils for good playing by drawing the curtain which usually covered the picture and permitting them to look upon it. It is, perhaps, the portrait, recently discovered by Dr. Fritz Volbach, which is reproduced at p. 92 of this volume.

[3] Nothing seems to be known of him.

[4] Johann Martin Schubart succeeded Bach at Weimar in 1717. He was born in 1690 and died in 1721. See Spitta, i. 343.

[5] In addition to those mentioned by Forkel, the following pupils of Bach are known: Johann Gotthilf Ziegler, of St. Ulrich's Church, Halle; J. Bernhard Bach, of Ohrdruf; Heinrich Nikolaus Gerber, Organist at Sondershausen; Samuel Anton Bach, of Meiningen; Johann Ernst Bach, of Saxe-Weimar; Johann Elias Bach, Cantor at Schweinfurt; Johann Tobias Krebs, organist at Buttelstädt, and his sons, Johann Ludwig, Johann Tobias, and Johann Carl; Johann

I have said already that Bach's sons were his most distinguished pupils. The eldest, WILHELM FRIEDEMANN BACH, came nearest to his father in the originality of his genius. His melodies have quite a different character from those of other composers. They are exceedingly clever, elegant, and spontaneous. When performed with delicacy, as he played them, they cannot fail to charm every hearer. It is greatly to be regretted that he preferred to follow his fancy in extemporisation and to expend his genius on fugitive thoughts rather than to work them out on paper. The number of his compositions therefore is small, but all are beautiful.

CARL PHILIPP EMMANUEL BACH, who comes next, went out into the world sufficiently early to discover that it is a good thing for a composer to have a large public behind him. Hence, in the clearness and easy intelligibility of his compositions, he approaches the popular style, though he scrupulously avoids the commonplace.[1] Both he and his elder brother admitted that they were

Schneider, organist of St. Nicolas', Leipzig; Georg Friedrich Einicke, Cantor at Frankenhausen; Johann Friedrich Doles, Bach's second successor in the Cantorate of St. Thomas'; Rudolph Straube, who afterwards settled in England; Christoph Nichelmann, cembalist to Frederick the Great; Christian Gräbner, and Carl Hartwig.

For full information upon Bach's pupils see Spitta, i. 522 ff., ii. 47 ff., iii. 116 ff., 239 ff., and the relative articles in Grove's 'Dictionary.'

[1] Forkel does not do justice to his friend. C. P. E. Bach is recognised as the immediate precursor of Haydn and as the link between the latter and J. S. Bach.

driven to adopt a style of their own by the wish to avoid comparison with their incomparable father.

JOHANN CHRISTOPH FRIEDRICH BACH, Concertmeister at the Court of Bückeburg, imitated Carl Philipp's style, but was not his equal. According to Wilhelm Friedemann, he was the best player among the brothers, and the most effective performer of their father's Clavier compositions.

JOHANN CHRISTIAN BACH, called 'Bach of Milan,' and afterwards 'Bach of London,' was the youngest son of Bach's second marriage and of too tender an age when his father died ever to have had lessons from him. Hence, perhaps, the absence of Bach's style in his music. He was, in fact, a popular composer universally admired in his day.[1]

---

[1] Mozart had a very particular regard for him. See Schweitzer i. 220 on his brothers' abilities as composers.

CHAPTER VIII

PERSONAL CHARACTERISTICS

DISTINGUISHED as a player, composer, and teacher, Bach was also an indulgent father, a good friend, and a loyal citizen. His paternal devotion is shown by his care for his children's education, and he was equally assiduous in the performance of his civil and social duties. His acquaintance was agreeable to everybody. Every lover of music, whatever his nationality, was sure of a friendly reception at his house, and his sociability and reputation caused him to be seldom without visitors.

As an artist Bach was exceptionally modest. Notwithstanding his pre-eminence in his profession, a superiority of which he could not but be conscious, and in spite of the admiration and respect daily shown him, he never gave himself airs. If he was asked the secret of his mastership he would answer, ' I was made to work ; if you are equally industrious you will be equally successful,' [1] a

---

[1] Spitta (iii. 262) quotes a characteristic anecdote. To some one who praised his skill on the Organ Bach replied : ' There is nothing wonderful about it. You merely strike the right note at the right moment and the Organ does the rest.'

remark which made no allowance for his own
exceptional genius.   His opinion of other composers and their work was invariably fair and
generous.   Naturally, much of their work struck
him as somewhat trivial, viewed from his own
altitude.   But he never uttered a harsh criticism,
unless it were to a pupil, to whom he held himself
bound to say what he thought.   Still less did
he presume on his acknowledged superiority to
indulge in braggadocio, as often happens with
performers brought into touch with those whom
they regard as their inferiors.   Herein Bach's
modesty went so far that he never spoke
voluntarily of his frustrated contest with
Marchand, though the latter was the challenger.[1]
Many absurd stories are told of Bach; for instance
that, dressed up as a village schoolmaster, he
liked to enter a church and ask the organist to
let him play a Choral, in order to enjoy the astonishment excited by his playing, or to hear the Organist
declare, ' This must be Bach or the Devil.'[2]
He always ridiculed such stories, and indeed
had too much respect for his art to make it cloak
his vanity.

[1] See *supra*, p. 19.   Bach himself certainly was the challenger.

[2] When Handel was at Venice in 1708, Domenico Scarlatti, hearing
a stranger touching the Harpsichord at a masquerade, exclaimed,
' That must either be the famous Saxon or the Devil ' (Rockstro's
' George Frederick Handel,' p. 48).   Streatfield (p. 145) mentions a
similar event which took place in 1737.   Hearing a stranger playing
a Fugue in one of the Flemish churches, the organist embraced him,
saying, ' You can be no other but the great Handel.'

At musical parties where Quartet or other instrumental music was performed, Bach liked to play the Viola, an instrument which put him, as it were, in the middle of the harmony in a position from which he could hear and enjoy it on both sides. On those occasions he would sometimes join in a Trio or other piece on the Harpsichord. If he was in the mood and the composer was agreeable, he would, as has been told already, extemporise a new Trio from the Continuo part, or, adding a new part, convert the Trio into a Quartet. But these were the only occasions on which he was ready to display his great powers before others. One Hurlebusch, of Brunswick,[1] a conceited and arrogant Clavier player, once visited Bach at Leipzig, not to hear him play, but to play to him. Bach received him politely and listened patiently to his very indifferent performance. On taking leave Hurlebusch made Bach's eldest sons a present of his published Sonatas, exhorting them to study them diligently. Bach, knowing the kind of music his sons were wont to play, smiled at Hurlebusch's naïveté but did not permit him to suspect his amusement.[2]

Bach was fond of listening to the music of other composers. If he and one of his elder sons hap-

[1] Heinrich Lorenz Hurlebusch was organist of three churches in Brunswick. His visit to Bach took place in 1730, seemingly. See Schweitzer, i. 154.

[2] Schweitzer prints an appreciation of Hurlebusch which suggests that he was a man of distinct ability and ' a paragon of politeness.'

pened to be in church when a Fugue was played, directly the subject had been stated he always pointed out how it ought to be developed. If the composer knew his business and fulfilled Bach's anticipations, he was pleased and nudged his son to draw his attention to the fact. Is this not evidence of his impartial interest in other people's compositions ?

I have mentioned already the composers whom in his youth Bach esteemed, loved, and studied. Later, when experience ripened his critical faculty, he had other favourites, among them Imperial Kapellmeister Fux, Handel, Caldara,[1] Reinhard Keiser, Hasse,[2] the two Grauns,[3] Telemann,[4] Zelenka,[5] Benda,[6] etc., and, in general, the distinguished musicians at Dresden and Berlin. He was acquainted with all except the first four of those I mention. In his youth Bach was intimate with Telemann.[7] He also had a very warm regard

[1] Antonio Caldara, b. *circ.* 1670 ; vice-Kapellmeister at Vienna, 1716-36 ; d. 1736.

[2] Johann Adolph Hasse, b. 1699, d. 1783 ; Kapellmeister and Director of the Opera, Dresden.

[3] Johann Gottlieb Graun, b. *circ.* 1698, d. 1771 ; conductor of the royal Kapelle, Berlin.

Carl Heinrich Graun, b. 1701, d. 1759 ; like his brother, in Frederick the Great's service.

[4] Georg Philipp Telemann, b. 1681, d. 1767 ; Cantor and Musikdirektor in Hamburg.

[5] Johann Dismas Zelenka, b. 1679 or 1681, d. 1745 ; Court Composer at Dresden.

[6] Franz Benda, b. 1709, d. 1786 ; Concertmeister to Frederick the Great upon the death of J. G. Graun.

[7] On Telemann's influence on Bach see Spitta, ii. 437.

for Handel and often expressed a desire to know him. As Handel, like himself, was a famous performer on the Organ and Clavier, many in Leipzig and its neighbourhood wished to bring the two great men together. But Handel, then living in London, never found time for a meeting during the visits he paid to Halle, his native town. On his first visit in 1719, Bach was at Cöthen, only some twenty miles distant. As soon as he was informed of Handel's arrival he lost not a moment in setting out to visit him, but on his arrival found that Handel had returned to England. At the time of Handel's second visit, between 1730 and 1740,[1] Bach was prevented from leaving Leipzig by indisposition. But no sooner was he advised of Handel's arrival at Halle than he sent his eldest son, Wilhelm Friedemann, to beg him to visit Leipzig, an invitation which Handel was unable to accept. In 1752 or 1753, when Handel paid his third visit to Germany,[2] Bach was dead. He had always expressed the strongest desire to know Handel, and the Leipzig people were disappointed in their wish to hear the two great men together.

While Hasse was Kapellmeister at Dresden both the Opera and Kapelle flourished. Bach

---

[1] Handel's second visit to Halle took place in June 1729. His mother's illness detained him. See Streatfield, p. 110.

[2] Handel's third visit took place in July–August 1750. He was laid up by a severe accident in the course of it, and appears to have not recovered from it at the time of Bach's death.

had many friends at Dresden, who held him in high regard. Among them may be mentioned Hasse and his wife, the celebrated Faustina.[1] They often visited Leipzig and were admirers of the Cantor's rare talents. Hence, at Dresden he was always received in the most respectful manner and often visited the Opera, generally accompanied by his eldest son. When the time for their journey approached Bach would say in fun, ' Well, Friedemann, shall we go to Dresden to hear the pretty tunes [2] again ? ' Innocent as the jest was, I am sure Bach would not have uttered it to any but his son, who already could distinguish between great music and agreeable trifles.

Bach was never in a position to make what is called a brilliant fortune.[3] He held a fairly lucrative office, but his income had to maintain and educate a large family. He neither possessed nor sought other means of livelihood, and was too absorbed in his art and work to think of accepting engagements which, in those days, and to a man of his genius, certainly would have brought riches. Had he possessed a taste for travel he would, as even one of his detractors admits, have ' drawn

---

[1] Faustina Bordoni, b. 1693, d. 1783 ; m. Hasse in 1730. She was one of the most famous singers of the day.

[2] The original has ' Liederchen.'

[3] See *supra*, p. 37. Compare Handel's case. He received a royal pension of £600 per annum, and though he was twice ι bankrupt, left £20,000.

upon himself the admiration of the whole world.' But he preferred a quiet domestic life, constant occupation in his work, with contentment and a moderate competence, like his forbears.

His modesty, however, did not prevent him from receiving manifold proofs of regard and affection and marks of honourable distinction. Prince Leopold of Cöthen, Duke Ernst August of Weimar,[1] and Duke Christian of Weissenfels, all showed sincere regard for him, which must have been the more agreeable to him seeing that they were all sound judges of music. At Berlin, as at Dresden, he was universally honoured and respected. If we add to these testimonies the fact that he captured the admiration of all who heard him play or were acquainted with his music, then we may be sure that Bach, 'singing for himself and the Muses,' received at the hands of Fame the recognition he valued most, and cherished it far more than the trivial honour of a ribbon or gold chain.

I add that, in 1747, Bach became a member of the 'Society of the Musical Sciences,' founded by Mizler, only because we owe to the circumstance his admirable Choral Variations on 'Vom Himmel hoch.' [2]   He presented them to the

---

[1] The Duke was the nephew of, and succeeded, Duke Wilhelm Ernst in 1728.

[2] The Canonic Variations on the melody are published by Novello bk. 19, p. 73. For the Mizler Society, see *supra*, p. xxiv.

Society on his admission and they were engraved subsequently.[1]

[1] Spitta (iii. 294) regards the statement as incorrect and holds that the work was engraved before Bach joined Mizler's Society in June 1747. Pirro (p. 215) supports Spitta and regards the Variations as having been engraved at Nürnberg ' vers 1746.'

CHAPTER IX

To have produced so many great works in all
forms of musical expression Bach necessarily must
have been a prolific writer. For if a composer be
the greatest genius in the world, unless he constantly exercises his art he cannot hope to produce
real masterpieces. Superlative excellence is the
fruit of indefatigable application. Yet in Bach's
case we should be wrong to acclaim as masterpieces all the products of his great activity just
because masterpieces at length were the fruit of
it. Already in his early compositions we find
undeniable evidence of genius. But they are
blemished by faults, passages poor in quality,
extravagant, insipid, that are hardly worth preserving, though of interest to the student who
wishes to trace from its source the development
of Bach's genius.

It is not difficult to distinguish with exactitude those of Bach's early compositions which
are of the first excellence ; for he has been at
pains to give us the clue. As he did not publish
his first work until he was about forty years

old,[1] we are justified in assuming the merit of
what, at so mature an age, he thought worthy
to put into print, and in concluding generally
that all his engraved works are of first-rate
merit.[2]

With respect to his unpublished compositions,
and they are by far the most numerous, we must
in order to distinguish their merit rely partly
on a critical examination of their texts, partly on
Bach's own judgment.   Like all great composers,
he was continually working on his compositions
with a view to making them still more finished.
Indeed, he actually attempted to improve some
of them that were already perfect.   Any that were
susceptible of improvement he improved, even
those already engraved.   Such is the origin of the
variant readings of his works found in older and
more recent texts.   By constantly retouching his
compositions Bach aimed at making them in-
disputable masterpieces.   In this category I place
most of what he wrote before the year 1725, as I
show in detail in the following catalogue.   A great

---

[1] The first of Bach's works to be engraved was the Mühlhausen
Cantata, ' Gott ist mein König ' (parts only).   It was published in
1708, when Bach was twenty-three years old.   Forkel refers to
Partita I. in the first Part of the 'Clavierübung' (P. bk. 205 p. 4).   It
was engraved in 1726, when Bach was forty-one years old.   In 1731
he republished it, with five others that had appeared in the interval,
in the first Part of the ' Clavierübung ' (P. bks. 205, 206).

[2] Forkel's rather casual critical axioms seem to be as follows :
' Publication postulates excellence ' ; ' An amended MS. implies that
the original text was not a finished work of art.'

many compositions subsequent to 1725, which for reasons easily understood are still in MS., bear too evidently the stamp of perfection to leave us in doubt whether to class them as early essays or as the finished work of an accomplished master.

The following are those of Bach's works which have been engraved :

1. *Clavierübung,* or ' Exercises for the Clavier, consisting of Preludes, Allemandes, Courantes, Sarabandes, Gigues, Minuets, etc., for the Diversion of Amateurs. Opus I. Published by the Composer, 1731.' This was Bach's first published work and contains six Suites. The first of them came out in 1726 ; [1] the others followed in successive years until all were engraved together in 1731.[2] The work was much noticed at the time. Such compositions for the Clavier had not been seen or heard before, and the man who could play them was sure of a success. Our young players to-day would profit by the study of them, so brilliant, agreeable, expressive, and original are they. In the new edition [3] they are entitled, ' Exercises for the Clavier.'

---

[1] It was the first work engraved by Bach himself, though the parts of the Cantata ' Gott ist mein König ' had been published by the Town Council at Mühlhausen in 1708.

[2] The work was published at Leipzig ' in Commission bey Boetii Seel. hinderlassenen Tochter, unter den Rath-hause.' The Suites, or Partitas (P. bks. 205, 206), are in B flat major, C minor, A minor, D major, G major, E minor.

[3] In 1801 Hoffmeister and Kühnel unsuccessfully attempted to publish Bach's works by subscription.

2. *Clavierübung*, or 'Exercises for the Clavier, Part II., consisting of a Concerto in the Italian style and an Overture in the French manner [1] for a Clavier with two manuals. Published by Christopher Weigel, Junior, in Nürnberg.' [2]

3. *Clavierübung*, or 'Exercises for the Clavier, Part III., consisting of various Organ Preludes to the Catechism and other Hymns, composed for the diversion of amateurs and particularly of competent judges of such works. Published by the Composer.' Besides the Preludes and Fugues for the Organ, all of which are masterly, the book contains four Duetti for the Clavier,[3] models of their kind.

4. *Sechs Choräle*, or 'Six Choral Melodies of different kinds, for an Organ with two manuals and pedal. Zella, in the Thuringian Forest. Published by Johann G. Schübler.' [4] They are full of dignity and religious feeling. In some of them, too, we have instances of Bach's original manage-

---

[1] The Partita in B minor (P. bk. 208 p. 20).

[2] The work was published in 1735. The Italian Concerto in F major is published by Novello and P. bk. 207.

[3] The work appeared in 1739. It was intended to contain works for the Organ only; the four Duetti are incongruous and seem to have crept in by mistake. See the scheme of the work discussed in Terry, 'Bach's Chorals,' Part III. The Choral Preludes are in Novello's ed., bk. xvi.

[4] The work was published *circ.* 1747-50. Five of the six movements certainly, and the sixth with practical certainty, are adaptations to the Organ of movements out of Bach's Church Cantatas. See Parry, 'Bach,' p. 535. The Chorals are in Novello's ed., bk. xvi.

ment of the stops.[1] Thus, in the second Choral,
' Wo soll ich fliehen hin,' he gives to the first
manual an 8 foot, to the second a 16 foot, and to
the pedal a 4 foot stop.   The pedal has the *cantus
firmus*.[2]

5. *Clavierübung*, or ' Exercises for the Clavier,
consisting of an Aria with several Variations, for
a Clavier with two manuals.   Published by
Balthasar Schmidt at Nürnberg.' [3]   This admirable work consists of thirty Variations, some
in canon, in a variety of movements and at all
intervals from the unison to the ninth, with easy
flowing melody. It includes a regular four-
part Fugue,[4] several extremely brillant Variations
for two Claviers,[5] and concludes with a Quodlibet,
as it is called, which alone would render its composer immortal, though it is not the best thing in
the volume.[6]

The Variations are models of what such compositions ought to be, though no one has been
so rash as to attempt to follow Bach's footsteps.

[1] See *supra*, p. 65.

[2] Thus the pedal sounds above the part given to the second manual
and is often the topmost part. See Novello's ed., bk. xvi. 4.

[3] Published *circ.* 1742 ; the so-called ' Goldberg Variations.' They
are in P. bk. 209.

[4] Variation No. 10 is a Fughetta in four parts.

[5] Ten of the Variations are marked ' a 2 Clav.,' that is, for two keyboards or manuals: Nos. 8, 11, 13, 14, 17, 20, 23, 25, 26, 28.   Nos. 5,
7, 29 are marked ' a 1 ovvero 2 Clav.'

[6] The movement is constructed upon two merry folk-songs, ' Kraut
and Rüben haben mich vertrieben,' and ' Ich bin so lang nicht bei dir
gewest.'

We owe them to Count Kaiserling, formerly Russian Ambassador at the Saxon Electoral Court, who frequently visited Leipzig with Goldberg, already mentioned [1] among Bach's pupils. The Count was a great invalid and suffered from insomnia. Goldberg lived in the Ambassador's house, and slept in an adjoining room, to be ready to play to him when he was wakeful. One day the Count asked Bach to write for Goldberg some Clavier music of a soothing and cheerful character, that would relieve the tedium of sleepless nights. Bach thought a set of Variations most likely to fulfil the Count's needs, though, on account of the recurrence of the same basic harmony throughout, it was a form to which he had hitherto paid little attention. Like all his compositions at this period, however, the Variations are a masterpiece, and are the only example he has left us of this form. [2] The Count always called them 'my Variations' and was never weary of hearing them. For long afterwards, when he could not sleep, he would say, 'Play me one of my Varia-

[1] See *supra*, p. 101.

[2] In fact Bach wrote the early 'Aria variata alla maniera Italiana' (Peters bk. 215, p. 12) for the Clavier. For the Organ he wrote four sets of Variations upon as many Choral melodies (Novello bk. xix.). But all except the Goldberg Variations are youthful works, and in his maturity Bach clearly had no liking for the form. The theme of the Goldberg Variations, moreover, is itself a youthful idea ; at least it dates back to as early as 1725, and is found in A. M. Bach's 'Notenbuch' (No. 26, Aria in G major).

tions, Goldberg.' Perhaps Bach was never so well rewarded for any composition as for this. The Count gave him a golden goblet containing one hundred louis d'ors, though, as a work of art, Bach would not have been overpaid had the present been a thousand times as large. It may be observed, that in the engraved copy of the Variations there are serious mistakes, which the composer has corrected in his own copy.[1]

6. *Einige kanonische Veränderungen*, ' Canonic Variations on the Christmas Hymn ' Vom Himmel hoch da komm ich her,' for an Organ with two manuals and pedal. Published at Nürnberg by Balthasar Schmidt.' The work contains five canonic variations of the utmost ingenuity.[2]

7. *Musikalisches Opfer*, or ' A Musical Offering,' dedicated to Frederick II., King of Prussia. The theme received by Bach from the King [3] is treated first as a three-part Fugue under the acrostic title ' Ricercare ' (*Regis iussu cantio et reliqua canonica arte resoluta*). There follows a six-part ' Ricercare ' and ' Thematis regii elaborationes canonicae '

---

[1] There is no reference to these corrigenda in the B.G. edition.

[2] The work has been referred to already in connection with Bach's membership of Mizler's Society (*supra*, p. 112). It was composed presumably *circ.* 1746 and in point of technical skill is the most brilliant of Bach's instrumental works. Forkel states that it was engraved after June 1747, when Bach joined Mizler's Society. Spitta (iii. 295) is of opinion that it was already engraved by then. It is in bk. xix. of Novello's edition.

[3] *Supra*, p. 25.

of various kinds.[1]   The work includes a Trio for Flute, Violin, and Clavier upon the same subject.[2]

8. *Die Kunst der Fuge*, or ' The Art of Fugue.' This work, unique of its kind, did not appear till about 1752, after Bach's death, though the greater part of it had been engraved by his sons during his lifetime.[3] Marpurg,[4] the leading German musical critic of that day, contributed a preface to this edition which contains many just observations on the value and utility of such treatises.[5] But, being too good for the general public, the work found only a small circulation among those who discerned its merit and eagerly bought copies.

The presentation copy of the work, which Bach sent to Frederick along with a dedicatory letter (July 7, 1747), is in the Berlin Amalienbibliothek and proves that only the first third of the work, as far as the ' Ricercare a sei voci' (see B.G. XXXI. (2)) was sent then. The latter and the remaining canons were dispatched subsequently probably by the hand of C. P. E. Bach. The six-part Ricercare was a particular compliment to the King. Frederick had desired Bach on his visit to play a Fugue in six parts but left it to the player to select his theme. Bach now employed the ' thema regium ' for the purpose. The first reissue of the work was by Breitkopf and Haertel in 1832. Peters (bk. 219) brought it out in 1866. See Schweitzer, i. 417 ff. and Spitta, iii. 191 ff. and 292.

[2] In C minor (P. bk. 237 p. 3).

[3] The statement is inaccurate. The work was written for the most part in 1749 and the greater part of it was prepared for engraving by Bach himself during his last illness. None of his elder sons was with him at his death, and the blunders that disfigure the engraved copy show that they clumsily finished their father's work. It is in P. bk. 218.

[4] Friedrich Wilhelm Marpurg, b. 1718, d. 1795.

[5] The work was published shortly after Bach's death, but had no sale. C. P. E. Bach then commissioned Marpurg to write a preface, and the new edition was published at the Leipzig Fair, Easter, 1752. In four years only about thirty copies were sold. See Spitta, iii. 197 ff. and Schweitzer, i. 423 ff.

The plates were never used again and eventually were sold [1] by Bach's heirs at the price of old copper. Written by a man of Bach's transcendent genius, and commended as a masterpiece by a critic so highly regarded as Marpurg, a work of this kind, if published in any other country than Germany, would have passed through at least ten editions by now, if only at the bidding of patriotism. But in Germany not a sufficient number of copies was sold to pay for the plates used in engraving the work !

The work consists of fugal Variations planned on the most elaborate scale.[2] The composer's intention was to show in what a variety of ways the same theme can be treated fugally. The Variations (here called 'Contrapunctus')[3] are complete Fugues upon the same theme. The last Fugue of all has three subjects, in the third of which the composer signs his name, B A C H.[4]

[1] In 1756. See C. P. E. Bach's advertisement in Felix Grenier, p. 232.

[2] The work contains six Fugues and four canons upon the same theme; an unfinished Fugue 'a tre soggetti,' the first four notes of the third of which spell B A C H; and the Choral Prelude 'Wenn wir in höchsten Nöthen sein.'

[3] Schweitzer explains: 'His purpose in this work being a purely theoretical one, Bach writes the Fugues out in score, and calls them "counterpoints."'

[4]

B   A   C   H

Bach was prevented from finishing it by the disorder of his eyes, and as an operation brought no relief the movement was never completed. It is said that Bach intended to introduce four themes into it and to bring it to an impressive conclusion by inverting them all. All the Fugues in the work are equally smooth and melodious.

To make up for the unfinished Fugue Bach concluded the work with a Choral Prelude upon the tune ' Wenn wir in höchsten Nöthen sein,' which he dictated to his son-in-law, Altnikol, a few days before his death.[1] Of the extraordinary skill it displays I do not speak, save to remark that even in his last illness it proclaims Bach's skill undiminished. The pious resignation and devotion that characterise it move me deeply whenever I play it. Nor should I find it easy to say which I had rather had been omitted, the Choral Prelude, or the conclusion of the unfinished Fugue.

9. Lastly, after Bach's death, his four-part Chorals were collected by his son, Carl Philipp Emmanuel, and were published by Birnstiel (Berlin and Leipzig), Part I. in 1765, Part II. in 1769.[2] Each Part contains one hundred Chorals,

---

[1] *Supra,* p. 27. The movement is in N. bk. 17 p. 85. It is not certain that Bach intended the Prelude or the unfinished Fugue to be included.

[2] C. P. E. Bach was only concerned with the first volume. Erk, in his edition of the ' Choralgesänge,' conjectures that Kirnberger was responsible for the second.

mostly taken from the composer's church Cantatas.

More recently Kirnberger edited, in four volumes, a collection of Bach's Chorals. They are published by Breitkopf.[1]

Bach's works, still in MS., consist of compositions for the Clavier, Organ, with and without other instruments, Strings, and the voice. I will enumerate them in that order.

I. Compositions for the Clavier

1. *Six Little Preludes for Beginners.*[2]

2. *Fifteen Two-part Inventions.* An Invention is a musical theme so constructed that by imitation and inversion a whole movement can be evolved from it. The subject having been first stated, the rest develops naturally out of it. For the instruction of a young Clavier player these fifteen Inventions are of great value, seeing that the composer has been careful not only to provide exercises for both hands but for every finger as

---

[1] The four volumes were published at Leipzig between 1784-87. Spitta states that C. P. E. Bach was the editor. Erk joins Kirnberger with him in that position. As C. P. E. Bach died in 1788 Kirnberger's association with the work is probable, especially if he had already been responsible for the 1769 volume.

[2] Bach's Clavier school consisted of eighteen Preludes for beginners (all in B.G. xxxvi.); the two-part and three-part Inventions; and the 'Well-tempered Clavier.' The six Preludes mentioned by Forkel, and which alone he knew, were published by him for the first time. Seven more are found in Wilhelm Friedemann's 'Clavierbüchlein' (B.G. xlv (1)), and the remaining five have survived in texts handed down by others of Bach's pupils. The eighteen are in P. bk. 200.

well. They were composed at Cöthen in 1723, with a long title which begins : ' An honest Guide, in which lovers of the Clavier are shown a clear method of playing correctly in two parts,' etc.[1]

It cannot be denied that, among other blemishes, the Inventions occasionally exhibit melodic poverty and roughness. But finding them useful to his pupils, Bach eventually revised them and removed from them everything that offended his maturer taste, so that they now stand as masterpieces of pure music. Moreover they are invaluable exercises for the fingers and hands and are sound instructors of taste. There is no better introduction to Bach's larger works than they afford.

3. *Fifteen three-part Inventions*, also called Symphonies. They were written for the same purpose as the Inventions, but are more advanced.[2]

4. ' *The Well-tempered Clavier*, or, Preludes and Fugues in all tones and semitones, composed for the profit and use of young musicians desirous of knowledge, as also for those who are skilled already in this *studio*.' Part I. was finished in 1722. Part II., like Part I., contains twenty-four Preludes and twenty-four Fugues in every key,

---

[1] The Autograph was written at Cöthen and is dated 1723. It also contains the fifteen Symphonies, or three-part Inventions mentioned in paragraph 3. Both Inventions and Symphonies are in P. bk. 201. According to Spitta (ii. 57 n.) the Inventions were published at Leipzig in 1763. See also Schweitzer, i. 328 ff.

[2] See the previous note.

and was composed at a later period.[1] Every number of it, from first to last, is a masterpiece. In Part I., however, certain Preludes and Fugues bear marks of immaturity and are included probably only in order to complete the series. But here again Bach eventually corrected whatever seemed to him lacking in finish. He altered or rewrote entire passages, so that in the later texts few movements are not perfect. Among these few I reckon the Fugues in A minor,[2] G major and G minor,[3] C major,[4] F major and F minor.[5] The rest are excellent, some of them so superlatively good as to be not inferior to those in Part II.[6] Even Part II., for all its original perfection, has been improved by the composer, as may be observed by comparing the original and later texts. Both Parts contain treasures of art not to be found outside Germany.

[1] The second Part was compiled in 1744 and Bach's Autograph of it, though not the earliest Autograph, is in the British Museum. See Schweitzer, i. 331 ff. and Spitta, ii. 161 ff. The whole work is in P. bks. 1. 2; or 1*a*, 1*b*; or 2790*a*, 2790*b*.

[2] No. 20. Spitta (ii. 164) attributes it to the years 1707 or 1708. Schweitzer (i. 332) also regards it as a youthful piece written, moreover, for the pedal Clavicembalo.

[3] Nos. 15 and 16. Spitta, admitting that the two do not rank with the most interesting in the collection, finds no indication of their being of different date from the best movements.

[4] No. 1. Here Spitta (ii. 165 n.) challenges Forkel.

[5] Nos. 11 and 12. In regard to No. 12 (F minor) Spitta holds Forkel to be in error. As to No. 11, he expresses the same opinion as in note 3, *supra*.

[6] The date 1744 places the second Part among Bach's latest compositions. On the other hand, like the first Part, it contained work of earlier date.

5. *Chromatic Fantasia and Fugue.*[1] I have taken considerable pains to discover a similar piece of music by Bach, but without success. The Fantasia is unique and unequalled. Wilhelm Friedemann sent it to me from Brunswick inscribed with these words by a mutual friend : 'Anbey kommt an etwas Musik von Sebastian, sonst genannt : *Fantasia chromatica* ; bleibt schön in alle Saecula.'

It is remarkable that this piece, for all its technical skill, appeals to the most unpractised hearer, if it is performed at all tolerably.

6. A *Fantasia in C minor.* It is not of the same character as the preceding work, but resembles rather the Allegro of a Sonata. It is divided into two parts, but must be played as a single movement. It is an excellent work, and in old copies an unfinished Fugue follows, which, however, cannot belong to it.[2] The first thirty bars certainly are by Bach, for they are marked by an extremely bold use of augmented and diminished intervals and their inversions, in three-part harmony. None but Bach attempted such things.

[1] Chromatic Fantasia and Fugue in D minor (P. bk. 207 p. 4). It probably dates from *circ.* 1720-23.

[2] The MS. was discovered in 1876 and is now at Dresden. It was written *circ.* 1738 and disproves Forkel's conjecture that the Fugue did not belong to the Fantasia and is only partially by Bach. The Fugue contains forty-seven bars. As the Autograph is a fair copy the Fugue cannot be called unfinished. See Spitta, iii. 182. The Fantasia is in P. bk. 207 p. 50; the Fugue in P. bk. 212 p. 88. See B.G. xxxvi., xxxviii., and xlii. for other Clavier Fantasias.

The rest of the movement seems to have been added by another hand and bears no trace of Bach's style.

7. *Six large Suites,* consisting of Preludes, Allemandes, Courantes, Sarabandes, etc. They are known as the 'English Suites,' because the composer wrote them for an Englishman of rank.[1] All of them are of great merit as works of art, and some movements, in particular the Gigues of the fifth and sixth Suites, are perfect masterpieces of harmony and melody.

8. *Six small Suites,* consisting of Allemandes, Courantes, etc. They are generally called the 'French Suites,' because they are written in the French style.[2] The composer is intentionally less academic in them than in his larger Suites, and their melodies are more than usually pleasant and agreeable. In particular the fifth Suite deserves to be noticed : all its movements are most melodious, and in the concluding Gigue

[1] The true explanation seems to be that the Prelude of the first Suite (A major) is based upon a Gigue by Charles Dieupart (d. *circ.* 1740), a popular teacher and composer in England. The words 'fait pour les Anglois,' which head the A major Suite in an early MS., have been wrongly interpreted as applying to the whole set of six. They merely indicate Dieupart's borrowed Gigue. See Grove, vol. i. 701, and Parry, 'J. S. Bach,' p. 463. A copy of the work exists, of date 1724-27, made by one of Bach's pupils. But the composition of the Suites may certainly be assigned to the Cöthen period. They are published in P. bks. 203, 204.

[2] The French Suites undoubtedly date back to the Cöthen period, since they figure, though incomplete, in the 'Notenbuch' of A. M. Bach (1722). They are published in P. bk. 202.

only consonant intervals, especially thirds and sixths, are used.

These are Bach's principal works for the Clavier which can be considered classics.[1] A great number of single Suites,[2] Toccatas and Fugues,[3] besides those already mentioned, have great and varying merit, but are youthful works.[4] At the most, ten or twelve of them seem to me worth preserving, some of them because they would be useful as finger exercises, for which their author originally intended them, others because they are at least better than similar works by other composers. As an exercise for the fingers of both hands I particularly single out a Fugue in A minor,[5] in which the composer has been at great pains to write florid passages in order to give equal strength and suppleness to both hands. For beginners a little two-part Fugue [6] should also prove useful. It is melodious, flowing, and not at all old-fashioned.

---

[1] Forkel's incomplete catalogue may be compared with the Bachgesellschaft volumes III., XIII. (2), XIV., XXV. (1), XXXI. (2), XXXVI., XLII., XLIII. (1 and 2), XLV. (1). See generally Schweitzer, ch. 15, and Pirro, pp. 218 ff.

[2] P. bks. 205, 206, 208, 212 (fragment in F minor), 214, 215, 1959.

[3] P. bks. 200, 210, 211, 212, 214, 215, 1959.

[4] For the most part these youthful works will be found in B.G. XXXVI.

[5] P. bk. 207 p. 16.

[6] In C minor (P. bk. 200 p. 10).

II. Music for the Clavier with other Instruments

1. *Six Sonatas for Clavier with Violin obbligato.*
Composed at Cöthen, they are among Bach's
masterpieces in this form and display fugal and
canonic writing which is both natural and full of
character. The Violin part needs a master to
play it ; for Bach knew the capabilities of the
instrument and spared it as little as the Clavier.
The six Sonatas are in the keys of B minor, A
major, E major, C minor, F minor, and G major.[1]

2. *Several Sonatas for Harpsichord and Violin,*[2]
Harpsichord and Flute,[3] *Harpsichord and Viol
da Gamba.*[4] They are admirably written and
most of them are pleasant to listen to even to-
day.[5]

3. *Several Concertos for the Clavier and other
instruments.* They contain real gems of art
but are antiquated in form.[6]

[1] In P. bks. 232, 233.

[2] Suite in A major (P. bk. 236), Sonata in E minor (P. bk. 236),
Fugue in G minor (P. bk. 236), four Inventions (P. bk. 2957), Sonata
in G minor (BG. IX. 274 ; not in P.), Sonata in C major for 2 Violins
and Clavier (P. bk. 237).

[3] There are six Sonatas for Flute and Clavier, in B minor, E flat
major, A minor, C major, E minor, E major (P. bks. 234, 235).

[4] There are three Sonatas for Clavier and Gamba, in G major,
D major, G minor (P. bk. 239).

[5] Forkel omits two Sonatas for Violin, Flute, and Clavier, in G major
and C minor (both in P. bk. 237).

[6] As Forkel mentions in secs. 4, 5, 6 the Concertos for two, three,
and four Claviers, perhaps he had in mind here seven Concertos for
Clavier and Orchestra (P. bks. 248-254). A Concerto for Clavier,

4. *Two Concertos for two Claviers,* with an accompaniment of two Violins, Viola, and Violoncello. The first, in C minor,[1] has an antique flavour. But the second, in C major,[2] is as fresh as if it had been written yesterday.[3] It may be played without the String quartet and still sounds admirable. The final Allegro is a majestic movement and strictly fugal. Compositions of this form were first perfected, indeed, we may conjecture, were first attempted, by Bach. At least, I have met with only a single example by another composer that may perhaps be older— namely, Pachelbel of Nürnberg's Toccata, as he called it. Pachelbel, however, was a contemporary of Bach and may have taken the idea from him. However, his work is not worth considering. One instrument merely repeats the other's phrases without being at all concertante. It almost seems as if Bach at this period had made up his mind to discover what could be done with any number of parts. Having already written for a

Violin, Flute, and Orchestra (P. bk. 255 p. 4) in A minor also should be mentioned. Also an Overture, in G minor, for Clavier and Strings (B.G. XLV. (1) p. 190; not in P.)

[1] P. bk. 257 p. 4.   [2] P. bk. 256 p. 4.

[3] There are, in fact, three Concertos for two Claviers and Orchestra : two in C minor and one in C major. Forkel refers to only one of the former and regards it as antiquated by comparison with the one in C major. Spitta (iii. 144) attributes the C major to 1730. Forkel's C minor in its original form was a Concerto for two Violins, now lost. The other C minor Concerto is identical with the Concerto in D minor for two Violins and is in P. 257b. Spitta (iii. 138) dates it 1736. See Schweitzer, i. 413.

single solo instrument music which required no accompaniment, he next experimented in dividing his material between as large a number of solo instruments as possible. Hence the Concertos for two Claviers were followed by

5. *Two Concertos for three Claviers* with an accompaniment of Strings.[1] These Concertos present a remarkable characteristic: besides the concertante combination of three Claviers, the stringed instruments also have concertante parts distinct from the accompaniment. It is difficult to realise the art involved in this achievement. For, in spite of their technical skill, the two works are so delicate, full of character, and expressive, that the composer might be treating a simple melody (note particularly the Concerto in D minor). Words are inadequate to express the admiration they arouse. But Bach was not satisfied. Hence he wrote

6. *A Concerto for four Claviers* and four stringed instruments.[2] I cannot judge the effect of this composition, for I have never been able to get together the four instruments and four performers

[1] In D minor and C major (P. bks. 258, 259). The tradition is that Bach wrote these two Concertos in order to play them with his elder sons. Spitta (iii. 144) finds the tradition trustworthy. Hence the two works must have been written by *c.* 1733 at latest, before the sons left home. See also Schweitzer, i. 414.

[2] In A minor (P. bk. 260). This is not an original composition, but is an arrangement by Bach of a Vivaldi Concerto for four Violins. Spitta (iii. 149) assigns it to the same period as the Concertos for three Claviers, *c.* 1733. See B.G. XLIII. (1) *infra.*

it requires.   But that it is admirably written can be seen from the parts.

III. COMPOSITIONS FOR THE ORGAN

The pedal is the distinctive feature of the Organ which places it above all other instruments, and gives it its magnificence, sonority, and majesty. Deprive it of the pedal and you take from it the solemn and imposing tones which are its distinctive utterance, reducing it to the level of a ' positiv,' or Chamber-organ, an instrument relatively insignificant.

But an Organ equipped with a pedal must be able to employ it in its full compass,[1] and both composer and organist must know the proper use of it.   No one excelled Bach in this knowledge. Not only is his rich harmony and melody singularly adapted to the instrument, but he gave the pedal a part of its own, even in his early compositions.   Yet it was only gradually that he mastered its technique; for his Organ masterpieces belong to the period in which those for the Clavier began to be classics.   His early and immature Organ works are widely dispersed; for as soon as a composer begins to be distinguished everybody is anxious to possess a specimen of his art.   Public curiosity, however, generally dies down long before a composer comes to maturity,

[1] The pedal on the small German Organ had only the compass of an octave.

particularly if his work is over the heads of the public. And this seems to have been Bach's fortune. Consequently his mature Organ works are less familiar than his early efforts. The latter, however, cannot possibly be admitted to a 'correct and critical' edition of his works, and I mention here only those whose merit is as incontestable as that of the Clavier works enumerated in the preceding paragraphs.

Bach's finest Organ music falls into three groups :

1. *The Great Preludes and Fugues,* with obbligato pedal. Their number cannot be stated, but I believe it not to exceed a dozen.[1] At least, after prolonged search I have not been able to collect more than that number.[2] To these I must add a very clever and original Passacaglia, which,

[1] The Great Preludes and Fugues are, with one exception, in B.G. xv. The Prelude and Fugue in E flat was published by Bach in the third Part of the 'Clavierübung.' Its Fugue is known as the 'St. Anne's.'

[2] From the figures printed by Forkel the twelve can be identified as follows (the references in parentheses are to the Novello edition of Bach's Organ works) :

Prelude and Fugue in C minor, the ' Great ' (bk. vii. 64).
    Do.   do.   A minor,   do.   (bk. vii. 42).
    Do.   do.   G major,   do.   (bk. viii. 112).
    Do.   do.   E minor.   do.   (bk. viii. 98).
    Do.   do.   B minor,   do.   (bk. vii. 52).
    Do.   do.   C major.   do.   (bk. ix. 156).
    Do.   do.   D minor (bk. ix. 150).
    Do.   do.   C major (bk. iii. 70).
Toccata and Fugue in D minor (bk. x. 196).
    Do.   do.   F major (bk. ix. 176).
Prelude and Fugue in G minor (bk. viii. 120).
    Do.   do.   E minor (bk. ii. 44).

however, seems suitable rather for a two-manual Clavicembalo and pedal than for the Organ.[1]

2. *Preludes on Choral Melodies.* It was at Arnstadt that Bach began to compose Variations on Choral melodies, under the title 'Partite diverse.'[2] Most of them can be played on the manuals alone. Those which I include here are an exception and require the obbligato pedal. Their number may amount to one hundred. I myself possess above seventy, and more survive elsewhere.[3] No other Choral Preludes approach

[1] The Passacaglia in C minor (Novello bk. 10 p. 214) was written originally for the Clavicembalo and pedal. It belongs to the later Weimar period, *i.e. circ.* 1715. See Spitta, i. 588 and Schweitzer, i. 280.

[2] They are all printed in Novello bk. 19, and are three in number, on the melodies 'Christ, der du bist der helle Tag,' 'O Gott, du frommer Gott,' and 'Sei gegrüsset, Jesu gütig.' The pedal is only required in one movement of the first, in none of the second, and considerably in the third. Without question all three date from Bach's earliest period, but whether they were written at Arnstadt or Lüneburg cannot be stated.

[3] The fullest collection of these miscellaneous Organ Choral Preludes is in B.G. XL. Not counting variant readings they number fifty-two, besides two fragments and thirteen of doubtful authenticity, of which two are sets of Variations. The Novello edition contains fifty-two in bks. 18 and 19. To these must be added the 'Eighteen' Preludes on Choral Melodies, which Forkel nowhere mentions, as well as the third Part of the 'Clavierübung,' the 'Schübler Chorals,' and the Variations on 'Vom Himmel hoch,' to which he has already made reference in the first section of this chapter. As he does not mention it specifically, it is to be inferred that Forkel was ignorant of the existence of the 'Orgelbüchlein'; otherwise he could hardly have failed to introduce it in this section. All Bach's Choral Preludes, miscellaneous and in collections made by himself, are in Novello's edition, bks. 15-19. A useful key to their melodies is provided by bk. 20. For more detailed information see Terry, 'Bach's Chorals,' Part III.

them in religious feeling, dignity, and sublimity of expression. I cannot notice them individually ; they are too numerous. Besides the larger, there is a great number of shorter and easier ones, particularly useful for young players. MSS. of them exist in considerable number.[1]

3. *Six Sonatas*, or Trios, for two manuals and an obbligato pedal.[2] Bach wrote them for his eldest son, Wilhelm Friedemann, whom they helped to become the great performer he was when I knew him. It is impossible to overpraise their beauty. Bach composed them when he was in the full vigour of his powers, and they may be considered his *chef d'œuvre* in this form.[3] He also wrote other Organ Sonatas, the MSS. of which are in various collections. They are fine compositions, though they do not equal the Six in merit.[4]

---

[1] The large number of MSS. of many of the miscellaneous Preludes is made evident in the introduction to B.G. XL.

[2] The Sonatas in E flat major, C minor, and D minor are in N. bk. 4 ; E minor, C major, G major in N. bk. 5.

[3] The so-called ' Sonatas ' were actually written for a Clavicembalo with two manuals and a pedal. Bach's Autograph of them belonged to his second son and an earlier copy of them to Wilhelm Friedemann. Both are now in the Berlin Royal Library. Friedemann went to Dresden as Organist in 1733 and Spitta is of opinion that the whole of the six Sonatas were in existence by or soon after 1727. If so, they must be regarded as the outcome of Bach's early years at Leipzig. See Spitta, iii. 212 ff. and Schweitzer, i. 278.

[4] None are extant. Spitta, iii. 213 n., conjectures that Forkel refers to the Trios in D minor and C minor (N. bks. 2 p. 54, 12 p. 108) and the Pastorale in F major (N. bk. 12 p. 102.) His incomplete knowledge of the Organ works is revealed by Appendix v. *infra.*

IV. INSTRUMENTAL MUSIC

There are few instruments for which Bach did not write. In his day it was usual to play a Concerto or instrumental Solo during the Communion office.[1] Bach composed many of these pieces himself, and always with a view to their improving the technique of the player. Most of them are lost. But two important works of another kind survive and to some extent compensate us. They are :

1. *Six Solos for Violin,* unaccompanied.[2]
2. *Six Solos for Violoncello,* unaccompanied.[3]

The Violin Solos have long been considered by the finest players to be the best instructor for the instrument. The Violoncello Solos are equally effective.[4]

---

[1] This is a pure conjecture and Schweitzer scouts it (i. 416 n.).

[2] The oldest copy of them dates from *circ.* 1720; they belong therefore to the late Cöthen period. The 1720 MS. is in A. M. Bach's handwriting and was discovered in 1814 at Petrograd among old papers about to be sent away to a butter dealer. The Sonatas are in P. bk. 228.

[3] They also date from the Cöthen period and are in P. bk. 238a, 238b.

[4] Forkel omits to mention the Brandenburg Concertos (P. bks. 261-266) ; the Overtures in C major (P. bk. 267), B minor (P. bk. 268), D major (P. bk. 269), D major (P. bk. 2068) ; and the Violin Concertos in A minor (P. bk. 229), E major (P. bk. 230), and (for two Violins) in D minor (P. bk. 231). In B.G. xxi. (1) is a Symphonic movement, in D major, for Violin and orchestra. A Sinfonia in F major (B.G. xxxi. 96) is another version of the first Brandenburg Concerto. The Clavier Concertos have been mentioned *supra.*

V. Vocal Music

1. Five complete sets of church Cantatas for the Sundays and Festivals of the year.[1]

2. Five compositions for Holy Week, one of which is for double chorus.[2]

3. Several Oratorios,[3] Masses,[4] a ' Magnificat,'

[1] The set of five is complete only for Christmas Day, Feast of the Circumcision, Whitsunday (one of the five is of doubtful authenticity), Purification of the B.V.M., and Feast of St. Michael the Archangel. See Terry, ' Bach's Chorals,' Part II. 2 ff.

[2] In giving the number of ' Passions ' as five, Forkel repeats the statement of the ' Nekrolog.' The number corresponds with the five sets of Church Cantatas which Bach is known to have written. It is, however, exceedingly doubtful whether Bach wrote more than four ' Passions.' Only those according to St. Matthew and St. John have come down to us from C. P. E. Bach, who was left the Autographs of both by his father. The ' St. John Passion ' was first performed in 1724 and the ' St. Matthew Passion ' in 1729. Picander, Bach's librettist, certainly wrote two other Passion texts, one of which was written for Good Friday 1725, and the second, based on St. Mark's Gospel, was actually performed at St. Thomas', Leipzig, on Good Friday 1731. Spitta (ii. 505) gives good reason to hold that Bach's music for this Passion was adapted from the ' Trauer-Ode,' which he had written in 1727 in memory of Queen Christiane Eberhardine. But of the 1725 ' Passion ' there is no trace. If it ever existed, its loss probably may be assigned to Wilhelm Friedemann's carelessness, to whom presumably it was assigned in the division of Bach's property after his death. But even so, we have no more than four ' Passions.' There exists, however, a fifth ' Passion according to St. Luke,' which is undoubtedly in Bach's Autograph, and which Spitta is inclined to attribute to Bach himself. It is published by Breitkopf and Haertel, but is generally regarded as being by another composer than Bach, who probably copied it for use at Leipzig. On the whole matter see Spitta, ii. 504 ff., Schweitzer, chap. xxvi., and the Bach-Jahrbuch for 1911 (Publications of the New Bachgesellschaft xii. (2)).

[3] Other than the ' Passions,' the only Oratorios are the ' Christmas Oratorio' (1734), the ' Easter Oratorio ' (c. 1736), and ' Ascension Oratorio ' (c. 1735).

[4] Besides the B minor Mass (1733-? 38) Bach wrote four miscalled

settings of the ' Sanctus,[1] compositions for birthdays and Saints' Days,[2] funerals,[3] marriages,[4] and
some Italian Cantatas.[5]

4. Several Motets for single and double
chorus.[6]

Most of these works are now dispersed. The
Church Cantatas were divided between his elder
sons after their composer's death. Wilhelm
Friedemann had the larger share because, being
organist at Halle, he could make use of them.
Later, circumstances compelled him to part with
them gradually. I know of no other collection of
Bach's larger choral works. There exist, however,
eight or ten Motets for double chorus, but they
are dispersed in various hands.[7] In the collection

' short ' Masses, in F major, A major, G minor, and G major. They
all belong to the Leipzig period (c. 1739).

[1] Besides the setting of the Sanctus in the B minor Mass there are
four detached settings, in C major, D major, D minor, and G major.
Of these only that in D major is probably by Bach (c. 1723).

[2] The music for Saints' Days is included in the church Cantatas.
For the Birthday Odes see supra, Chap. IIA.

[3] Besides the ' Trauer-Ode,' three or four of the church Cantatas
and certainly three of the Motets were written for funerals. See
Terry, op. cit., pp. 24, 44.

[4] Among the church Cantatas there are at least five for use at
weddings. Bach wrote also three secular wedding Cantatas: ' Weichet
nur, betrübte Schatten' (c. 1730); ' O holder Tag' (? 1749); the third
(1728) has disappeared.

[5] Two Italian Cantatas—' Amore traditore ' and ' Non sa che sia
dolore '—have come down to us. A third, ' Andro dall colle al prato,'
is lost. See B.G. XI. (ii.), XXIX.

[6] Only six are genuine. See infra, p. 141.

[7] Of the Motets that have come down to us as his, only six are
Bach's. Forkel mentions five of them in secs. 7 and 8 of the next

bequeathed by the Princess Amalia of Prussia to the Joachimsthal Gymnasium at Berlin there are some of Bach's vocal compositions.[1] Their number is not considerable, but among them are the following :

1. Twenty-one Church Cantatas.[2] In one of them, set to the words, ' Schlage doch, gewünschte Stunde,' [3] the composer introduces a bell obbligato. From that fact we may conclude that the Cantata was not composed in the period of Bach's maturity,[4] for the use of bells is of doubtful taste.

2. Two Masses for five voices with instrumental accompaniment.[5]

3. A Mass for double chorus, the first being

paragraph ; he omits ' Lobet den Herrn, alle Heiden.' In 1802-3 Breitkopf and Haertel published six Motets—the five mentioned by Forkel and another, ' Ich lasse dich nicht,' of which Bach made a copy, but whose composer actually was Johann Christoph Bach. We know that Bach composed at least one Latin Motet for double chorus, and Friedemann's share of his father's autographs may have contained it and others known to Forkel but no longer extant.

[1] The Amalienbibliothek of the Joachimsthal Gymnasium, Berlin, contains one of the most important Bach collections, but it has long been superseded by the Royal Library there as the chief repository of Bach's Autographs.

[2] The Amalienbibliothek has only one Autograph, namely, Cantata 34, ' O ewiges Feuer.' The rest are early copies.

[3] Cantata 53. No Autograph of this Cantata exists, and the copies from which the B.G. edition was printed are in the Amalienbibliothek.

[4] On the contrary, the Cantata belongs to the Leipzig period, 1723-34.

[5] None of the four ' short' Masses is in five parts. All have instrumental accompaniments. The autograph scores of the Masses in A major and G major are in Messrs. Breitkopf and Haertel's possession. Copies of the other two scores, in Altnikol's handwriting, are in the Berlin Royal Library. See Introduction to B.G. VIII.

accompanied by Strings and the second by wind instruments.[1]

4. A ' Passion,' for double Chorus,[2] the text by Picander.[3]

5. A ' Sanctus,' for four voices and instrumental accompaniment.[4]

6. A Motet, for four voices, ' Aus tiefer Noth schrei ich zu dir.' [5]

7. A Motet for five voices, ' Jesu, meine Freude.'

8. Four Motets, for eight voices in double chorus :

    (a) ' Fürchte dich nicht, ich bin dei dir.'

    (b) ' Der Geist hilft unserer Schwachheit auf.'

    (c) ' Komm, Jesu, komm.'

    (d) ' Singet dem Herrn ein neues Lied.' [6]

9. A detached four-part fugal chorus, ' Nimm was dein ist, und gehe hin.' [7]

---

[1] An eight-part Mass in G was performed at a Leipzig Gewandhaus Concert on March 7, 1805, and was published later in the year by Breitkopf and Haertel. The score is admittedly, for the greater part of the work, in Bach's hand and is in the Berlin Royal Library. The publication of the work was under consideration by the Bachgesellschaft in 1858. That it is not by Bach is generally held. It has been attributed to Johann Ludwig Bach (d. 1741). See Genealogical Table II.

[2] The ' St. Matthew Passion.'

[3] A *nom de plume* for Christian Friedrich Henrici (1700-64), who wrote a large number of Bach's Leipzig texts.

[4] Perhaps Forkel indicates the short *Sanctus* in Richter's edition of the *Choralgesänge*, No. 123, or that in B.G. XLI. p. 177.

[5] This is the first Chorus of Cantata No. 38. It is printed as a separate Motet in Erk, No. 150.

[6] Forkel's list is complete except for ' Lobet den Herrn, alle Heiden.'

[7] The opening Chorus of Cantata 144.

10. A bucolic Cantata, with Recitatives, Aria, Duet, and Chorus.   A note is prefixed to it.[1]

On the MS. of the last-named Cantata and of the Mass for double chorus (No. 3 *supra*) there is a note by Kirnberger analysing the skill and merit of the compositions.

---

[1] Forkel refers to the ' Peasant Cantata,' or ' Mer hahn en neue Oberkeet,' performed on August 30, 1742. Forkel clearly was not familiar with Bach's other secular Cantatas. See B.G. XI. (ii.), XX. (ii.), XXIX. The Autograph score of the Peasant Cantata is in the Berlin Royal Library.

CHAPTER X

BACH'S MANUSCRIPTS

IT has been remarked more than once that Bach, throughout his life, devoted much thought to the improvement of his compositions. I have had frequent occasion to compare the original and subsequent texts of his works, and confess to have experienced both surprise and pleasure in observing his care to improve whatever he thought faulty, to make good better, and better perfect. Nothing is more instructive than a collation of this kind, whether to the experienced musician or the instructed amateur. I should like to see a supplement to the complete edition of Bach's works showing these variant readings.[1] The collation would be in the highest degree instructive, and to attempt it is as appropriate to the works of the composer, a poet in sound, as to those of the poet in words.

In Bach's early texts he often repeats a phrase to other words with some melodic variety, in a

---

[1] Forkel's suggestion was carried out, with varying thoroughness, in the Bachgesellschaft edition.

lower or even in the same octave. In his riper
experience he could not tolerate such poverty of
workmanship, and cut out these passages remorse-
lessly, without regard for the number and quality
of the persons who had approved them in their
original state. There occur to me two good
examples of this, the C major and C sharp minor
Preludes in the first part of the ' Well-tempered
Clavier.' Bach revised them so drastically as to
cut them down by one-half, sacrificing passages
that he thought redundant.[1]

In other places Bach tends to be over-concise ;
he expresses an idea, but does not fully develop it.
The best illustration that occurs to me is the
D minor Prelude in the second part of the ' Well-
tempered Clavier.' I possess several texts of it.
In the oldest the first transposition of the theme
in the Bass and several other details essential to
a complete development of the idea are wanting.
A second MS. gives the theme to the Bass wherever
the latter is in a key nearly related to that of the
tonic. In a third MS. these addenda are developed more fully and are joined more skilfully.
But melodic details are present of doubtful
relevance to the rest of the composition. In a
fourth MS. these disappear or are amended, so
that, as we have it, the Prelude stands as one of
the most beautiful and least faulty in the ' Well-
tempered Clavier.' Many people, no doubt, pre-

---

[1] Forkel's judgment is at fault. See Schweitzer, i. 336.

ferred the movement in its original form.   But
Bach was not a man to be influenced by approbation or criticism.   He went on correcting until
he satisfied himself.

In the early part of the seventeenth century it
was the fashion in instrumental music to overload
single notes with ornaments and add florid runs.
Lately it has become the fashion to do so in vocal
music as well.   That Bach shared this disposition
may be inferred from certain pieces that he wrote
in this style.   An instance is the Prelude in
E minor in the first part of the ' Well-tempered
Clavier.'   But he soon returned to his natural
better taste, and altered the movement to the
form in which it is engraved.[1]

Every decade has its own style of melody, distinctive of itself and evanescent.   A composer
must carefully avoid it if he hopes to be listened
to by posterity.   In his young days even Bach
ran upon this rock.   His early compositions for
the Organ, and the two-part ' Inventions ' in their
original form, are full of *fiorituri* such as the taste
of his period approved.   His Organ compositions
remain comparatively untouched, but the ' Inventions ' he closely revised.   The public will soon
be able to compare them in their first and later
forms, as the publishers, with admirable spirit,
have resolved to discontinue the present edition

[1] Also in Wilhelm Friedemann's 'Clavierbüchlein.'   See Schweitzer,
i. 279; Spitta, ii. 165.

and to send out to subscribers a revised one based on Bach's corrected text.

Bach's processes of revision so far mentioned, however, merely correct faults of form, that is, diffuseness or incomplete development of a musical thought. But Bach employed other methods which are less easy to describe because they are more subtle. He often rivets the style and character of a piece by changing a single note, strictly correct grammatically and yet disagreeable to an artist such as himself. Even commonplace passages he could convert into phrases of beauty by the addition or alteration of a single note. Only the most sensitive taste and trained experience can decide in such cases, and Bach possessed both in the highest perfection. He developed them to such a pitch, indeed, that his brain eventually rejected any idea which, in all its properties and relations, did not accord inevitably and naturally with the whole composition. Consequently his later works display such consistency of merit that all of them seem to have been cast complete in a mould, so smooth, facile and abundant is the flow of his rich fancy. It is on the highest summits of the art that harmony and melody find their ideal union, and as yet Bach dwells there in majestic isolation.

CHAPTER XI

IT is surely unnecessary to ask whether that artist is a genius who, in every form of his art, has produced masterpiece after masterpiece, of an originality which sets them above the achievements of all other ages, distinguished also by a wealth of originality and agreeableness that enslaves every hearer. The most fertile fancy, invention inexhaustible, a judgment so nice as to reject intuitively every irrelevant and jarring detail, unerring ingenuity in employing the most delicate and minute resources of his art, along with an unrivalled technique—these qualities, whose expression demands the outpouring of a man's whole soul, are the signboards of genius. The man who cannot find them in Bach's music either is not acquainted with it at all or knows it imperfectly. One needs to be steeped in it thoroughly to appreciate the genius of its author. For the greater the work the closer study is demanded for its apprehension. The butterfly method, a sip here and there, is of little use.

But admirable as were the gifts Bach received

from nature, he could never have become an accomplished genius had he not learned betimes to avoid the rocks on which many artists, some of them perhaps not less gifted than he, too often founder. I will communicate to the reader some scattered thoughts on the subject and conclude this essay with an indication of the characteristics of Bach's genius.

Even the largest natural gifts, coupled with the strongest propensity for a particular art, offer no more than fruitful soil on which that art may thrive by patient cultivation. Industry, the true begetter of every art and science, is an indispensable factor. Not only does it enable genius to master technique, but it stimulates the critical and reflective faculties also. The very ease with which genius acquires and applies the apparatus of musical composition frequently entices it to leap over root principles in its plunge into deeper waters, or to fly before its wings are grown. In such a case, unless genius is guided back to neglected fundamentals and forced to build itself upon the great examples of the past, it will inevitably expend its treasure uselessly and never attain to its promised dimensions. For it is an axiom, that real progress can never be made, nor the highest perfection be attained, if the foundations are insecure. If arduous heights are to be achieved, the easier obstacles must first be approached and overcome. Guided by his own

inexperience no one ever can hope to become
great. He must profit by the practice and example of others.

Bach did not founder on this rock. His soaring
genius attended an equally ardent industry which
incessantly impelled him, whenever he found his
own equipment insufficient, to seek guidance from
others. Vivaldi and his Concertos were the first
from whom he sought counsel. From them he
turned to the principal Organ and Clavier composers of the period. Nothing is more intel-
lectually stimulating than counterpoint, and the
composers Bach studied were distinguished by
their mastery of it, as their fugal writing attests.
Hence Bach's diligent study and imitation of them
pointed his taste and imagination to perceive
wherein himself was lacking and what steps were
needed to take him farther in his art.

A second rock upon which genius often comes
to grief is the public's undiscriminating applause.
To be sure, I do not undervalue public approval
or commend without reserve the remark of a
Greek teacher to his pupil, ' You performed badly,
otherwise the audience would not have applauded
you.' Yet it is none the less true that many
artists are thrown off their balance by exaggerated
and often unmerited plaudits, particularly in their
early careers before they have acquired self-discipline and sound judgment. The public merely
asks for what it can understand, whereas the true

artist ought to aim at an achievement which cannot be measured by popular standards. How, then, can popular applause be reconciled with the true artist's aspirations towards the ideal ? Bach never sought applause, and held with Schiller :

> Kannst du nicht allen gefallen durch deine That und
>   dein Kunstwerk,
> Mach' es wenigen recht ; vielen gefallen ist schlimm.[1]

Like every true artist, Bach worked to please himself in his own way, obeying the summons of his own genius, choosing his own subjects, and finding satisfaction only in the approval of his own judgment. He could count on the applause of all who understood good music, and never failed to receive it. Under what other conditions can sound works of art emerge ? The composer who debases his muse to the popular mood either lacks real genius or, having it, abuses it. For to catch the ear of the public is not a difficult task and merely connotes an agreeable facility. Composers of that class are like artisans who frankly fashion their goods to suit their market. But Bach never condescended to such artifices. The artist, in his judgment, is the dictator of public taste, not its slave. If, as often happened, he was asked to write something simple for the Clavier

---

[1] ' Since you cannot please everybody by your actions and work, strive at least to satisfy a few ; popular appreciation encourages bad art.'—Schiller's ' Votiftafeln.'

he would answer, 'I will do what I can.' He
would choose an easy theme.   But when he began
to develop it he always found so much to say
that the piece soon became anything but simple.
If his attention was drawn to the fact, he would
answer smilingly, 'Practise it well and you will
find it quite easy.   You have as many good fingers
on each hand as I have.'   Nor was he prompted
in this by mere contradictoriness, but exhibited
the true artist spirit.

It was, in fact, the artist temperament that led
Bach to make the great and sublime his goal.
For that reason his music is not merely agreeable,
like other composers', but transports us to the
regions of the ideal.   It does not arrest our attention momentarily but grips us the stronger the
oftener we listen to it, so that after a thousand
hearings its treasures are still unexhausted and
yield fresh beauties to excite our wonder.   Even
the beginner who knows but the A B C of his art
warms with pleasure when he hears Bach's music
and can open his ear and heart to it.   It was the
true artist spirit, too, that guided Bach to unite
majesty and grandeur of design with meticulous
care for detail and the most refined elegance,
characteristics which we rather seek, perhaps, in
works whose object is merely to give pleasure.
Bach held strongly that if the strands are imperfect, the whole design is faulty.   His genius
is sublime and impressive, and he never conde-

scends to be frivolous even when he touches the lighter forms of art.

To conclude : it was the union of astounding genius and indefatigable application that enabled Bach to widen at every point the domain of musical expression. His successors have failed to maintain the art at the level to which he raised it. If Bach was more successful, if he was able to produce great work of convincing beauty and imperishable as a model for those who came after him, we owe it as much to his application as to his genius.

This man, the greatest orator-poet that ever addressed the world in the language of music, was a German ! Let Germany be proud of him ! Yes, proud of him, but worthy of him too !

THE BACH STATUE AT LEIPZIG.

APPENDIX I

CHRONOLOGICAL CATALOGUE OF BACH'S COMPOSITIONS [1]

I. CATALOGUE OF BACH'S COMPOSITIONS PRIOR TO HIS APPOINTMENT TO WEIMAR IN JUNE 1708, in his twenty-fourth year.

VOCAL :—

Motet : Lobet den Herrn, alle Heiden.

CLAVIER [2] :—

Capriccio sopra la lontananza del suo fratello dilettissimo (bk. 208 p. 62) (1704).

Capriccio in honorem Joh. Christoph Bachii, Ohrdruf (bk. 215 p. 34) (c. 1704).

Sonata in D major (bk. 215 p. 44) (c. 1704).[3]

B.G. xxxvi. prints a number of pieces which, in general, may be assigned to Bach's immature years. They are reproduced in Peters' edition :

Book 200 : Fughetta in C minor (p. 10).

Prelude and Fughetta in D minor (p. 40).

Do.   do.   E minor (p. 42).

Do.   do.   A minor (p. 47).

---

[1] The Cantatas are classified under Appendix II.

[2] The references are to Peters' edition. Excepting bk. 1959, which contains pieces of doubtful authenticity, every number printed by Peters is entered in the Chronological Catalogue.

[3] There are three other Sonatas, in A minor, C major, D minor, none of which is an original composition. They are printed in P. bk. 213. The first and second are adaptations of material in Reinken's 'Hortus Musicus.' The third is a transcription of the second Solo Sonata for Violin.

154   JOHANN SEBASTIAN BACH

Fugue in C major (p. 54).
Do.   do.   (p. 56).
Book 207 : Fantasia in C minor (p. 50).
Book 212 :   Do.   do.   (p. 58).
Fugue in D minor (p. 59).
Do.   do.   (p. 61).
Do.   E minor (p. 68).
Book 214 : Prelude and Fughetta in F major (p. 76).
Do.   do.   G major (p. 78).
Prelude in G major (p. 80).
Book 215 : Three Minuets (p. 62).
To these may be added (? authentic) from B.G. xlii. :
Book 212 : Fantasia and Fughetta in B flat major (p. 58).
Do.   do.   D major (p. 60).

ORGAN ¹ :—

Prelude and Fugue in C minor (bk. 2 p. 48) (c. 1704).
Do.   do.   C major (bk. 8 p. 88) (? 1707).²
Do.   do.   the ' Short,' A minor (bk. 10 p. 208).
Fugue in C minor (bk. 12 p. 95) (c. 1704).
Do.   C minor, on a theme by Legrenzi (bk. 10 p. 230)
        (c. 1708).
Do.   B minor, on a theme by Corelli (bk. 3 p. 60).
Do.   D major (bk. 12 p. 83).
Do.   G major (bk. 12 p. 55).
Do.   G major (bk. 12 p. 86).
Do.   G minor (bk. 2 p. 41).
Prelude in A minor (bk. 10 p. 238) (by 1706).
Do.   C major (bk. 12 p. 94).

¹ The references are to Novello's twelve Books of Bach's Organ
Works, edited by J. F. Bridge and J. Higgs. The edition is complete,
and contains every movement included in Alfred Dörffel's ' Thematisches Verzeichniss ' (second edition, 1882) except his No. 24 on p.
72 ; Nos. 6 and 8 on page 85 ; the ' Kleines harmonisches Labyrinth '
(Dörffel, p. 88, figs. 131-33), the genuineness of which is questioned
by Spitta (ii. 43) ; and figs. 136-37 on p. 88. The Novello edition also
follows Rust, against Spitta's judgment, in printing tho ' Fantasia con
Imitazione ' (bk. 12 p. 71) as an Organ instead of as a Clavier piece.
Books 15-19 print the Choral Preludes. See the Peters and Novello
editions collated in Appendix V.
² Printed as a ' Toccata ' in E major in B.G. xv. p. 276.

Fantasia and Fugue in A minor (bk. 12 p. 60).
Fantasias in G major (bk. 9 p. 168 ; bk. 12 p. 75).
Pastorale in F major (bk. 12 p. 102).
Choral Partita : Christ, der du bist der helle Tag (bk. 19 p. 36).
 Do. O Gott, du frommer Gott (bk. 19 p. 44).
 Do. Sei gegrüsset, Jesu gütig (bk. 19 p. 55).
Generally speaking, the Choral Preludes, other than those in the maturer collections made by Bach himself, may be regarded as youthful works (bks. 18, 19).

II. CATALOGUE OF BACH'S COMPOSITIONS AT WEIMAR, 1708-17, from his twenty-fourth to his thirty-third year.

VOCAL :—
 Secular Cantata : Was mir behagt (1716), or, Verlockender Götterstreit.

CLAVIER :—
 Sixteen Concertos after Vivaldi (bk. 217) (c. 1708-12).
 Toccatas in D major (bk. 211 p. 28), G major (bk. 215 p. 19), D minor (bk. 210 p. 68), G minor (bk. 211 p. 4), E minor (bk. 210 p. 23) (c. 1708-12).
 Aria variata alla maniera Italiana (bk. 215 p. 12) (c. 1708-12).
 Prelude and Fugue in A minor (bk. 211 p. 14) (c. 1715).
 Fugues in A major (bk. 215 pp. 52, 57).
 Do. B minor (bk. 214 p. 48).
 Do. A major (bk. 212 p. 66).
 Do. A minor (bk. 212 p. 70).
 Fantasia in G minor (bk. 215 p. 32).
 Do. B minor (bk. 215 p. 41). (For Organ, N. bk. 12 p. 71.)
 Do. D major (bk. 211 p. 28).
 Do. A minor (bk. 215 p. 5) (c. 1710).

ORGAN :—
 Passacaglia and Fugue in C minor (bk. 10 p. 214).
 Four Concertos after Vivaldi (bk. 11).

Eight Short Preludes and Fugues (bk. 1).
Orgelbüchlein (bk. 15) (1717).
Aria in F major (bk. 12 p. 112).
Fantasia con Imitazione (bk. 12 p. 71)
Do.   C major (bk. 12 p. 92).
Do.   C minor (bk. 3 p. 57).
Trio in C minor (bk. 12 p. 108).
Do. D minor (bk. 2 p. 54).
Canzona in D minor (bk. 2 p. 34) (c. 1714).
Allabreve in D major (bk. 2 p. 26).
Prelude and Fugue in C major (bk. 7 p. 74).
Do.   do.   the ' Short,' E minor (bk. 2 p. 44).
Do.   do.   D major (bk. 6 p. 10).
Do.   do.   the ' Great,' A minor (bk. 7 p. 42).
Do.   do.   A major (bk. 3 p. 64).
Do.   do.   the ' Great,' C minor (bk. 7 p. 64).
Do.   do.   F minor (bk. 6 p. 21).
Do.   do.   G major (bk. 7 p. 80).
Do.   do.   G minor (bk. 8 p. 120) (c. 1712).
Toccata and Fugue in D minor (bk. 6 p. 2).
Do.   do.   the ' Great,' C major (bk. 9 p. 137).
Do.   do.   the ' Great,' F major (bk. 9 p. 176).
Do.   do.   the Dorian, D minor (bk. 10 p. 196).
Fantasia and Fugue in C minor (bk. 3 p. 76).
Prelude in G major (bk. 2 p. 30).
Do.   C major (bk. 12 p. 91).
Fugue, the ' Short,' in G minor (bk. 3 p. 84).
Do.   C major (bk. 12 p. 100).

III. CATALOGUE OF BACH'S COMPOSITIONS AT CÖTHEN, 1717-23, from his thirty-third to his thirty-ninth year.

VOCAL :—

Secular Cantata : Durchlaucht'ster Leopold (1717).
Do.   Mit Gnaden bekröne der Himmel die Zeiten (? 1721).
Do.   Weichet nur, betrübte Schatten (?1717-23).[1]

[1] Spitta (ii. 620, 718) mentions a Birthday Cantata written in 1717-1721 (?), the title of which is lost.

CLAVIER :—

Clavier-Büchlein vor Wilhelm Friedemann Bach (1720).
Chromatic Fantasia and Fugue (bk. 207 p. 4) (c. 1720-23).
Clavier-Büchlein vor A. M. Bachin (bk. 1959) (1722).
The Well-tempered Clavier (Part I.) (bk. 2790a) (1722).
Six French Suites (bks. 202 and 2793) (c. 1722).
Six English Suites (bks. 203-4 and 2794-95) (before 1726).
Fantasia and Fugue in A minor (bk. 208 p. 50).
Fugue in A minor (bk. 207 p. 16) (B.G. III. p. 334).
Twelve Little Preludes and Six Preludes for Beginners
    (bks. 200 and 2791) (c. 1722).
Inventions and Symphonies (bks. 201 and 2792) (1723).
Toccatas in F sharp minor and C minor (bk. 210 pp. 30
    and 40).
Suites in A minor, E flat major, E minor, F major, and
    F minor (fragment) (bk. 214 pp. 54, 62, 68; bk. 215 p. 27;
    bk. 212 p. 84).
Prelude and Fugue in E flat major (bk. 214 p. 40).

CHAMBER : [1]—

Six Sonatas (Suites) for Violin Solo (bk. 228) (c. 1720).[2]
Six Sonatas (Suites) for Violoncello Solo (bk. 238a) (c. 1720).
Six Sonatas for Violin and Clavier (bks. 232-33-232a-33a).
Suite in A major for Violin and Clavier (bk. 236).
Four Inventions for Violin and Clavier (bk. 2957).
Sonata in E minor and Fugue in G minor for Violin and
    Clavier (bk. 236) (? early work).
Six Sonatas for Flute and Clavier (bks. 234-35).
Sonata in C major for two Violins and Clavier (bk. 237).
Three Sonatas for Viol da Gamba and Clavier (bk. 239).
Sonata in G major for two Flutes and Clavier (bk. 239 p. 2).
Sonata in G major for Violin, Flute, and Clavier (bk. 237).

ORCHESTRAL : [3]—

Six Brandenburg Concertos (bks. 261-66) (1721).

[1] The references are to Peters' edition.
[2] The D minor contains the famous Chaconne.
[3] The references are to Peters' edition. In the B.G. edition the
Orchestral music is included in the Chamber Music volumes.

Four Suites (Overtures) (bks. 267-69, 2068).[1]
Three Concertos for Violin and Orchestra (bks. 229, 230).[2]
Concerto in D minor for two Violins and Orchestra (bk. 231).[3]

ORGAN :—
Prelude (Fantasia) and Fugue, the ' Great,' in G minor
(bk. 8 p. 127) (? 1720).

IV. CATALOGUE OF BACH'S COMPOSITIONS AT LEIPZIG,
1723-34, from his thirty-ninth to his fiftieth year.

VOCAL :—
Magnificat in D (? 1723).[4]
Sanctus in C major, D major (c. 1723), D minor, and
G major (P. bk. 29b).[5]
St. John Passion (1723).
Trauer-Ode (1727).
St. Matthew Passion (1729).
Mass in B minor (1733-?1738).
Christmas Oratorio (1734).
Three Wedding Chorals (P. bk. 1654).
Motet : Jesu, meine Freude (1723).
Do.   Der Geist hilft unsrer Schwachheit auf (1729).
Do.   Fürchte dich nicht.
Do.   Singet dem Herrn ein neues Lied.

[1] Pirro, p. 228, holds that the first two (C major and B minor) were written at Cöthen and the last two (D major and D major) at Leipzig. Schweitzer (i. 402) regards it as not clear in which period the Overtures were written.

[2] In A minor, E major, G major. The G major figures as the fourth Brandenburg (bk. 264) and as the Clavier Concerto in F major (bk. 248). The A minor and E major were also converted into Clavier Concerti (G minor and D major) (bks. 249, 251). The D minor Clavier Concerto (bk. 254) preserves a lost Violin Concerto in the same key, and the one in F minor (bk. 250) corresponds with a lost Violin Concerto in G minor (bks. 3068, 3069).

[3] Also arranged as a Concerto for two Claviers (C minor) in P. bk. 257b.

[4] Bach wrote another Magnificat, the music of which is lost. See Spitta, ii. 374.

[5] All except the Sanctus in D major are of doubtful authenticity. See Schweitzer, ii. 328 and Spitta, iii. 41 n.

Motet : Komm, Jesu, komm.

Secular Cantata : Der zufriedengestellte Aeolus (1725) ; *also entitled* Blast Lärmen, ihr Feinden (1734).

Do   Vereinigte Zwietracht der wechselnden Saiten (1726), *or,* Auf schmetternde Töne der muntern Trompeten (after 1733).

Do.   Schwingt freudig euch empor ; *also entitled* Die Freude reget sich, *or* Steigt freudig in die Luft (1726).

Do   Entfernet euch, ihr heitern Sterne (1727 ; music lost).

Do.   Vergnügte Pleissenstadt (1728 ; music lost).

Do.   Von der Vergnügsamkeit, *or* Ich bin in mir vergnügt (*c.* 1730).

Do.   Weichet nur, betrübte Schatten (*c.* 1730).

Do.   Der Streit zwischen Phoebus und Pan (1731).

Do.   Froher Tag, verlangte Stunden (1732 ; music lost).

Do.   Schweigt stille (Coffee Cantata) (*c.* 1732).

Do.   Herkules auf dem Scheidewege, *or* Die Wahl des Herkules (1733).

Do.   Tönet, ihr Pauken ! Erschallet, Trompeten (1733).

Do.   Preise dein Glücke, gesegnetes Sachsen (1734).

Do.   Schleicht, spielende Wellen (1734).

Do.   Thomana sass annoch betrübt (1734 ; music lost).

Graduation Cantata : Siehe, der Hüter Israels (music lost).

CLAVIER :—

Notenbuch vor Anna Magdalena Bach (bk. 1959) (1725).

Clavierübung, Part I. containing the six Partitas, or German Suites (bks. 205-6 or 2796-97) (1731).

ORCHESTRAL :—

Concertos in C major, C minor, and C minor for two Claviers and Orchestra (bks. 256, 257, 257b) (1727-36).[1]

Seven Concertos for Clavier and Orchestra (bks. 248-54) (1729-36).

Concerto in A minor for Violin, Flute, Clavier, and Orchestra (bk. 255) (c. 1730).[2]

Concerto in A minor for four Claviers and Orchestra (bk. 260) (c. 1733).

Concertos in D minor and C major for three Claviers and Orchestra (bks. 258, 259) (c. 1733).

ORGAN :—

Prelude and Fugue, the Great, in G major (bk. 8 p. 112) (1724 or 1725).[3]

Six Sonatas in E flat major, C minor, D minor, E minor, C major, G major (bks. 4 and 5) (1727-33).[4]

Prelude and Fugue in C major (bk. 3 p. 70) (c. 1730).[3]

Do.   do.   D minor (bk. 9 p. 150).

V. CATALOGUE OF BACH'S COMPOSITIONS AT LEIPZIG, 1735-50, from his fifty-first year to his death.

VOCAL :—

Ascension Oratorio (Cantata 11) (c. 1735).

Schemelli's Hymn-book (1736).

Easter Oratorio (c. 1736).

---

[1] The Concerto in C minor (P. bk. 257) is an arrangement of one for two Violins now lost. The third, also in C minor, is identical with the D minor Concerto for two Violins and is published in that key in the Peters edition. The remaining Concerto, in C major, is the only one originally written for the Clavier. See Schweitzer, i. 413.

[2] The work is an amplification of the Prelude and Fugue in A minor, already catalogued among the Clavier works of the Cöthen period. Schweitzer (i. 340) concludes that it was rearranged as an orchestral Concerto early in the thirties, when Bach needed Concertos for the Telemann Society's Concerts.

[3] The scheme of the G major and C major Preludes and Fugues dates back to the Weimar period. See Spitta, iii. 208 ; Parry, p. 67.

[4] These so-called ' Organ ' Sonatas were written for the Pedal Clavi-cembalo.

Four Masses, in F major, A major (*c.* 1739), G minor, G major (*c.* 1739).

Secular Cantata : Angenehmes Wiederau (1737).

Do.	Willkommen, ihr herrschenden Götter der Erden (1738) (music lost).
Do.	Mer hahn en neue Oberkeet (Peasant Cantata) (1742).
Do.	O holder Tag (? 1749), *or*, O angenehme Melodei.

Italian Cantata : Amore traditore.

Do.	Andro dall' colle al prato (lost).
Do.	Non sa che sia dolore.

CLAVIER :—

Clavierübung, Part II. containing the Italian Concerto (bk. 207) and Partita in B minor (bk. 208) (1735).

Fantasia and Fugue in C minor (bk. 207 p. 50 and bk. 212 p. 88) (*c.* 1738).

Clavierübung, Part III. containing the four Duetti (bk. 208) (1739).

Clavierübung, Part IV. containing the Goldberg Variations (bk. 209) (*c.* 1742).

The Well-tempered Clavier, Part II. (bk. 1b or 2790b) (1744).

CHAMBER :—

Sonata for Violin, Flute, and Clavier, in C minor (in the 'Musical Offering') (bk. 237 p. 3) (1747).

Three Partitas for the Lute (? 1740).[1]

ORGAN :—

The Catechism Choral Preludes (in Clavierübung, Part III.) (bk. 16) (1739).

Fugue in D minor (in ditto) (bk. 16 p. 49) (1739).

Prelude and Fugue in E flat major (in ditto) (bk. 6 p. 28) (1739).

Do.	do.	the 'Great,' in C major (bk. 9 p. 156).
Do.	do.	the 'Great,' in B minor (bk. 7 p. 52) (1727-36).
Do.	do.	the 'Great,' in E minor (bk. 8 p. 98).

[1] The Clavier Suites in E minor, E major, and C minor are arrangements of these, otherwise lost, Lute Partitas. See Schweitzer, i. 344.

Canonic Variations on ' Vom Himmel hoch ' (bk. 19) (1746).
The Schübler Choral Preludes (bk. 16) (c. 1747-50).
The Eighteen Choral Preludes (bk. 17) (c. 1747-50).

The Musical Offering (P. bk. 219) (1747).
The Art of Fugue (P. bk. 218) (1749).

APPENDIX II

THE CHURCH CANTATAS ARRANGED CHRONOLOGICALLY

WE have the statement of Carl Philipp Emmanuel Bach,[1] confirmed by Forkel,[2] Bach's earliest biographer, that his father composed five Cantatas for every Sunday and Festival of the ecclesiastical year. Concerted music was sung at Leipzig annually on forty-three Sundays and sixteen week-days.[3] Bach therefore must have written at least 295 Cantatas. Of this number he composed at least thirty before 1723. Hence approximately 265 were written at Leipzig. But Bach's fertility does not appear to have outlived the year 1744. We have reason, therefore, to conclude that the 265 Leipzig Cantatas were written in the course of twenty-one years, that is, between 1723 and 1744. To complete that number Bach must have composed a new Cantata every month, a surprising but demonstrable conclusion.

Of the 295 Cantatas only 202 have come down to us, three of them in an incomplete state.[4] Of those written before 1723 the survivors are too scanty to indicate a rate of productivity. But thereafter we have fuller materials for a calculation. Bach, as Cantor, conducted his first Leipzig Cantata on May 30, 1723, and in the following sixteen months produced twenty-four Cantatas, at the

---

[1] In Mizler's ' Nekrolog.'
[2] *Supra*, p. 138.
[3] See the present writer's ' Bach's Chorals,' Part II. p. 1.
[4] *Ibid.*, p. 4. Four more Cantatas, of doubtful authenticity, are published by the Bachgesellschaft, Jahrgang XLI.

rate of more than one a month.[1] Beginning at the New
Year of 1725 he wrote eighteen Cantatas in nine months,
some of which, however, may belong to the years
1726-7-8-9. But even so, his monthly average seems to
have been maintained. For 1730 we have, perhaps, ten
Cantatas. For 1731 about twenty survive, of which
half a dozen may belong to 1732, a deduction which still
preserves Bach's steady average. In 1735 he produced
actually nineteen Cantatas between the New Year and
the following November, though not all of them are
positively dated. Thereafter his activity is less certainly
measured. But from 1736 till the end of 1744 he composed fifty-three Cantatas, at the rate, that is, of at least
six every year, without making allowance for Cantatas
written and lost.

There are few phenomena in the record of art more
extraordinary than this unflagging cataract of inspiration,
in which masterpiece followed masterpiece with the
monotonous periodicity of a Sunday sermon. Its musical
significance has been presented with illuminating exegesis
by more than one commentator. But its literary apparatus
has captured little attention. Yet Bach's task must have
been materially eased or aggravated according as the
supply of libretti was regular or infrequent, while the
flow of his inspiration must have been governed by their
quality. Moreover, the libretto was the medium through
which he offered the homage of his art to the service of
God. The subject therefore deserves attention. However trivial, measured against the immensities of Bach's
genius, the study will at least provide a platform from
which to contemplate it.

At the outset the opinion may be hazarded that the
provision of his weekly libretti caused Bach greater
anxiety than the setting of them to music, a task which
he accomplished with almost magical facility. It is

[1] See the Table of Cantatas set out in chronological order.

true that from the early part of the 18th century cycles of Cantata texts for the Church's year were not infrequently published. Bach was in more or less intimate touch with the authors of four, perhaps five, printed collections of the kind. But he used them with surprising infrequency. Neumeister's published cycles provided him with seven libretti,[1] Franck's with sixteen,[2] Picander's with ten,[3] Marianne von Ziegler's with nine,[4] and Helbig's with two.[5] He took three libretti from the Bible,[6] and the hymn-book furnished him with eleven more.[7] But all these published sources together only account for fifty-eight texts. Bach possessed only one book that could assist his own efforts at authorship—Paul Wagner's eight-volumed Hymn-book—whence he took the stanzas which decorate his Cantatas like jewels in the rare settings he gave them. It was, therefore, mainly upon writers with whom he was brought into occasional or official contact that Bach depended for his texts.

At the beginning of his career Bach was thrown upon his inexperience. His earliest libretti, consequently, are tentative and transitory in their construction. His first Cantata was written at Arnstadt for the Easter Festival of 1704.[8] The core of the libretto is a seven-stanzaed Easter song by an unknown poet, eked out by two passages of Scripture, a Recitativo, Aria, and a verse of a congregational hymn. The Aria and Recitativo are the only original numbers of the libretto, and there is little

---

[1] Nos. 18, 24, 28, 59, 61, 142, 160.

[2] Nos. 31, 70, 72, 80, 132, 147, 152, 155, 161, 162, 163, 164, 165, 168, 185, 186 (part).

[3] Nos. 145, 148 (part), 156, 157, 159, 171, 174, 188, 190 (one version), 'Ehre sei Gott' (incomplete).

[4] Nos. 68, 74, 87, 103, 108, 128, 175, 176, 183.

[5] Nos. 47, 141.

[6] Nos. 50, 191, 196.

[7] Nos. 4, 97, 100, 107, 112, 117, 118, 129, 137, 177, 192.

[8] No. 15: 'Denn du wirst meine Seele nicht in der Hölle lassen.'

doubt that Bach wrote them himself.[1] But the whole libretto is stamped by his personality, and reveals the inveterate subjectivity of his religion. For, disregarding the general message of the Festival, the libretto opens on the soul's personal longing for immortality and closes on its song of victory over death. In construction it is archaic, a survival of traditions acquired from central and northern Germany through Bach's earlier residence at Lüneburg and intercourse with Hamburg.[2]

Three years passed before Bach produced his next extant Cantata. In the interval, on 29th June 1707, he resigned his Arnstadt appointment to become organist of the Church of St. Blasius at Mühlhausen.[3] Here, within the space of ten months, he produced three Cantatas, the uniform character of whose libretti points to local and transitory influence upon the composer. The first of them,[4] written in August 1707, is a setting of Psalm 130, with the addition of two hymn-stanzas. The second [5] was performed on 4th February 1708, at the inauguration of the Mühlhausen Town Council, and consists of Old Testament passages, a verse of a hymn, and three original stanzas. The third,[6] a wedding Cantata, was performed at Dornheim, near Arnstadt, on 5th June 1708, at the marriage of Pastor Johann Lorenz Stauber to Frau Bach's aunt, and is set to four verses of Psalm 115.

We can have little doubt regarding the authorship of these singularly austere libretti, so far removed in atmosphere from those of Bach's subsequent periods. In fact, the clue is furnished by Bach himself. A note in his handwriting on the score of the first of the three

---

[1] The intimate personal note of the opening words of the Recitativo— ' Mein Jesus ware tot '—reveals him.

[2] Spitta, i. 231.   [3] Schweitzer, i. 103.

[4] No. 131 : ' Aus der Tiefe rufe ich, Herr, zu dir.'

[5] No. 71 : ' Gott ist mein König.'

[6] No. 196 : ' Derr Herr denket an uns.'

Cantatas (No. 131) states that he composed it at the request of Georg Christian Eilmar. The man was a close friend, godfather of Bach's eldest daughter, Katharina Dorothea (b. 1708), chief pastor of the Church of the Blessed Virgin, and Consistorial Assessor, at Mühlhausen. He was, moreover, an aggressive foe of Pietism, of which Mühlhausen was the citadel, and Bach's minister, Frohne, the protagonist. Indeed, the two men waged so public and wordy a warfare [1] that Bach's social relations with the one and official connection with the other must have been rendered difficult. To his settled convictions regarding the fellowship of music and worship Pietism offered Puritan opposition. In fact, its lack of sympathy eventually drove him from Mühlhausen, in hope, in his own words, ' to realise my views upon the right ordering of Church music without vexation from others.' [2] Eilmar, on the other hand, though he admitted the æsthetic value of music, conspicuously lacked the warmth and emotionalism of Bach's religious temperament. To him undoubtedly we must attribute the cold austerity of the three Mühlhausen libretti and the suppression of the personal note already sounded in Bach's Arnstadt Cantata. Nor did Eilmar's influence pass with Bach's departure from Mühlhausen.[3] It is to be traced in the early libretti of the Weimar period.

The Weimar Cantatas are twenty-two in number, of which all but three were written subsequently to Bach's appointment as Concertmeister early in 1714. He had been organist to the Ducal Court of Weimar since June 1708, a position which did not require him to compose for the Ducal Chapel. On the other hand, three Cantatas are attributed to the early Weimar years. But they

[1] See Spitta, i. 359 ff.

[2] *Ibid.*, i. 374. On the other hand, Bach's art was visibly affected by Pietistic influences, as Schweitzer, i. 169, shows.

[3] Eilmar died in 1715 (Spitta, i. 361).

cannot be positively dated, and their libretti bear such clear traces of Eilmar's influence that their composition may belong rather to the Mühlhausen period. Their texts display Eilmar's preference for strictly Biblical material and a disinclination to employ secular forms. The first of them [1] is a paraphrase of the Magnificat. The second [2] consists of four verses of Psalm 25, along with three simple rhymed stanzas which we have no difficulty in attributing to Bach himself. The third, ' Gottes Zeit ist die allerbeste Zeit ' (No. 106), was composed, Spitta conjectures,[3] for the funeral of Philipp Grossgebauer, Rector of Weimar School, in 1711. But more recently, and more probably, Pirro [4] has expressed the opinion that Bach wrote it for the funeral of his uncle, Tobias Lämmerhirt, who was buried at Erfurt in September 1707. The theory accords with the suggestion that all three Cantatas belong to the Mühlhausen period. If so, it is probable that the libretto, a very ingenious mosaic of Scripture texts, was written by Eilmar for the occasion. It is the last in which we detect his influence.

Bach's appointment as Ducal Concertmeister at Weimar can be placed between 14th January and 19th March 1714 [5] and, it is probable, was nearer the former date. He seems to have produced the first Cantata his new post required him to write on Sexagesima Sunday, which fell on 4th February in that year. From thence to the end of 1716 he produced nineteen Cantatas and collaborated with a writer whose libretti at length gave him a satisfactory literary medium.

The new poet, Erdmann Neumeister, four of whose libretti Bach set to music immediately after his appoint-

---

[1] No. 189 : ' Meine Seele rühmt und preist.'
[2] No. 150 : ' Nach dir, Herr, verlanget mich.'
[3] Vol. i. 456.
[4] ' J.-S. Bach,' p. 87.
[5] The conclusion is based on letters printed by Spitta, i. 517.

ment, and a fifth a year later,[1] was considerably Bach's
senior.[2] As far back as 1700 he had begun to write a
cycle of Cantata texts for the Ducal Chapel at Weissenfels,
and published it in 1704, with an explanatory Preface
referred to later.[3] In 1708 he issued a second cycle for
the Court of Rudolstadt, while in 1711 and 1714 third
and fourth cycles were written for the Ducal Chapel
at Eisenach. All four cycles were reissued in 1716,[4] with
the addition of a fifth and a Preface, which lauded
Neumeister as ' the first German to give sacred music its
fitting position by introducing and perfecting the Church
Cantata.' [5]

Spitta has dealt exhaustively [6] with the evolution and
construction of the Neumeister libretto. It need only
be remarked that it adapted a secular or operatic
apparatus to the service of religion, and that the innova-
tion, hateful to many, triumphed because of Neumeister's
delicate handling of it. He perfected the new form, however, in stages. ' A Cantata,' he insisted in his 1704
Preface, ' is simply a fragment of Opera made up of
Aria and Recitativo.' But the restriction excluded from
the Cantata its most appropriate material. In his 1708
cycle he found a place for the chorus. Finally, he
admitted the Bible stanza and congregational hymn.
With their inclusion the Cantata libretto assumed the
form familiar to us in Bach's use. It represents a combination of secular Opera and ecclesiastical Motet. The
free Arias and Recitativi are derived from the one, the
Bible stanzas and congregational hymns perpetuate the
traditions of the other. Unity of design is stamped on

---

[1] Nos. 18, 61, 142, 160, and 59. See Table.

[2] He was born May 12, 1671 (Spitta, i. 470).

[3] The volume is entitled ' Erdmann Neumeisters Geistliche Cantaten
statt einer Kirchen-Musik. Die zweyte Auflage.'

[4] Entitled 'Herrn Erdmann Neumeisters Fünffache Kirchen-
Andachten,' Leipzig, 1716.

[5] Spitta, i. 474.   [6] Vol. i. 466 ff.

the whole by its general subordination to the Gospel for the Day. Thus, at the moment when Bach was about to devote his genius to the Cantata, Neumeister opportunely provided him with a libretto singularly adapted to the end Bach had in view, and appropriate to the musical expression by which he proposed to secure it. He adhered to it almost to the end of his life, and found unfailing inspiration in Neumeister's sincerity, delicacy, and uniformly religious outlook. Neumeister's Arias, with a single exception,[1] are hymn-like in mood and metre. His Recitativi are reflective and prayerful, rarely oratorical or pictorial, simple communings upon the Gospel themes which the libretto handles.[2]

Bach's early introduction to Neumeister's texts is explained by the close relations between the Courts of Weimar and Eisenach, by his associations with his own birthplace, and his intimacy with Georg Philipp Telemann, Kapellmeister there, for whose use Neumeister's third and fourth cycles were written.[3]   Bach set, in all, seven of the libretti—four from the fourth cycle,[4] one from the third,[5] and two from the first,[6] one of which (No. 142) differs so much from the published version as to raise the question whether Bach did not receive it direct from Neumeister in the form in which he set it.[7]

That Bach should have set no more than seven of Neumeister's texts [8] is strange. He shrank, perhaps, from appropriating libretti on which his friend Telemann had a prior claim.[9]   But the reason is found rather in the fact that at Weimar Bach discovered in 1715 a local

[1] See the Aria (Duetto) of Cantata No. 28.

[2] See particularly the Litanei in Cantata No. 18.

[3] Telemann was Carl Philipp Emmanuel Bach's godfather (Spitta, i. 486).

[4] Nos. 24, 28, 59, 61.   [5] No. 18.

[6] Nos. 142, 160.   [7] See Spitta, i. 630.

[8] His influence is also detected in Nos. 27, 56, 199.

[9] Telemann also set the libretti of Bach's Nos. 18 and 142.   See Spitta, i. 487.

poet of first-rate ability who, with perhaps but one exception, wrote the libretti of all the Cantatas he composed during the last two years of his Weimar appointment.

Salomo Franck, Bach's new collaborator, was Curator of the Ducal Museum of Coins and Medals at Weimar. He was twenty-six years older than Bach. But Spitta's conjecture,[1] that the two men were not acquainted, is hardly tenable. Both resided in the same small provincial town, both were in the Duke's service, and throughout 1715 and 1716 collaborated in at least ten Cantatas performed in the Ducal Chapel. Moreover, though the Preface of Franck's first cycle is dated 4th June 1715,[2] Bach had already set one of its libretti for Easter of that year. A second cycle of texts, of which Bach made little use,[3] was published by Franck in 1717.[4]

Schweitzer, no doubt, is correct in his conclusion [5] that Bach was drawn to Franck by his poetic insight, his mysticism, and innate feeling for nature. It must be remembered, too, that his libretti were, in some degree, official. On the other hand, Franck was Neumeister's inferior in ability to conceive a picture fit to express Bach's larger moods, and on occasion could descend to sheer bathos.[6] But his texts have a rhythmic swing and melody which Bach found agreeable. He set at least sixteen of them, and returned to them even after he settled at Leipzig.

The circumstances which terminated Bach's service at

---

[1] Vol. i. 530.

[2] Wustmann, 'Joh. Seb. Bach's Kantaten-Texte' (1913), p. xxii n. The cycle is entitled ' Evangelisches Andachts-Opffer.'

[3] Only Nos. 70, 147, and 186 are taken from it.

[4] Entitled ' Evangelische Sonn- und Fest-Tages Andachten.'

[5] Vol. ii. 131.

[6] For instance, the Aria in Cantata No. 168, beginning :

' Kapital und Interessen
Meiner Schulden gross und klein,
Müssen einst verrechnet sein.'

Weimar are familiar, and need not be restated. He received a new appointment at Cöthen on 1st August 1717, and took up his duties there, probably at Christmas, that year.[1] His position was that of Capellmeister to the princely Court. He never styles himself Court Organist,[2] and his duties severed him for five years from the service of the Church, to which he had declared his particular dedication in 1708. The Cöthen Court was unpretentious. The Prince was a Calvinist. Figurate music was not permitted in the Court Chapel, and its Organ was small and inadequate. Hence Bach devoted himself chiefly to chamber music, and only two genuine Church Cantatas belong to this period of his career. Both must have been written for performance elsewhere, possibly in connection with Bach's frequent Autumn tours as a performer.[3]

For both Cantatas Bach employed a librettist, otherwise little known, named Johann Friedrich Helbig, State Secretary to the Eisenach Court. In March 1720,[4] more than two years after Bach's arrival at Cöthen, Helbig published a cycle of ' Musical Texts on the Sunday and Saints' Day Gospels throughout the year,' for performance ' in God's honour by the Prince's Kapelle at Eisenach.' [5] How they came into Bach's hands we do not know, but can readily conjecture. They are indifferent poetry, judging them by the two specimens Bach made use of, and are uniform in construction. The first movement invariably is a Chorus upon a text from the Gospel for the Day, or a Scripture passage closely related to it. Two Arias separated by a Recitativo follow. A Choral brings the libretto to an end.[6]

The first of the two Cantatas written to Helbig's words

---

[1] Spitta, ii. 5 ; Schweitzer, i. 106.   [2] Spitta, ii. 3.
[3] The two Cantatas are Nos. 47 and 141.
[4] Wustmann, p. xxiii.   [5] Spitta, ii. 12 n.
[6] The Choral is absent from No. 141. It should be ' Christe, du Lamm Gottes.'

was designed for the Seventeenth Sunday after Trinity, which fell in 1720 on September 22.[1] Spitta conjectures [2] that Bach intended it for performance at Hamburg. In fact, his wife's death postponed Bach's visit to that town until November, by which date the Sunday appropriate to the Cantata had passed. Spitta holds that the Cantata may have been performed, after all, during the visit. Schweitzer is sceptical.[3] But Bach certainly expended great pains upon the score.

The second Helbig Cantata [4] is for the Third Sunday in Advent, and the date of it would appear to have been 1721. It is one of the least agreeable of Bach's works. Spitta [5] declares it a juvenile composition hastily adapted to a new libretto. Schweitzer [6] expresses the same opinion, and Sir Hubert Parry [7] finds the work ' rather commonplace.' Its genuineness is discussed by Max Schreyer in the ' Bach-Jahrbuch ' for 1912, and more recently Rudolf Wustmann has insisted that it does not bear the stamp of Bach's genius.[8] If it actually was composed in 1721, its production must have coincided with Bach's second marriage on December 3 of that year.[9] In that case, his resort to old material is explicable.

Only these two Cantatas were composed at Cöthen. But later, at Leipzig, two others were manufactured out of secular material written there.[10] It is unnecessary to refer to them, except to remark that in each case Bach appears to have been the author of the new libretto. In the first of them [11] it is clear that he was handicapped by the frankly secular metre of the original stanzas. The

---

[1] Schweitzer, ii. 147. The Cantata is No. 47, ' Wer sich selbst erhöhet.'

[2] Vol. ii. 13.   [3] Vol. ii. 147.

[4] No. 141 : ' Das ist je gewisslich wahr.'

[5] Vol. ii. 15.   [6] Vol. ii. 148.

[7] ' Johann Sebastian Bach,' p. 108.   [8] Op. cit., Note 195.

[9] Spitta, ii. 147.   [10] Nos. 134 and 173.

[11] No. 134 : ' Ein Herz, das seinen Jesum lebend weiss.'

second of them,[1] originally a Birthday Ode to Prince Leopold of Anhalt-Cöthen, is a masterly conversion into a Whit-Monday text which, assuming that Bach wrote it, puts his literary facility beyond question.

Bach made the last move in his professional career on May 31, 1723, when he was inducted Cantor of St. Thomas' School at Leipzig, with particular charge of the Churches of St. Thomas and St. Nicolas. Here by far the greater number of his Cantatas appeared, and 172 of them survive. They are too numerous to be considered individually, and their classification is rendered difficult by the fact that the authorship of most of their libretti is conjectural and not ascertained. They fall, however, into two large categories, each of which exhibits characteristics of its own.

The dividing year, clearly but not arbitrarily, is 1734. Before it and after it Bach was aided by new writers. But the earlier period pre-eminently was one of experiment, out of which emerged the glorified hymn-libretto, or Choral Cantata, of Bach's last years. That it sprang, in some degree, from the difficulty of finding good original texts in sufficient number may be granted. That it was adopted as an avenue of escape from Picander's coarser work is a conjecture based, apparently, upon a prevalent exaggeration of Bach's dependence on that writer. The fundamental reason which led Bach to the hymn-libretto undoubtedly was the fact that it most closely fulfilled the ideals which informed his work.

The first Cantata performed during Bach's Cantorship [2] reveals a new author, whose assistance, if the conclusion is well grounded, was at Bach's disposal throughout the whole of the earlier Leipzig period. Spitta's keen insight failed him in this instance. He betrays no recognition of

[1] No. 173 : ' Erhötes Fleisch und Blut.'
[2] No. 75 : ' Die Elenden sollen essen,' sung on May 30, the day preceding Bach's formal induction.

the new writer, and occasionally [1] attributes his libretti to Picander. The credit of the discovery belongs to Rudolf Wustmann, though he fails to work it out to its fullest conclusions.[2]

No one can read the early Leipzig libretti without being struck by the number of them that are not only uniform in structure, but similar in tone and point. They all begin with a Bible text, chosen frequently, but not invariably, from the Gospel for the Day. Every one of them ends with a hymn-stanza. Their Arias, with hardly an exception,[3] are written in what, compared with Picander's rollicking dactyls, may be held hymn-metres. Their Recitativi, almost invariably, are didactic or exegetical.[4] They do not display the vapid rhetoric of Picander. Nor do they express the reflective or prayerful mood that reveals Bach. They are essentially expository and, it is noticeable, are studded with direct or veiled references to Bible passages which expand or enforce the lesson of the initial text. In a word, they suggest the work of a preacher casting his sermon notes into lyrical form, an impression which is strengthened by the fact that the libretto invariably opens with a Scripture passage and frequently blends the Gospel and Epistle for the Day in one harmonious teaching. Spitta detected this characteristic. But he failed to follow up the clue. He speaks [5] of one of these texts [6] as a ' moralising homily,' a phrase concisely appropriate to them all. Moreover, a remark of his,[7] pointing the significance of

[1] For instance, Nos. 67 and 102.

[2] Wustmann, by implication, only associates eight libretti (Cantatas Nos. 37, 44, 75, 76, 86, 104, 166, 179) with Weiss. All of them belong to the early years, 1723-27.   [3] See Nos. 75 and 105.

[4] See Nos. 25, 42, 77. As an extreme illustration, the first Recitativo of No. 25 begins with the words, ' Die ganze Welt ist nur ein Hospital.'

[5] Vol. ii. 388.

[6] Cantata No. 65 : ' Sie werden aus Saba Alle kommen.'

[7] Vol. i. 361.

the god-parents chosen by Bach for his children—Eilmar, for instance—as revealing Bach's intimate associates at the moment, affords another clue to the personality of the new writer.

Among the clergy of St. Thomas' during Bach's Cantorate were two men, father and son, each of whom bore the name Christian Weiss. The elder was Pastor of the Church from 1714 till his death in 1737. He was a cultured man, in touch with the University, and possibly formed a link between it and Bach, to whom he showed greater cordiality than the Cantor received from other clerical colleagues. In 1732 his daughter, Dorothea Sophia stood godmother to Bach's son, Johann Christoph Friedrich, afterwards famous as the ' Bückeburg Bach.' [1] In 1737 his son stood sponsor to Bach's daughter, Johanna Caroline.[2] Nor can it be altogether without significance that the names Dorothea, Sophia, Christian, are borne by others of Bach's children by his second marriage. There is sufficient evidence, therefore, that Bach's relations with the elder Weiss were intimate enough to support a literary partnership. Moreover, circumstances lend weight to the inference. For some years before Bach's arrival in Leipzig, Weiss suffered from an affection of the throat which kept him from the pulpit. But, during the first year of Bach's Cantorate, he was able to resume his preaching. If he was, in fact, the author of the libretti, we can have little difficulty in concluding that they and his sermons were built on the same text.

So far as they can be identified—the attempt is somewhat speculative—Weiss provided Bach with at least thirty-three libretti. He set five of them in 1723, three in 1724, nine in or about 1725, one in 1727, two in 1730, six in 1731, three in 1732, and four in the later Leipzig period.[3] Fourteen others bear a constructional

[1] Wustmann, p. xxiv.   [2] *Ibid.*
[3] See the Table.

resemblance to Weiss's texts,[1] but their character refers them rather to Bach or Picander. Even so, if we do not exaggerate his activity, Weiss seems to have written at least one-sixth of the Leipzig libretti and more than a quarter of those of the earlier period. Without a doubt he eased a difficult situation in Bach's experience before his regular association with Picander began.

Apart from their revelation of Christian Weiss, the libretti of Bach's first year at Leipzig do not call for comment. Franck and Neumeister appear among them, and we trace Bach's hand in nine.[2] But at Easter, 1724, he broke new ground with a libretto whence developed the Cantata form of his latest period.

The Cantata for Easter Day 1724,[3] is Bach's earliest setting of an entire congregational hymn. Spitta suggests[4] that he felt the fitness of giving the libretto an antique character to match the hymn's melody. However that may be, Bach would appear already to have been groping towards the Choral Cantata of the late '30's. And though he did not repeat the experiment until the Easter of 1731,[5] he treated three hymn-libretti in the interval in a manner which shows him already to have worked out the essentials of the Choral Cantata form.[6]

Another landmark meets us a year and a half after the Easter experiment. On September 23, 1725 (?)—the Seventeenth Sunday after Trinity—Bach produced a Cantata [7] whose Arias are set to words which had appeared in print in the preceding year. Their author was a hack writer named Christian Friedrich Henrici, or, as he preferred to style himself, Picander. His hand probably

---

[1] They are Nos. 6, 17, 22, 43, 48, 57, 144, 148, 157, 159, 171, 190, 195, and the incomplete Cantata, ' Ehre sei Gott in der Höhe.'
[2] Nos. 16, 23, 63, 81, 83, 153, 154, 184, 194. See the Table.
[3] No. 4 : ' Christ lag in Todesbanden.' [4] Vol. ii. 393.
[5] See the Table : No. 112, ' Derr Herr ist mein getreuer Hirt.'
[6] Nos. 8, 20, 93.
[7] No. 148 : ' Bringet dem Herrn Ehre seines Namens.'

is also traced in the libretto used by Bach on the preceding
Sunday [1] and again in that for Sexagesima in the same
year.[2] But the evidence is only inferential. That he
collaborated with Bach on September 23, 1725 (?), is
incontestable, and the work defines the beginning of a
long and fruitful partnership.

Spitta,[3] who tells us all that is known of Picander, has
sufficiently exposed his superficial literary facility. He
commenced to write sacred poetry in 1724, and on Advent
Sunday of that year began a cycle of 'Profitable Thoughts,'
so he termed them, upon the Sunday and Saints' Day
Gospels. He published them in 1725, when the cycle was
complete.[4] Three years later he issued a cycle of Cantata
texts for 1728-29 in the Neumeister form.[5] That he
intended them for Bach's use is apparent in the fact
that he expressly dedicated them to the service of ' our
incomparable Capellmeister.' But Bach made the sparest
use of them and of the earlier ' Profitable Thoughts ' alike.
From the latter he took not one libretto.[6] Of the 1728-29
cycle he used only eight texts.[7] One more libretto can be
referred to Picander's later publications,[8] and of six others
we can be sure that they are based upon his texts.[9] In
other words, of the original libretti of the Leipzig period
we can trace Picander's hand positively in no more than
fifteen.

It is necessary to emphasise this point. For Spitta [10]
has stated positively that Picander wrote ' most ' of the
Leipzig libretti, and his opinion has been generally

---

[1] No. 8 : ' Liebster Gott, wann werd' ich sterben.'

[2] No. 181 : ' Leichtgesinnte Flattergeister.'   [3] Vol. ii. 340 ff.

[4] The volume is entitled ' Sammlung Erbaulicher Gedancken, Bey
und über gewöhnlichen Sonn- und Festtags-Evangelien,' Leipzig.

[5] ' Cantaten auf die Sonn- und Fest-Tage durch das gantze Jahr,'
Leipzig, 1728. He reprinted them in 1732 in his ' Satyrische Gedichte.'

[6] But see Cantata No. 148 and Spitta, ii. 693. Also No. 19.

[7] Cantatas Nos. 145, 156, 159, 171, 174, 188, 190 (one version), and
the Cantata ' Ehre sei Gott.'   [8] No. 157.

[9] Nos. 19, 30, 36, 84, 148, 197.   [10] Vol. ii. 346.

accepted. But its correctness may be contested. It is suspicious, to begin with, that Picander never published the texts which Spitta asserts him to have poured out in such profusion. 'He placed no value,' Spitta answers readily, 'on these manufactured compositions, put together hastily to please his friend.' But the argument cannot stand. Why should Picander have thought less of libretti actually used by his 'incomparable Capell-meister' than of those published for and rejected by him ?—for Spitta does not venture to declare that as literature the rejected were superior to the accepted texts. If out of a published cycle of libretti expressly written for him Bach chose only eight texts, are Picander's 'manufactured compositions,' as Spitta calls them, likely to have attracted him to a greater degree ? We can detect his hand perhaps in six Cantatas [1] besides those already mentioned, and Bach relied on him exclusively for his secular texts. One concludes, none the less, that Bach rarely accepted an original Cantata libretto from Picander, and employed him chiefly on the Choral Cantatas of his latest period. Excluding them, and adding the probable to the actual original Picander texts, they total only twenty-one, a fraction inadequate to support Spitta's sweeping statement.

From the advent of Picander in 1725, to the end of the first Leipzig period nine years later, Bach does not seem to have gone outside the circle of familiar authors for his regular Cantata texts. On October 17, 1727, however, he produced a funeral Cantata, or 'Trauer-Musik,' in memory of the late Queen of Poland, the libretto of which was written by Professor J. C. Gottsched. The partner-ship, in fact, was accidental : the libretto was supplied to Bach with the commission to set it to music, and, so far as is known, Gottsched and he did not collaborate again.

[1] Nos. 32, 48, 57, 90, 144, 181.

So, reviewing Bach's activities during his first eleven years at Leipzig, we find that of the hundred libretti set by him to music Christian Weiss heads the list as the presumed author of twenty-nine. Bach follows him with eighteen.[1] Picander's hand appears in fifteen, Franck's in eight,[2] Neumeister's and Gottsched's in one each. Fifteen libretti are congregational hymns in their original or paraphrased form. One is the ' Gloria in Excelsis ' of the B minor Mass adapted as a Christmas Cantata (No. 190). Twelve are by authors not identified.

Passing to the later Leipzig period, seventy-two surviving Cantatas are attributed to the years 1735-50. They reveal one, perhaps two, new writers. The first of them, Marianne von Ziegler, was identified by Spitta in 1892. She was the widow of an officer, resident in Leipzig, a cultured woman, in touch with University life, her house a salon for music and musicians.[3] There is no reason to suppose Bach to have been of her circle, or that he was acquainted with her literary gifts. Indeed the contrary is to be inferred from the fact that, though she published her poems in 1728,[4] he does not seem to have known them until seven years later, when he used them for nine consecutive Sundays and Festivals in 1735, beginning on the Third Sunday after Easter, and ending on Trinity Sunday.

In addition to these nine libretti, both Spitta [5] and Schweitzer [6] attribute to her the text of Bach's Cantata for the Second Sunday after Easter in the same year.[7] It is uniform in construction with the authentic nine, but is not among the authoress's published works. Wustmann [8]

---

[1] Nos. 16, 22, 23, 27, 35, 51, 56, 58, 63, 66, 81, 82, 83, 153, 154, 194, 195. No. 184 is an adaptation. See also Nos. 19, 36, 84, 144, 145, 148, for Bach's collaboration with Picander.
[2] Besides No. 80, a Choral Cantata.   [3] Schweitzer, ii. 332 ff.
[4] Entitled ' Versuch in gebundener Schreibart.'   [5] Vol. iii. 71.
[6] Vol. ii. 331 n.   [7] No. 85 : ' Ich bin ein guter Hirt.'
[8] Note 60.

finds the tone of the libretto less ardent and its rhythm rougher than those published under her name. Admitting the soundness of Wustmann's criticism, one hazards the opinion that the challenged text was written at the period when Bach set it, namely, in 1735, eight years after the poetess published her earlier texts. The difference of time may account for the difference of texture to which Wustmann draws attention, but leaves undecided the question whether Bach was drawn to the earlier through the later and unpublished texts or *vice versa*. It is quite probable that he set other libretti by the same writer, though Schweitzer's [1] attribution to her of a second text for Ascension Day, 1735, must be rejected.[2]

It is worth noticing, since it certainly reveals Bach's preference, that Marianne von Ziegler's libretti are constructed almost invariably in the Weiss form. Every one of them but three [3] opens with a Bible passage, invariably taken from St. John's Gospel, which provides the Gospel for the Day from the First Sunday after Easter down to Trinity Sunday, excepting Ascension Day. All but one (No. 68) of the libretti conclude with a Choral, and their Arias are hymn-like in metre. The tone of them, however, is warmer, more personal, less didactic than the Weiss texts. That Bach regarded them with particular favour is apparent in the circumstance that he took the trouble to revise all but one of them.[4] That they stirred his genius deeply is visible in the settings he gave them.

After 1735 the chronology of the Cantatas is not certainly ascertained. Of those that fall after the Ziegler year, as we may term it, the majority can only be dated approximately as *circa* 1740, that is, anywhere between 1735 and 1744. Nor, except rarely, can we detect in their libretti the work of those on whom Bach elsewhere

---

[1] Vol. ii. 331 n.   [3] No. 33 : ' Gott fähret auf mit Jauchzen.'
[2] See Table.   [4] No. 74.

relied. Weiss, who died late in 1737, is only an occasional contributor. The texts of this period, in fact, are the outcome of Bach's own experiments in libretto form. Thirty-three of them are Choral Cantatas, whose evolution it remains to trace concisely.

That Bach should have turned to Lutheran hymnody, chiefly of the fifteenth and sixteenth centuries, and that the Cantatas built upon it should be his most perfect religious work is not surprising. The hymns and their melodies were the foundations upon which the temple of German Protestantism had been reared. They appealed vividly and powerfully to Bach's spiritual nature, and profoundly influenced his musical utterance. His whole career, as Sir Hubert Parry points out,[1] was an effort to widen his means for self-expression. And the Choral Cantata, in effect, was the reconciliation or blending of this self-discipline. It was the supreme achievement of Bach's genius to assert the faith and idealism of Lutheran hymnody with the fullest resources of his technique.

It is not our task to consider the hymn libretto in its relation to the structure of Bach's latest Cantatas. Necessarily it tied him to a stereotyped design, which he clung to with greater persistency because it exactly fulfilled his devotional purpose. But experience compelled him, after a brief trial, to discard the simple hymn libretto. In the earlier Leipzig years as many as eight Choral Cantatas [2] are set to the unaltered text of a congregational hymn. In the later Leipzig period only two [3] libretti are of that character. Bach, in fact, soon realised that, while the unaltered hymn-stanza, with its uniform metre and balanced rhyme, was appropriate to the simple Choral or elaborate Fantasia, it was unmalleable for use as an Aria or Recitativo. Hence, retaining the unaltered Hymn-stanza for the musical movements

---

[1] *Op. cit.*, p. 377.   [2] See Table.
[3] Nos. 100 and 107, both of them *c.* 1735.

congruous to it, he was led to paraphrase, in free madrigal
form, those stanzas which he selected for the Arias and
Recitativi.

As early as September 16, 1725,[1] Bach was moving
towards this solution. And it is significant that Picander's
hand is visible in the libretto. The next example [2]
occurs three years later, and again reveals Picander's
authorship. Two other instances also occur in the early
Leipzig period.[3] To that point, however, it is clear that
Bach was not satisfied as to the most effective treatment
of the hymn-libretto. But in the second Leipzig period,
after his collaboration with Marianne von Ziegler, he
arrived at and remained constant to a uniform design.
Of the thirty-nine Choral Cantatas of the whole period
only two exhibit the earlier form. Of all the others the
libretto consists partly of unaltered hymn-stanzas—invariably used for the first and last movements, and
occasionally elsewhere—but chiefly of paraphrased stanzas
of the hymn, whose accustomed melody, wherever else
it may be introduced, is associated invariably with the
hymn when the text is used in its unaltered form. We,
to whom both words and melody are too frequently
unfamiliar, may view the perfections of the Choral
Cantata with some detachment. But Bach's audience
listened to hymns and tunes which were in the heart of
every hearer and a common possession of them all. The
appeal of his message was the more arresting because it
spoke as directly to himself as to those he addressed.

It would be satisfactory and interesting to point
positively to Bach's own handiwork in these libretti, of
which he set fifty-four in the period 1724-44. Unfortunately it is impossible to do so, except, perhaps, in a
single case,[4] where we can reasonably infer that the

---

[1] No. 8, for the Sixteenth Sunday after Trinity.
[2] No. 93, for the Fifth Sunday after Trinity (1728).
[3] Nos. 9 (? 1731), 99 (c. 1733).   [4] No. 122.

libretto is his. Of the rest, one is by Franck.[1] In
eighteen of them the hand of Picander is more or less
patent.[2] Nineteen [3] we can only venture to mark
'anonymous,' though Picander is probably present in
most of them. Ten are unaltered congregational
hymns.[4] There remain, however, five [5] in which, perhaps, we detect another, and the last, of Bach's literary
helpers.

Wustmann draws attention [6] to the libretto of Cantata
No. 38, a paraphrase of Luther's Psalm 130. He finds
in it, and reasonably, an expression of ' Jesus religion '
very alien to Picander's muse, and suggests the younger
Christian Weiss as the author of it. Like his father, he
was Bach's colleague, the godfather of his daughter, and
undoubtedly on terms of close friendship with him. But
if he wrote the libretto of Cantata No. 38, probably it is
not the only one. The same note rings in four more of
the Choral Cantatas,[7] which may be attributed tentatively
to Weiss, though their ascription to Bach would be
equally congruous.

Returning, however, to the seventy-two libretti of the
later Leipzig period we reach this result : More than half
of them (thirty-nine) are congregational hymns, all but
two of which are of the paraphrased type in which we
detect the work of Picander, Bach himself, and perhaps
the younger Weiss. Of the remaining thirty-three
original libretti Marianne von Ziegler heads the list with
nine, and perhaps ten.[8]   Bach follows with a problematical

---

[1] No. 80.

[2] Nos. 1, 2, 5, 8, 20, 26, 62, 78, 91, 92, 93, 96, 115, 121, 124, 127,
138, 140.

[3] Nos. 7, 9, 10, 14, 33, 41, 94, 99, 101, 111, 113, 114, 116, 125, 126,
130, 139, 178, 180.

[4] Nos. 4, 97, 100, 107, 112, 117, 129, 137, 177, 192.

[5] Nos. 3, 38, 123, 133, 135.

[6] P. xxiv.

[7] Nos. 3, 123, 133, 135.   [8] See *supra*, p. 180.

six,[1] Picander with five,[2] the elder Weiss with four,[3] Neumeister with one.[4] One text is taken from the Bible.[5] Another consists of a single stanza of a hymn by Martin Behm.[6] Five are by authors unknown or undetected.[7]

But, as was said at the outset, the attribution of particular libretti to individual writers is conjectural, except in comparatively few cases. Yet, unsatisfying as it is, this guess-work reveals with approximate correctness the extent to which Bach drew upon his own and other people's abilities for the texts he needed. Summarising our conclusions, we discover that about one-quarter (fifty-four) of the 202 libretti set by Bach between the years 1704 and 1744 were provided by the hymn-book. It is shown elsewhere [8] that all but eleven of them are taken from Paul Wagner's volumes. The elder Weiss comes next with thirty-three libretti. Bach follows with thirty, Salomo Franck with twenty-one, Picander with twenty (exclusive of his arrangements of Choral Cantata texts). Marianne von Ziegler contributes ten, Neumeister seven, Eilmar and Helbig two each, Gottsched and Martin Behm one each. Three libretti are taken from the Bible or Church liturgy. Eighteen remain anonymous.

The literary qualities of the libretti are not under discussion here. They have a characteristic, however, on which one cannot forbear from remarking. Indifferent literature as, for the most part, they are—children of their period and blemished with its imperfections—they enshrine an extraordinarily interesting anthology of the religious poetry of the sixteenth, seventeenth, and eighteenth centuries. They expose the evangelical thought of Germany from the age of Luther to that of Bach, and are

[1] Nos. 17, 34, 43, 151, 197, and 'Herr Gott, Beherrscher aller Dinge.'

[2] Nos. 30, 32, 48, 57, 90.   [3] Nos. 45, 79, 110, 143.

[4] No. 28.   [5] No. 50.   [6] No. 118.

[7] Nos. 6, 11, 13, 146, 193.

[8] See 'Bach's Chorals,' Part II., Introduction.

particularly rich in the lyrical fervour of the Reformation itself. Of the seventy-seven hymn-writers whom Bach includes in his collection, so many as forty-four belong to the sixteenth century. Only thirteen of them touch Bach's own period. And a similar bias to the Reformation epoch is observable in his choice of the tunes of the Chorals, which are absent from only twenty-one of the Cantatas. By far the greater number of them are coeval with the hymns themselves ; that is, they date from the Reformation and behind it.

Here clearly is the source of Bach's inspiration, the master-key of his art. He touches Luther, is in a sense his complement, his art builded on the foundations Luther laid, consecrated to the ends Luther vindicated, inspired by a dedication of himself to God's service not less exalted—a great artist, a great Protestant, a great man.[1]

[1] The above article and the Table that follows were communicated originally to the Musical Association on March 28, 1918.

THE CHURCH CANTATAS ARRANGED CHRONOLOGICALLY

NOTE.—Cantatas distinguished by an asterisk (*) are for Soli voices only (S.A.T.B. unless the particular voices are stated); those marked (†) include, in addition, simple four-part Chorals: the rest contain concerted Choruses.

No.	Date.	Title.	Author of Libretto.	Composition of the Text.
		(1) COMPOSED AT ARNSTADT		
15	1704. Easter Day (revised for subsequent performance).	Denn du wirst meine Seele nicht in der Hölle lassen (Psalm xvi. 10).	? Bach.	*Part I.*: Psalm xvi. 10; St. Mark xvi. 6; *Part II.*: seven (six) stanzas of the anonymous hymn, 'Auf, freue dich, Seele, du bist nun getröst'; Stanza iv. of Nikolaus Herman's hymn, 'Wenn mein Stündlein vorhanden ist.' The rest of the libretto perhaps is by Bach.
		(2) COMPOSED AT MÜHLHAUSEN. (See also Nos. 106, 150, 189.)		
131	1707. ? for 11th, 19th, 21st, or 22nd S. after Trinity.	Aus der Tiefe rufe ich, Herr, zu dir (Psalm cxxx.).	? Georg Christian Eilmar.	Psalm cxxx.; Stanzas ii. and v. of Bartholomäus Ringwaldt's hymn, 'Herr Jesu Christ, du höchstes Gut.' T. B. Soli.
71	1708. Feb. 4. Town Council Inauguration.	Gott ist mein König (Psalm lxxiv. 12).	? Bach (or Eilmar).	Psalm lxxiv. 12, 16, 17, 19; 2 Sam. xix. 35, 37; Deuteronomy xxxiii. 25; Gen. xxi. 22; Stanza vi. of Johann Heermann's hymn, 'O Gott, du frommer Gott'; rest of libretto original. A. T. B. Soli.

No.	Date.	Title.	Author of Libretto.	Composition of the Text.
196	1708. June 5. Wedding of Johann Lorenz Stauber (at Dornheim).	Der Herr denket an uns (Psalm cxv. 12).	Psalm cxv. 12-15.	The libretto consists exclusively of the Psalm verses. S. T. B. Soli.

(3) COMPOSED AT WEIMAR. (See also Nos. 12, 72, 80, 164, 168, 186.)

No.	Date.	Title.	Author of Libretto.	Composition of the Text.
*189	c. 1707-10. Visitation of the B.V.M.	Meine Seele rühmt und preist.	Author unknown. ? Composed at Mühlhausen.	A paraphrase of the 'Magnificat.' Tenor Solo.
150	c. 1710. ? Occasion.	Nach dir, Herr, verlanget mich (Psalm xxv. 1).	? Bach. ? Composed at Mühlhausen.	Psalm xxv. 1, 2, 5, 15; rest of libretto perhaps by Bach. See 'Bach-Jahrbuch' for 1913, p. 39, on authenticity of Cantata.
106	? 1711. Funeral of Rector Philipp Grossgebauer (Weimar); or ? 1707 (Sept.) funeral of Thomas Lämmerhirt (Erfurt).	Gottes Zeit ist die allerbeste Zeit (Actus tragicus).	? G. C. Eilmar (or Bach). ? Composed at Mühlhausen.	Acts xvii. 28; Psalm xc. 12; Isaiah xxxviii. 1; Ecclesiasticus xiv. 17; Rev. xxii. 20; Psalm xxxi. 5; St. Luke xxiii. 43; Stanza i. of Luther's hymn, 'Mit Fried' und Freud' ich fahr' dahin'; Stanza vii. of Adam Reissner's hymn, 'In dich hab' ich gehoffet, Herr.' A. B. Soli.
18	1714 (or 1713). Sexagesima.	Gleich wie der Regen und Schnee vom Himmel fällt (Isaiah lv. 10-11).	Erdmann Neumeister 'Fünffache Kirchen-Andachten', (Leipzig, 1716) (Ser. III.).	Isaiah lv. 10, 11; four clauses of the Litany; Stanza viii. of Lazarus Spengler's hymn, 'Durch Adams Fall ist ganz verderbt'; rest of libretto original. S. T. B. Soli.

*160	1714 (or 1713). Easter Day.	Ich weiss, dass mein Erlöser lebt.	Erdmann Neumeister (Ibid., Ser. I.). Slight verbal alterations by Bach.	Original throughout. Tenor Solo.
21	1714. Third S. after Trinity and General Use.	Ich hatte viel Bekümmernis (Psalm xciv. 19)	Spitta (i. 531) attributes text to Salomo Franck.	Part I.: Psalm xciv. 19; Psalm xlii. 5. Part II.: Psalm cxvi. 7; Rev. v. 12, 13; Stanzas ii. and v. of Georg Neumark's hymn, 'Wer nur den lieben Gott lässt walten'; rest of libretto original.
*199 N.B.G.	c. 1714. Eleventh S. after Trinity.	Mein Herze schwimmt im Blut.	The title is from a Neumeister text for this Sunday. ? By Bach.	Stanza iii. of Johann Heermann's hymn, 'Wo soll ich fliehen hin'; rest of libretto original. Soprano solo.
61	1714. First S. in Advent.	Nun komm, der Heiden Heiland.	Erdmann Neumeister, 'Fünffache Kirchen-Andachten', (Leipzig, 1716), (Ser. IV).	Stanza i. of Luther's hymn, 'Nun komm, der Heiden Heiland'; Rev. iii. 20; part of stanza vii. of Philipp Nicolai's hymn, 'Wie schön leuchtet der Morgenstern'; rest original. S. T. B. Soli.
142	1714 (or 1712). Christmas Day.	Uns ist ein Kind geboren (Isaiah ix. 6).	Erdmann Neumeister (Ibid., Ser. I.). Textually, the last three movements are altered, perhaps by Bach, whose authorship of the Cantata, however, is questioned ('Bach-Jahrbuch,' 1912, p. 132).	Isaiah ix. 9; Psalm lxix. 30; Stanza v. of Caspar Fuger's hymn, 'Wir Christenleut'; rest of libretto original (see Spitta i. 630 on Bach's emendations). A. T. B. Soli.

No.	Date.	Title.	Author of Libretto.	Composition of the Text.
182	1715 (or 1714). Palm Sunday (used also for the Annunciation).	Himmelskönig, sei willkommen.	Spitta (i. 539) suggests Salomo Franck, whose characteristics it displays.	Psalm xl. 7, 8; Stanza xxxiii. of Paul Stockmann's hymn, 'Jesu Leiden, Pein und Tod'; rest of libretto original. A. T. B. Soli.
31	1715. Easter Day. Revised in ? 1723. (Schweitzer, ii. 141n).	Der Himmel lacht, die Erde jubiliret.	Salomo Franck ('Evangelisches Andachts-Opffer' Weimar, 1715, p. 75).	Stanza v. (posthumous) of Nikolaus Herman's hymn, 'Wenn mein Stündlein vorhanden ist'; rest of libretto original. S. T. B. Soli.
†185	1715. Fourth S. after Trinity.	Barmherziges Herze der ewigen Liebe.	Salomo Franck (Ibid., p. 128).	Stanza i. of Johannes Agricola's hymn, 'Ich ruf' zu dir, Herr Jesu Christ'; rest of libretto original.
161	1715. Sixteenth S. after Trinity (also for Purification).	Komm, du süsse Todesstunde.	Salomo Franck (Ibid., p. 162); verbal alterations by Bach.	Stanza iv. of Christoph Knoll's hymn, 'Herzlich thut mich verlangen'; rest original. A. T. Soli.
†162	1715. Twentieth S. after Trinity.	Ach, ich sehe, jetzt da ich zur Hochzeit gehe.	Salomo Franck (Ibid., p. 172).	Stanza vii. of Johann Georg Albinus' hymn, 'Alle Menschen müssen sterben'; rest of libretto original.
†163	1715. Twenty-third S. after Trinity.	Nur Jedem das Seine.	Salomo Franck (Ibid., p. 182).	Stanza xi. (suggested by Spitta i. 557) of Johann Heermann's hymn, 'Wo soll ich fliehen hin'; rest of libretto original.
*132	1715. Fourth S. in Advent.	Bereitet die Wege, bereitet die Bahn.	Salomo Franck (Ibid., p. 8)	Stanza v. of Elisabethe Cruciger's hymn, 'Herr Christ, der einig' Gott's Sohn'; rest of libretto original.

No.	Date and Occasion	First line	Librettist	Notes
*152	1715 (or 1714). S. after Christmas.	Tritt auf die Glaubens-bahn.	Salomo Franck (*Ibid.*, p. 19).	Original throughout. S. and B. Soli.
†155	1716. Second S. after the Epiphany.	Mein Gott, wie lang', ach lange.	Salomo Franck (*Ibid.*, p. 32).	Stanza xii. of Paul Speratus' hymn, 'Es ist das Heil uns kommen her'; rest of libretto original.
†59	1716. Whit Sunday. Expanded in ? 1735 (No. 74 *infra*).	Wer mich liebet, der wird mein Wort halten (St. John xiv. 23).	Erdmann Neumeister ('Fünffache Kirchen-Andachten,' Ser. IV.).	St. John xiv. 23; Stanza i. of Luther's hymn, 'Komm, heiliger Geist, Herre Gott'; rest of libretto original. S. and B. Soli.
70	1716. Second S. in Advent; later (c. 1723). Twenty-sixth S. after Trinity.	Wachet, betet, betet, wachet.	Salomo Franck ('Evangelische Sonn- und Festtages Andachten,' Weimar, 1717, p. 4) (opening chorus and Arias only). Recitativi added by a later (? Bach) hand (c. 1723)	*Part I.*: Stanza x. of the anonymous hymn, 'Freu dich sehr, O meine Seele.' *Part II.*: Stanza v. of Christian Keimann's hymn, 'Meinen Jesum lass' ich nicht.' Rest of libretto, both parts, original.
147	1716. Fourth S. in Advent; later (c. ? 1727). Feast of the Visitation.	Herz und Mund und That und Leben.	Salomo Franck (*Ibid.*). (Opening chorus and first three Arias only). Recitativi and fourth Aria added by a later hand (? Bach).	*Part I.*: Stanza vi. of Martin Janus' hymn, 'Jesu, meiner Seelen Wonne.' *Part II.*: Stanza xvii. of the same hymn. Rest of libretto, both parts, original.

No.	Date.	Title.	Author of Libretto.	Composition of the Text.
†158	c. 1708-16. Purification of the B.V.M.; later (at Leipzig) adapted to Easter Tuesday.	Der Friede sei mit dir.	Spitta (ii. 688) suggests Franck as author of the Aria and following Recitativo, both of which bear on the Gospel for the Purification. The opening Recitativo and choice of the concluding Choral, both of which are relevant to the Gospel for Easter Tuesday, must be attributed to a later hand (? Bach).	Stanza i. of Johann Georg Albinus' hymn, 'Welt, ade! ich bin dein müde'; Stanza v. of Luther's hymn, 'Christ lag in Todesbanden'; rest of libretto original. S. and B. Soli.

(4) COMPOSED AT CÖTHEN. (See also Nos. 22 and 23.)

No.	Date.	Title.	Author of Libretto.	Composition of the Text.
173	c. 1718. Birthday Serenade; new text (c. 1730) for Whit Monday.	Erhötes Fleisch und Blut.	The music of the Cantata is that of the Birthday Serenade, 'Durchlaucht'-ster Leopold' (omitting numbers 5 and 6). Cantata text probably by Bach.	Original throughout.
47	? 1720. Seventeenth S. after Trinity.	Wer sich selbst erhöhet, der soll erniedriget werden (St. Luke xiv. 11).	Johann Friedrich Helbig ('Aufmunterung zur Andacht,' Eisenach, 1720, p. 114.	St. Luke xiv. 11; Stanza xi. of anonymous (? Hans Sachs) hymn, 'Warum betrübst du dich, mein Herz'; rest original. S. B. Soli.

No.	Date / Season	First line	Author	Notes
141	1721 or 1722. Third S. in Advent.	Das ist je gewisslich wahr (I. Timothy i. 15).	Johann Fr. Helbig (Ibid., p. 5). Bach's authorship of the music is questioned ('Bach-Jahrbuch,' 1912).	1 Timothy i. 15; rest of libretto is original. The concluding Choral is omitted by Bach. It should be 'Christe, du Lamm Gottes' (Spitta. ii. 15n.). A. T. B. Soli.
134	c. 1717-22. Secular Cantata; later adapted for Easter Tuesday (c. 1731).	Ein Herz, das seinen Jesum lebend weiss.	? Bach.	Text original throughout. A. T. Soli.

(5) COMPOSED AT LEIPZIG. 1723-34. (See also Nos. 31, 70, 134, 147, 158, 173.)

No.	Date / Season	First line	Author	Notes
22	1723. Quinquagesima. ('Estomihi').	Jesus nahm zu sich die Zwölfe (St. Luke xviii. 31). [See No. 31 (1715).]	? Bach (composed at Cöthen). Trial Cantata (February 7, 1723).	St. Luke xviii. 31, 34; Stanza v. of Elisabethe Cruciger's hymn, 'Herr Christ, der einig' Gott's Sohn'; rest original. A. T. B. Soli.
75	1723 (May 30). First S. after Trinity.	Die Elenden sollen essen (Psalm xxii. 26).	? Christian Weiss, senr.	Part I.: Psalm xxii. 26; Stanza v. of Samuel Rodigast's hymn, 'Was Gott thut, das ist wohlgethan'; Part II.: Stanza v. of the same hymn (repeated); rest of libretto, both parts, original.
76	1723. Second S. after Trinity. Also for Reformation Festival.	Die Himmel erzählen die Ehre Gottes (Psalm xix. 1, 3).	? Christian Weiss, senr.	Part I.: Psalm xix. 1, 3; Stanza i. of Luther's hymn, 'Es woll' uns Gott genädig sein'; Part II.: Stanza iii. of the same hymn; rest of libretto original. See Spitta ii. 357n.
24	1723. Fourth S. after Trinity.	Ein ungefärbt Gemüthe.	Erdmann Neumeister ('Fünffache Kirchen-Andachten') (Ser. IV.).	St. Matthew vii. 12; Stanza i. of Johann Heermann's hymn, 'O Gott, du frommer Gott'; rest of libretto original. A. T. B. Soli.

No.	Date.	Title.	Author of Libretto.	Composition of the Text.
186	1723. Seventh S. after Trinity.	Aergre dich, O Seele, nicht.	The opening chorus and first two Arias are by Salomo Franck ('Evangelische Sonn- und Fest-Tages,' p. 6), written for the Third S. in Advent, perhaps composed by Bach at Weimar. The remainder of the libretto was added in 1723 for the Seventh S. after Trinity. Both Gospels relate Christ's miracles.	*Part I.*: Stanza xii. of Paul Speratus' hymn, 'Es ist das Heil uns kommen her.'
†164	1723 (or 1724). Thirteenth S. after Trinity.	Ihr, die ihr euch von Christo nennet.	Salomo Franck ('Evangelisches Andachts-Opffer,' 1715, p. 152).	Stanza v. of Elisabethe Crueiger's hymn, 'Herr Christ, der einig' Gott's Sohn'; rest of libretto original. Perhaps written at Weimar.
119	1723. Inauguration of Town Council (Aug. 30).	Preise, Jerusalem, den Herrn (Psalm cxlvii. 12.	? Christian Weiss, senr.	Psalm cxlvii. 12-14; clauses xxii. and xxiii. of the 'Te Deum'; rest of libretto original.
194	1723. Opening of the Organ at Störmthal (November 2); later (1731) for Trinity Sunday. [See No. 70 (1716).]	Höchsterwünschtes Freudenfest.	? Bach.	*Part I.*: Stanzas vi. and vii. of Johann Heermann's hymn, 'Treuer Gott, ich muss dir klagen'; *Part II.*: Stanzas ix. and x. of Paul Gerhardt's hymn, 'Wach auf, mein Herz, und singe.' Rest of libretto original. S. T. B. Soli.

63	? 1723. Christmas Day.	Christen ätzet diesen Tag.	? Bach. The opening two lines suggested by a poem in Joh. Jakob Rambach's 'Geistliche Poesien' (Halle, 1720).	Original throughout.
40	? 1723. Feast of St. Stephen.	Dazu ist erschienen der Sohn Gottes (1 John iii. 8).	? Christian Weiss, senr. Wustmann (note 8) suggests Bach. Certainly same author as Nos. 64, 65 *infra*.	1 John iii. 8; Stanza iii. of Caspar Fuger's hymn, 'Wir Christenleut'; Stanza ii. of Paul Gerhardt's hymn, 'Schwing' dich auf zu deinem Gott'; Stanza iv. of Christian Keimann's hymn, 'Freuet euch, ihr Christen alle'; rest of libretto original. A. T. B. Soli.
64	? 1723. Feast of St. John the Evangelist.	Sehet, welch' eine Liebe hat uns der Vater erzeiget (1 John iii. 1).	? Christian Weiss, senr. Certainly same author as Nos. 40 *supra* and 65 *infra*.	1 John iii. 1; Stanza vii. of Luther's hymn, 'Gelobet seist du, Jesu Christ'; Stanza i. of Georg Michael Pfefferkorn's hymn, 'Was frag ich nach der Welt'; Stanza v. of Johann Franck's hymn, 'Jesu, meine Freude'; rest of libretto original. S. A. B. Soli.
16	? 1724. New Year's Day. Spitta (ii. 386, 413) regards No. 190 (*infra*) as Bach's first Leipzig New Year Cantata, and dates No. 16, 1723-27.	Herr Gott dich loben wir.	? Bach.	Clauses i. and ii. of Luther's 'Te Deum'; Stanza vi. of Paul Eber's hymn, 'Helft mir Gott's Güte preisen'; rest of libretto original. A. T. B. Soli.

No.	Date.	Title.	Author of Libretto.	Composition of the Text.
†153	1724. Sunday after the Circumcision.	Schau', lieber Gott, wie meine Feind'.	? Bach.	Stanza i. of David Denicke's (?) hymn, 'Schau', lieber Gott, wie meine Feind'; Isaiah xli. 10; Stanza v. of Paul Gerhardt's hymn, 'Befiehl du deine Wege'; Stanzas xi. and xii. (as three verses) of Martin Moller's (?) hymn, 'Ach Gott, wie manches Herzeleid'; rest of libretto original. A. T. B. Soli.
65	1724. Feast of the Epiphany.	Sie werden aus Saba Alle kommen (Isaiah lx. 6).	? Christian Weiss, senr. Wustmann (note 23) attributes text to author of Nos. 40 and 64 supra, i.e. Bach.	Isaiah lx. 6; Stanza iv. of the anonymous hymn, 'Ein Kind geborn zu Bethlehem'; Stanza x. of Paul Gerhardt's hymn, 'Ich hab' in Gottes Herz und Sinn'; rest original. A. T. B. Soli.
†154	1724. First S. after the Epiphany.	Mein liebster Jesus ist verloren.	? Bach. Wustmann (note 25) attributes it to an anonymous author.	Stanza ii. of Martin Janus' hymn, 'Jesu, meiner Seelen Wonne'; St. Luke ii. 49; Stanza vi. of Christian Keimann's hymn, 'Meinen Jesum lass' ich nicht'; rest original. A. T. B. Soli.
†81	1724. Fourth S. after the Epiphany.	Jesus schläft, was soll ich hoffen?	? Bach. Wustmann regards texts of Nos. 81 and 154 as being by the same hand (note 35).	St. Matthew viii. 26; Stanza ii. of Johann Franck's hymn, 'Jesu, meine Freude'; rest of libretto original. A. T. B. Soli.
†83	?1724. Feast of the Purification.	Erfreute Zeit im neuen Bunde.	? Bach.	St. Luke ii. 29, 30; Stanza iv. of Luther's hymn, 'Mit Fried' und Freud' ich fahr' dahin'; rest of libretto original. A. T. B. Soli.

23	1724. Quinquagesima ('Estomihi'). ? Composed at Cöthen. Spitta (ii. 679) holds this, and not No. 22, to have been Bach's first Quinquagesima Cantata at Leipzig.	Du wahrer Gott und Davids Sohn.	? Bach.	Three stanzas of 'Christe, du Lamm Gottes'; rest of libretto original. S. A. T. Soli.
4	1724. Easter Day ('Am Osterfeste')	Christ lag in Todesbanden	Luther.	Choral Cantata. The seven stanzas of the hymn are set in their original form.
12	1724 (or 1725). Third S. after Easter ('Jubilate'). Composed c. 1714 at Weimar (Spitta ii. 404).	Weinen, Klagen, Sorgen, Zagen.	? Salomo Franck.	Acts xiv. 22; Stanza vi. of Samuel Rodigast's hymn, 'Was Gott thut, das ist wohlgethan'; rest of libretto original. A. T. B. Soli.
172	1724 (or 1725). Whit Sunday. Perhaps revised c. 1727-30 (see Schweitzer, ii. 162).	Erschallet ihr Lieder.	? Salomo Franck (Spitta ii. 398). Wustmann (note 73) does not support the conjecture.	St. John xiv. 23; Stanza iv. of Philipp Nicolai's hymn, 'Wie schön leuchtet der Morgenstern'; rest of libretto original. Organ obbligato.
184	? 1724. Whit Tuesday.	Erwünschtes Freudenlicht.	? Bach. An adaptation of an earlier secular Cantata (Spitta, ii. 399).	Stanza viii. of Anark of Wildenfels' (?) hymn, 'O Herre Gott, dein göttlich Wort'; rest of libretto original. S. A. T. Soli.

No.	Date.	Title.	Author of Libretto.	Composition of the Text.
†165	? 1724. Trinity Sunday.	O heil'ges Geist- und Wasserbad.	Salomo Franck ('Evangelisches Andachts-Opffer,' 1715, p. 111).	Stanza v. of Ludwig Helmbold's hymn, 'Nun lasst uns Gott dem Herren'; rest of libretto original.
179	? 1724. Eleventh S. after Trinity.	Siehe zu, dass deine Gottesfurcht nicht Heuchelei sei (Ecclesiasticus i. 28).	? Christian Weiss, senr.	Ecclesiasticus i. 28; Stanza i. of Christoph Tietze's hymn, 'Ich armer Mensch, ich armer Sünder'; rest original. S. T. B. Soli.
69	? 1724. Twelfth S. after Trinity; c. 1730 adapted as a Ratswahl Cantata.	Lobe den Herren, meine Seele (Psalm ciii. 2).	? Christian Weiss, senr.	Psalm ciii. 2; Stanza iii. of Luther's hymn, 'Es woll' uns Gott genädig sein'; rest of libretto original. (See B. G. xvi. 379 for the Ratswahl form.)
190	c. 1725 (or 1724). New Year's Day; revised to celebrate the Augsburg Confession Jubilee on June 25, 1730.	Singet dem Herrn ein neues Lied (Psalm cxlix. 1).	As extended in 1730 the text is in Picander's 'Cantaten,' 1728-29. His authorship of the 1725 text is not therefore established.	Psalm cxlix. 1; Psalm cl. 4, 6; Clauses i. and ii. of the 'Te Deum'; Stanza ii. of Johann Hermann's hymn, 'Jesu, nun sei gepreiset'; rest of libretto original. A. T. B. Soli.
†73	c. 1725. Third S. after the Epi-	Herr, wie du willt, so schick's mit mir.	Author unknown. Spitta's (ii. 414) attribution of	Stanza i. of Caspar Bienemann's hymn, 'Herr, wie du willt, so schick's mit mir'; Stanza ix.

No.	Occasion	First line	Author	Notes
	phany.		the text to Picander is inadequately founded.	of Ludwig Helmbold's hymn, 'Von Gott will ich nicht lassen'; rest original. S. T. B. Soli.
144	c. 1725. Septuagesima.	Nimm was dein ist, und gehe hin (St. Matthew xx. 14).	Wustmann (note 37) suggests Picander, with Bach's additions. Schweitzer (ii. 200) supposes that the music is adapted.	St. Matthew xx. 14; Stanza i. of Samuel Rodigast's hymn, 'Was Gott thut, das ist wohlgethan'; Stanza i. of Albrecht of Brandenburg-Culmbach's hymn, 'Was mein Gott will, das g'scheh' allzeit'; rest of libretto original. S. A. T. Soli.
181	c. 1725. Sexagesima.	Leichtgesinnte Flattergeister.	? Picander.	Original throughout.
67	c. 1725. First S. after Easter ('Quasimodogeniti').	Halt' im Gedächtniss Jesum Christ (2 Timothy ii. 8).	? Christian Weiss, senr. Certainly not Picander, as Spitta (ii. 417) suggests.	2 Timothy ii. 8; Stanza i. of Nikolaus Herman's hymn, 'Erschienen ist der herrlich' Tag'; Stanza i. of Jakob Ebert's hymn, 'Du Friedefürst, Herr Jesu Christ'; rest of libretto original. A. T. B. Soli.
104	c. 1725. Second S. after Easter ('Misericordias Domini').	Du Hirte Israel, höre (Psalm lxxx. 1).	? Christian Weiss, senr.	Psalm lxxx. 1; Stanza i. of Cornelius Becker's hymn, 'Der Herr ist mein getreuer Hirt'; rest of libretto original. T. B. Soli.
†166	c. 1725. Fourth S. after Easter ('Cantate').	Wo gehest du hin? (St. John xvi. 5).	? Christian Weiss, senr.	St. John xvi. 5; Stanza iii. of Bartholomäus Ringwaldt's hymn, 'Herr Jesu Christ, ich weiss gar wohl'; Stanza i. of Emilie Juliane of Schwarzburg-Rudolstadt's hymn, 'Wer weiss, wie nahe mir mein Ende'; rest of libretto original.

No.	Date.	Title.	Author of Libretto.	Composition of the Text.
†86	c. 1725. Fifth S. after Easter ('Rogate').	Wahrlich, wahrlich, ich sage euch (St. John xvi. 23).	? Christian Weiss, senr.	St. John xvi. 23; Stanza xvi. of Georg Grüenwald's hymn, 'Kommt her zu mir, spricht Gottes Sohn'; Stanza xi. of Paul Speratus' hymn, 'Es ist das Heil uns kommen her'; rest of libretto original.
44	c. 1725. Sixth S. after Easter (S. after the Ascension) ('Exaudi').	Sie werden euch in den Bann thun (St. John xvi. 2).	? Christian Weiss, senr.	St. John xvi. 2; Stanza i. of Martin Moller's (?) hymn, 'Ach Gott, wie manches Herzeleid'; Stanza xv. of Paul Flemming's hymn, 'In allen meinen Thaten'; rest of libretto original.
20	c. 1725. First S. after Trinity. In its existing form the work is c. 1735.	O Ewigkeit, du Donnerwort.	Johann Rist (arranged). (? Picander).	Choral Cantata (2 Parts). Stanzas i., xi., xvi. are retained in their original form. Stanzas ii.-x. are paraphrased in the Arias and Recitativi. A. T. B. Soli.
†167	c. 1725. Feast of St. John Baptist (Midsummer Day).	Ihr Menschen, rühmet Gottes Liebe.	Author unknown. Spitta (ii. 423) remarks on the 'vapid emptiness' of the text.	Stanza v. of Johann Graumann's hymn, 'Nun lob', mein' Seel', den Herren'; rest of libretto original. The Choral is extended.
136	c. 1725 (or later). Eighth S. after Trinity.	Erforsche mich, Gott, und erfahre mein Herz (Psalm cxxxix. 23).	? Christian Weiss, senr. Schweitzer (ii. 200) supposes that the music is adapted.	Psalm cxxxix. 23; Stanza ix. of Johann Heermann's hymn, 'Wo soll ich fliehen hin'; rest of libretto original. A. T. B. Soli.

No.	Date	First Line	Librettist	Notes
†168	c. 1725. Ninth S. after Trinity. Perhaps composed at Weimar.	Thue Rechnung! Donnerwort!	Salomo Franck ('Evangelisches Andachts-Opffer,' 1715, p. 141).	Stanza viii. of Bartholomäus Ringwaldt's hymn, 'Herr Jesu Christ, du höchstes Gut'; rest of libretto original.
105	c. 1725. Ninth S. after Trinity.	Herr, gehe nicht in's Gericht (Psalm cxliii. 2).	? Christian Weiss, senr.	Psalm cxliii. 2; Stanza xi. of Johann Rist's hymn, 'Jesu, der du meine Seele'; rest of libretto original.
46	c. 1725. Tenth S. after Trinity.	Schauet doch und sehet, ob irgend ein Schmerz sei (Lam. i. 12).	? Christian Weiss, senr.	Lamentations i. 12; Stanza ix. (apocryphal) of Balthasar Schnurr's hymn, 'O grosser Gott von Macht'; rest original. A. T. B. Soli.
77	c. 1725. Thirteenth S. after Trinity.	Du sollst Gott, deinen Herren, lieben (St. Luke x. 27).	? Christian Weiss, senr.	St. Luke x. 27; Stanza viii. of David Denicke's (?) hymn, 'Wenn einer alle Ding verstünd' (posthumously added to Bach's text); rest of libretto original.
8	c. 1725. Sixteenth S. after Trinity.	Liebster Gott, wann werd' ich sterben?	Caspar Neumann (arranged by ? Picander).	Choral Cantata. Stanzas i. and v. are retained in their original form. Stanzas ii.-iv. are paraphrased in the Arias and Recitativi.
148	c. 1725. Seventeenth S. after Trinity.	Bringet dem Herrn Ehre seines Namens (Psalm xcvi. 8).	The groundwork is by Picander ('Sammlung Erbaulicher Gedancken,' Leipzig, 1725, p. 428), arranged by Bach. This is the earliest ascertained association of Bach and Picander (date ? Sept. 23, 1725).	Psalm xcvi. 8, 9; Stanza xi. of Johann Heermann's hymn, 'Wo soll ich fliehen hin' (suggested by Spitta, ii. 694; wanting in the score); rest of libretto original. A. T. B. Soli.

No.	Date.	Title.	Author of Libretto.	Composition of the Text.
72	c. 1726 (or earlier). Third S. after the Epiphany.	Alles nur nach Gottes Willen.	Salomo Franck ('Evangelisches Andachts-Opffer,' 1715, p. 35).	Stanza i. of Albrecht of Brandenburg-Culmbach's hymn, 'Was mein Gott will, das g'scheh' allzeit'; rest original. A. S. B. Soli.
19	1726. Feast of St. Michael the Archangel.	Es erhub sich ein Streit.	The groundwork of the text is a libretto for the season published by Picander in 1725. The Cantata version probably is by Bach himself. Spitta's (ii. 344) attribution of it to Picander is ill-founded.	Stanza ix. of the anonymous hymn, 'Freu' dich sehr, O meine Seele'; rest of libretto original. S. T. B. Soli.
195	? c. 1726. For a Wedding.	Dem Gerechten muss das Licht (Psalm xcvii. 11).	? Bach. Spitta (ii. 469) supposes that the music is adapted.	Psalm xcvii. 11, 12; Stanza i. of Paul Gerhardt's hymn, 'Nun danket all' und bringet Ehr''; rest of libretto original.
†157	1727. Feast of the Purification. Also for a Funeral.	Ich lasse dich nicht, du segnest mich denn (Gen. xxxii. 26).	Picander ('Satyrische Gedichte,' vol. i. p. 210).	Genesis xxxii. 26; Stanza vi. of Christian Keimann's hymn, 'Meinen Jesum lass' ich nicht'; rest by Picander. T. B. Soli.
37	c. 1727. (Schweitzer ii. 260, dates it 1728-34). Ascension Day. [See Nos. 147 (1716) and 172 (1724).]	Wer da glaubet und getauft wird (St. Mark xvi. 16).	? Christian Weiss, senr.	St. Mark xvi. 16; Stanza v. of Philipp Nicolai's hymn, 'Wie schön leuchtet der Morgenstern'; Stanza iv. of Johann Kolross' hymn, 'Ich dank' dir, lieber Herre'; rest of libretto original.

			Prof. J. C. Gottsched.	Original throughout.
198	1727. October 17.	Trauer-Musik: for Queen Christiane Eberhardine of Poland * (d. Sept. 7, 1727).	Prof. J. C. Gottsched.	Original throughout.
93	? 1728. Fifth S. after Trinity.	Wer nur den lieben Gott lässt walten.	Georg Neumark (arranged by ? Picander).	Choral Cantata; Stanzas i., iv., v., vii. of Neumark's hymn are retained in their original form; Stanzas ii., iii., vi. are inserted or paraphrased in the Arias and Recitativi.
†Incomplete.	? 1728. Christmas Day.	Ehre sei Gott in der Höhe (St. Luke ii. 14).	Picander ('Cantaten,' 1728-29, p. 71).	St. Luke ii. 14; Stanza iv. of Caspar Ziegler's hymn, 'Ich freue mich in dir'; rest original. A. B. Soli.
†159	? 1729. Quinquagesima ('Estomihi').	Sehet, wir geh'n hinauf nach Jerusalem (St. Luke xviii. 31).	Picander (Ibid., p. 106).	St. Luke xviii. 31; Stanza vi. of Paul Gerhardt's hymn, 'O Haupt voll Blut und Wunden'; Stanza xxxiii. of Paul Stockmann's hymn, 'Jesu Leiden, Pein und Tod'; rest original.
145	1729 (or 1730). Easter Tuesday ('Am Osterfeste').	So du mit deinem Munde bekennest Jesum (Romans x. 9), or Auf, mein Herz! des Herren Tag, or Ich lebe, mein Herze.	Picander ('Cantaten,' 1728-29, p. 125), with the addition (by Bach) of the opening Choral and Bible verse. See Spitta, ii. 442 n.	Stanza i. of Caspar Neumann's hymn, 'Auf, mein Herz! des Herren Tag'; Romans x. 9; Stanza xiv. of Nikolaus Herman's hymn, 'Erschienen ist der herrlich' Tag'; rest of libretto by Picander. S. T. B. Soli.
171	1730 (or 1731). Feast of the Circumcision (New Year's Day).	Gott, wie dein Name, so ist auch dein Ruhm (Psalm xlviii. 10).	Picander (Ibid., p. 81).	Psalm xlviii. 10; Stanza iii. of Johann Heermann's hymn, 'Jesu, nun sei gepreiset'; rest of libretto original.

NOTE.—General mourning for the Queen lasted from Sept. 7, 1727, to Jan. 6, 1728. No Cantatas were sung in the period.

* General mourning for the Queen lasted from Sept. 7, 1727, to Jan. 6, 1728.

No.	Date.	Title.	Author of Libretto.	Composition of the Text.
†156	1730 (or 1729). Third S. after the Epiphany. [See No. 173 (1718).]	Ich steh' mit einem Fuss im Grabe.	Picander (*Ibid.*, p. 91).	Stanza i. of Joh. Hermann Schein's hymn, 'Mach's mit mir, Gott, nach deiner Güt'; Stanza i. of Caspar Bienemann's hymn, 'Herr, wie du will't, so schick's mit mir'; rest of libretto original.
120	1730. Inauguration of the Town Council (Aug. 24). Used also for Augsburg Confession celebration on June 26, 1730. [See Nos. 69 (1724), 190 (1725).]	Gott, man lobet dich in der Stille (Psalm lxv. 1).	? Christian Weiss, senr.	Psalm lxv. i.; clauses xx.-xxiii. of the 'Te Deum'; rest of libretto original.
†188	1730 (or 1731). Twenty-first S. after Trinity. Incorporates older instrumental material.	Ich habe meine Zuversicht.	Picander ('Cantaten,' 1728-29, p. 47). Music probably by Wilhelm Friedemann Bach to a large extent.	Stanza i. of Sigismund Weingärtner's (?) hymn, 'Auf meinen lieben Gott'; rest of libretto original. Organ obbligato.
80	1730. Reformation Festival (c. Oct. 31). Composed mainly at Weimar (1716).	Ein' feste Burg ist unser Gott.	Luther and Salomo Franck ('Evangelisches Andachts-Opffer,' p. 60).	Choral Cantata. Stanzas i., ii., iii., iv. of Luther's hymn, 'Ein' feste Burg ist unser Gott,' are set in their original form; rest of libretto by Franck.

†89	c. 1730. Twenty-second S. after Trinity.	Was soll ich aus dir machen, Ephraim? (Hosea xi. 8).	? Christian Weiss, senr.	Hosea xi. 8; Stanza vii. of Johann Heermann's hymn, 'Wo soll ich fliehen hin'; rest of libretto original. S. A. B. Soli.
†52	c. 1730. Twenty-third S. after Trinity. Incorporates older instrumental material.	Falsche Welt, dir trau ich nicht.	Author unknown.	Stanza i. of Adam Reissner's hymn, 'In dich hab' ich gehoffet, Herr'; rest of libretto original. Soprano Solo.
36	c. 1730. First S. in Advent.	Schwingt freudig euch empor.	The opening Chorus and three Arias are adaptations by Bach of a secular Ode, having the same title, written by Picander and performed Nov. 30, 1726. The four Chorals replace Picander's original Recitativi. The music (excepting the Recitativi and final Chorus of the Ode) of the two works is identical.	Part I.: Stanza i. of Luther's hymn, 'Nun komm, der Heiden Heiland'; Stanza vi. of Philipp Nicolai's hymn, 'Wie schön leuchtet der Morgenstern'; Part II.: Stanzas vi. and viii. of Luther's hymn; remaining movements adapted by Bach from Picander.
Incomplete	c. 1730? For a Wedding.	O ewiges Feuer, O Ursprung der Liebe.	Author unknown. See No. 34 infra (c. 1740).	Psalm cxxviii. 4, 5, 6; Benediction; rest of libretto original.
*82	c. 1731. Feast of the Purification.	Ich habe genug.	? Bach.	Original throughout. Spitta (ii. 346) points out that the Aria 'Schlummert ein', seems to have been suggested by a text by Johann Jakob Rambach for the same season. Bass Solo.

No.	Date.	Title.	Author of Libretto.	Composition of the Text.
†84	1731 (or 1732). Septuagesima.	Ich bin vergnügt mit meinem Glücke.	A revision (? by Bach) of a text by Picander ('Cantaten,' 1728-29, p. 101).	Stanza xii. of Emilie Juliane of Schwarzburg-Rudolstadt's hymn, 'Wer weiss, wie nahe mir mein Ende'; rest original. Soprano Solo.
66	1731 (not 1735). Easter Monday. [See No. 134 (1717-22).]	Erfreut euch, ihr Herzen.	? Bach.	Stanza iii. of the hymn, 'Christ ist erstanden'; rest of libretto original. A. T. B. Soli.
†42	1731 (not c. 1740). First S. after Easter. ('Quasimodogeniti').	Am Abend aber desselbigen Sabbaths (St. John xx. 19).	? Christian Weiss, senr. Wustmann (note 57) suggests Bach.	St. John xx. 19; Stanza i. of Joh. Michael Altenburg's hymn, 'Verzage nicht, du Häuflein klein'; Stanza i. of Luther's Antiphon, 'Verleih' uns Frieden' and addendum; rest original.
112	1731. Second S. after Easter ('Misericordias Domini').	Der Herr ist mein getreuer Hirt (Psalm xxiii.).	Wolfgang Meusel.	Choral Cantata. The five stanzas of the hymn are set in their original form.
†174	1731 (or 1732). Whit Monday. Incorporates older instrumental material. [See No. 194 (1723).]	Ich liebe den Höchsten von ganzem Gemüthe.	Picander ('Cantaten,' 1728-29, p. 147).	Stanza i. of Martin Schalling's hymn, 'Herzlich lieb hab' ich dich, O Herr'; rest of libretto original. A. T. B. Soli.

9	? 1731. Sixth S. after Trinity.	Es ist das Heil uns kommen her.	Paul Speratus (arranged).	Choral Cantata. Stanzas i. and xii. are set in their original form. The intermediate stanzas are paraphrased in the Arias and Recitativi.
102	? 1731. Tenth S. after Trinity.	Herr, deine Augen sehen nach dem Glauben (Jeremiah v. 3).	? Christian Weiss, senr. Spitta (ii. 464) suggests Picander.	*Part I.*: Jeremiah v. 3; Romans ii. 4, 5; *Part II.*: Stanzas vi. and vii. of Johann Heermann's hymn, 'So wahrich lebe, spricht dein Gott'; rest original. A. T. B. Soli.
*35	? 1731. Twelfth S. after Trinity.	Geist und Seele wird verwirret.	The probability that the Cantata is a converted chamber music composition supports the inference that Bach wrote the text. See Spitta, ii. 447.	Original throughout (2 parts). Alto Solo and Organ obbligato.
25	c. 1731. Fourteenth S. after Trinity.	Es ist nichts gesundes an meinem Leibe (Psalm xxxviii. 3).	? Christian Weiss, senr.	Psalm xxxviii. 3; Stanza xii. of Johann Heermann's hymn, 'Treuer Gott, ich muss dir klagen'; rest of libretto original. S. T. B. Soli.
29	1731. Inauguration of the Town Council (Aug. 27). Incorporates older instrumental material.	Wir danken dir, Gott (Psalm lxxv. i.).	? Christian Weiss, senr.	Psalm lxxv. 1; Stanza v. (posthumous) of Johann Graumann's hymn, 'Nun lob', mein' Seel', den Herren'; rest of libretto original. Organ obbligato.
*51	1731 (or 1732). Fifteenth S. after Trinity.	Jauchzet Gott in allen Landen.	? Bach. A version for Michaelmas (? 1737) also exists. See Spitta, ii. 473n.	Stanza v. of Johann Graumann's hymn, 'Nun lob', mein' Seel', den Herren'; rest of libretto original. Soprano Solo.

No.	Date.	Title.	Author of Libretto.	Composition of the Text.
†27	1731. Sixteenth S. after Trinity.	Wer weiss, wie nahe mir mein Ende.	? Bach. The first Aria is suggested by a Neumeister stanza ('Kirchen-Andachten,' p. 294). See Spitta, ii. 451.	Stanza i. of Emilie Juliane of Schwarzburg-Rudolstadt's hymn, 'Wer weiss, wie nahe mir mein Ende'; Stanza i. of Joh. Georg Albinus' hymn, 'Welt ade! ich bin dein müde; rest of libretto original. Organ obbligato. Choral extended.
†169	1731 (or 1732). Eighteenth S. after Trinity. Incorporates older instrumental material.	Gott soll allein mein Herze haben.	Author unknown.	Stanza iii. of Luther's hymn, 'Nun bitten wir den heiligen Geist'; rest of libretto original. Alto Solo and Organ obbligato.
149	1731. Feast of St. Michael the Archangel.	Man singet mit Freuden vom Sieg (Psalm cxviii. 15).	? Christian Weiss, senr. First Chorus borrowed from 'Was mir behagt.'	Psalm cxviii. 15, 16; Stanza iii. of Martin Schalling's hymn, 'Herzlich lieb hab' ich dich, O Herr'; rest of libretto original.
†56	1731 (or 1732). Nineteenth S. after Trinity.	Ich will den Kreuzstab gerne tragen.	? Bach, working on a Neumeister text ('Kirchen-Andachten,' p. 514).	Stanza vi. of Johann Franck's hymn, 'Du, O schönes Weltgebäude'; rest of libretto original. Bass Solo.
*49	c. 1731. Twentieth S. after Trinity. Incorporates older instrumental material.	Ich geh' und suche mit Verlangen.	Author unknown.	Stanza vii. of Philipp Nicolai's hymn, 'Wie schön leuchtet der Morgenstern'; rest of libretto original. S. B. Soli and Organ obbligato.

109	c. 1731. Twenty-first S. after Trinity.	Ich glaube, lieber Herre, hilf meinem Unglauben (St. Mark ix. 24).	? Christian Weiss, senr.	St. Mark ix. 24; Stanza vii. of Lazarus Spengler's hymn, 'Durch Adams Fall ist ganz verderbt'; rest original. A. T. Soli.
†55	1731 (or 1732). Twenty-second S. after Trinity.	Ich armer Mensch, ich Sündenknecht.	Author unknown.	Stanza vi. of Johann Rist's hymn, 'Werde munter, mein Gemüthe'; rest of libretto original. Tenor Solo.
140	1731 (or later). Twenty-seventh S. after Trinity.	Wachet auf, ruft uns die Stimme.	Philipp Nicolai (arranged by ? Picander).	Choral Cantata. All three stanzas of the hymn are set in their original form. The rest of the libretto is original. S. T. B. Soli.
129	1732. Trinity Sunday.	Gelobet sei der Herr.	Johannes Olearius.	Choral Cantata. The five stanzas of the hymn are set in their original form. S. A. B. Soli.
39	1732 (not c. 1740). First S. after Trinity.	Brich dem Hungrigen dein Brod (Isaiah lviii. 7).	? Christian Weiss, senr. Schweitzer (ii. 343) attributes the text to Picander.	Part I.: Isaiah lviii. 7, 8; Part II.: Hebrews xiii.16; Stanza vi. of David Denicke's hymn, 'Kommt, lasst euch den Herren lehren'; rest of libretto original. S. A. B. Soli.
177	1732. Fourth S. after Trinity.	Ich ruf' zu dir, Herr Jesu Christ.	Johannes Agricola.	Choral Cantata. The five stanzas of the hymn are set in their original form. S. A. T. Soli.
†88	1732. Fifth S. after Trinity.	Siehe, ich will viel Fischer aussenden (Jer. xvi. 16).	? Christian Weiss, senr.	Part I.: Jeremiah xvi. 16; Part II.: St. Luke v. 10; Stanza vii. of Georg Neumark's hymn, 'Wer nur den lieben Gott lässt walten'; rest of libretto original.
*170	? 1732. Sixth S. after Trinity.	Vergnügte Ruh, beliebte Seelenlust.	Author unknown.	Original throughout. See Spitta, ii. 453n. Alto Solo and Organ obbligato.

o

No.	Date.	Title.	Author of Libretto.	Composition of the Text.
187	1732. Seventh S. after Trinity.	Es wartet Alles auf dich (Psalm civ. 27).	? Christian Weiss, senr. Schweitzer (ii. 343) attributes the text to Picander.	*Part I.*: Psalm civ. 27, 28; *Part II.*: St. Matthew vi. 31, 32; Stanzas iv. and vi. of the anonymous hymn, 'Singen wir aus Herzensgrund'; rest original. S. A. B. Soli.
137	? 1732. Twelfth S. after Trinity.	Lobe den Herren, den mächtigen König der Ehren.	Joachim Neander.	Choral Cantata. The five stanzas of the hymn are set in their original form.
95	? 1732. Sixteenth S. after Trinity.	Christus, der ist mein Leben.	Author unknown.	Stanza i. of the anonymous hymn, 'Christus, der ist mein Leben'; Stanza i. of Luther's hymn, 'Mit Fried' und Freud' ich fahr' dahin'; Stanza i. of Valerius Herberger's hymn, 'Valet will ich dir geben'; Stanza iv. of Nikolaus Herman's hymn, 'Wenn mein Stündlein vorhanden ist'; rest original. S. T. B. Soli.
98	c. 1732. Twenty-first S. after Trinity.	Was Gott thut, das ist wohlgethan.	Author unknown.	Stanza i. of Samuel Rodigast's hymn, 'Was Gott thut, das ist wohlgethan'; rest of libretto original.
†60	1732. Twenty-fourth S. after Trinity.	O Ewigkeit, du Donnerwort.	Author unknown.	Stanza i. of Johann Rist's hymn, 'O Ewigkeit du Donnerwort'; Psalm cxix. 166; Revelation xiv. 13; Stanza v. of Franz Joachim Burmeister's hymn, 'Es ist genug'; rest of libretto original. A. T. B. Soli.

No.	Date / Occasion	Title	Author	Notes
192	c. 1732. Occasion not specified. Incomplete.	Nun danket alle Gott.	Martin Rinkart.	Choral Cantata. The three stanzas of the hymn are set in their original form. S. A. B. Soli.
*58	1733. Sunday after the Circumcision.	Ach Gott, wie manches Herzeleid.	? Bach.	Stanza i. of Martin Moller's (?) hymn, 'Ach Gott, wie manches Herzeleid'; Stanza ii. of Martin Behm's hymn, 'O Jesu Christ, mein's Lebens Licht'; rest original. S. B. Soli.
99	c. 1733. Fifteenth S. after Trinity.	Was Gott thut, das ist wohlgethan.	Samuel Rodigast (arranged).	Choral Cantata. Stanzas i. and vi. of the hymn are set in their original form. The intervening stanzas are paraphrased in the Arias and Recitativi.
191	c. 1733. Christmas Day ('Am Weihnachtsfeste').	Gloria in excelsis Deo.	St. Luke ii. 14.	The 'Gloria' of the B minor Mass.
117	c. 1733. Occasion not specified.	Sei Lob und Ehr' dem höchsten Gut.	Johann Jakob Schütz.	Choral Cantata. The nine stanzas of the hymn are set in their original form. A. T. B. Soli.
97	1734. ? For a Wedding, or general use.	In allen meinen Thaten.	Paul Flemming. See Schweitzer, ii. 242n.	Choral Cantata. The nine stanzas of the hymn are set in their original form.
*54	1723-34. Occasion not specified.	Widerstehe doch der Sünde.	Author unknown.	Original throughout. Alto Solo.
*53	1723-34. ? For a Funeral.	Schlage doch, gewünschte Stunde.	? Salomo Franck.	A single eight-lined original stanza. Alto Solo.

(6) COMPOSED AT LEIPZIG: 1735-50

No.	Date.	Title.	Author of Libretto.	Composition of the Text.
43	1735. New Year's Day.	Lobe den Herrn, meine Seele (Psalm cxlvi. 1).	? Christian Weiss, senr. Wustmann (note 19) suggests Bach.	Psalm cxlvi. 1, 5, 10; Stanzas i. and iii. of Jakob Ebert's hymn, 'Du Friedefürst, Herr Jesu Christ'; the rest of the libretto (two Arias) original. S. T. B. Soli.
14	1735. Fourth S. after the Epiphany.	Wär' Gott nicht mit uns diese Zeit (Psalm cxxiv.).	Luther (arranged).	Choral Cantata. Stanzas i. and iii. are set in their original form. Stanza ii. is paraphrased in the intervening Arias and Recitativo. S. T. B. Soli.
†85	1735. Second S. after Easter. ('Misericordias Domini').	Ich bin ein guter Hirt (St. John x. 11).	Spitta (iii. 71) and Schweitzer (ii. 331n) attribute the text to Marianne von Ziegler. Wustmann (note 60) disagrees.	St. John x. 11; Stanza i. of Cornelius Becker's hymn, 'Derr Herr ist mein getreuer Hirt'; Stanza iv. of Ernst Christoph Homburg's hymn, 'Ist Gott mein Schild und Helfersmann'; rest of libretto original.
103	? 1735. Third S. after Easter ('Jubilate').	Ihr werdet weinen und heulen (St. John xvi. 20).	Marianne von Ziegler ('Versuch in gebundener Schreibart,' Leipzig, 1728). Emended by Bach.	St. John xvi. 20; Stanza ix. of Paul Gerhardt's hymn, 'Barmherzger Vater, höchster Gott'; rest of libretto original. A. T. Soli.
108	? 1735. Fourth S. after Easter. ('Cantate').	Es ist euch gut, dass ich hingehe (St. John xvi. 7).	Marianne von Ziegler (Ibid.). Emended by Bach.	St. John xvi. 7, 13; Stanza x. of Paul Gerhardt's hymn, 'Gott Vater, sende deinen Geist'; rest of libretto original. A.T.B. Soli.

No.	Date and Occasion	First line	Author		Notes
†87	? 1735. Fifth S. after Easter ('Rogate').	Bisher habt ihr nichts gebeten in meinem Namen (St. John xvi. 24).	Marianne (*Ibid.*). Bach.	von Ziegler Emended by	St. John xvi. 24, 33; Stanza ix. of Heinrich Müller's hymn, 'Selig ist die Seele'; rest of libretto original. A. T. B. Soli.
43	1735. Ascension Day.	Gott fähret auf mit Jauchzen (Psalm xlvii. 5).	? Bach. Schweitzer (ii. 331n) wrongly attributes text to Marianne von Ziegler.		*Part I.*: Psalm xlvii. 5, 6; St. Mark xvi. 19; *Part II.*: Stanzas i. and xiii. of Johann Rist's hymn, 'Du Lebensfürst, Herr Jesu Christ'; rest of libretto original, excepting the second, third, and fourth Arias. Original portion perhaps by Bach.
11	c. 1735. Ascension Day.	Lobet Gott in seinen Reichen.	Author unknown.		St. Luke xxiv. 50-52; Acts i. 9-11; Stanza iv. of Johann Rist's hymn, 'Du Lebensfürst, Herr Jesu Christ'; Stanza vii. of Gottfried Wilhelm Sacer's hymn, 'Gott fähret auf gen Himmel'; rest of libretto original.
128	? 1735. Ascension Day.	Auf Christi Himmelfahrt allein.	Marianne (*Ibid.*). Bach.	von Ziegler Emended by	Stanza i. of Josua Wegelin's hymn, 'Auf Christi Himmelfahrt allein'; Stanza iv. of Matthäus Avenarius's hymn, 'O Jesu, meine Lust'; rest of libretto original. A. T. B. Soli.
†183	? 1735. Sunday after the Ascension ('Exaudi').	Sie werden euch in den Bann thun (St. John xvi. 2).	Marianne (*Ibid.*). Bach.	von Ziegler Emended by	St. John xvi. 2; Stanza v. of Paul Gerhardt's hymn, 'Zeuch ein zu deinen Thoren'; rest of libretto original.
74	? 1735. Whit Sunday. An expansion of No. 59 (1716).	Wer mich liebet, der wird mein Wort halten (St. John xiv. 23).	Marianne (*Ibid.*).	von Ziegler	St. John xiv. 23, 28; Romans viii. 1; Stanza ii. of Paul Gerhardt's hymn, 'Gott Vater, sende deinen Geist' rest of libretto original.

No.	Date.	Title.	Author of Libretto.	Composition of the Text.
68	? 1735. Whit Monday. Contains old (1716) secular material.	Also hat Gott die Welt geliebt.	Marianne von Ziegler (*Ibid.*). Emended by Bach. See 'Was mir behagt.'	Stanza i. of Salomo Liscow's hymn, 'Also hat Gott die Welt geliebt'; St. John iii. 18; rest of libretto original. S. B. Soli.
†175	? 1735. Whit Tuesday.	Er rufet seinen Schafen mit Namen (St. John x. 3).	Marianne von Ziegler (*Ibid.*). Emended slightly by Bach.	St. John x. 3, 6; Stanza ix. of Johann Rist's hymn, 'O Gottes Geist, mein Trost und Rath'; rest of libretto original. A. T. B. Soli.
176	? 1735. Trinity Sunday. [See No. 20 (1725).]	Es ist ein trotzig und verzagt Ding. (Cf. Jer. xvii. 9).	Marianne von Ziegler (*Ibid.*). Emended by Bach.	Stanza viii. of Paul Gerhardt's hymn, 'Was alle Weisheit in der Welt'; rest original. S. A. B. Soli.
107	c. 1735. Seventh S. after Trinity.	Was willst du dich betrüben.	Johann Heermann.	Choral Cantata. Six stanzas of the hymn are set in their original form. The final Choral is stanza xiv. of David Denicke's hymn, 'Ich will zu aller Stunde.' S. T. B. Soli.
94	? 1735. Ninth S. after Trinity.	Was frag ich nach der Welt.	Georg Michael Pfefferkorn (arranged).	Choral Cantata. Stanzas i., iii., v., vii., viii. are set in their original form. Stanzas ii., iv., vi. are paraphrased in the Arias.
133	1735 (or 1737). Feast of St. John the Evangelist.	Ich freue mich in dir.	Caspar Ziegler (arranged by ? Christian Weiss, junr.).	Choral Cantata. Stanzas i. and iv. of the hymn are set in their original form. The intervening stanzas are paraphrased in the Arias and Recitativi.

No.	Date and Occasion	First Line	Author	Notes
100	c. 1735. ? Fifteenth S. after Trinity, or for a Wedding.	Was Gott thut, das ist wohlgethan.	Samuel Rodigast.	Choral Cantata. The six stanzas of the hymn are set in their original form.
5	1735. Nineteenth S. after Trinity.	Wo soll ich fliehen hin.	Johann Heermann (arranged by ? Picander).	Choral Cantata. Stanzas i. and xi. of the hymn are set in their original form. The intervening Arias and Recitativi are based particularly on stanzas iii., iv., vii., viii., ix.
79	? 1735. Reformation Festival (Oct. 30).	Gott, der Herr, ist Sonn und Schild (Psalm lxxxiv. 11).	? Christian Weiss, senr.	Psalm lxxxiv. 11; Stanza i. of Martin Rinkart's hymn, 'Nun danket alle Gott'; Stanza viii. of Ludwig Helmbold's hymn, 'Nun lasst uns Gott dem Herren'; rest of libretto original. S. A. B. Soli.
41	? 1736. New Year's Day.	Jesu, nun sei gepreiset.	Johann Heermann (arranged).	Choral Cantata. Stanzas i. and iii. of the hymn are set in their original form. Stanza ii. is paraphrased in the intervening Arias and Recitativi.
†13	c. 1736. Second S. after the Epiphany.	Meine Seufzer, meine Thränen.	Author unknown.	Stanza ii. of Johann Heermann's hymn, 'Zion klagt mit Angst und Schmerzen'; Stanza xv. of Paul Flemming's hymn, 'In allen meinen Thaten'; rest original.
	[1736. Easter Day	Kommt, eilet und laufet.	? Picander.]	
6	1736. Easter Monday.	Bleib' bei uns, denn es will Abend werden (St. Luke xxiv. 29).	Author unknown. Wustmann (note 53) suggests Picander.	St. Luke xxiv. 29; Stanzas i. and ii. of Nikolaus Selnecker's hymn, 'Ach bleib' bei uns, Herr Jesu Christ'; Stanza ii. of Luther's hymn, 'Erhalt' uns, Herr, bei deinem Wort'; rest original.

No.	Date.	Title.	Author of Libretto.	Composition of the Text.
28	c. 1736. Sunday after Christmas. Spitta, ii. 433, dates it 1725-27.	Gottlob! nun geht das Jahr zu Ende.	Erdmann Neumeister ('Fünffache Kirchen-Andachten,' 1716. Ser. IV.).	Stanza i. of Johann Graumann's hymn, 'Nun lob', mein Seel', den Herren'; Jeremiah xxxii. 41; Stanza vi. of Paul Eber's hymn, 'Helft mir Gott's Güte preisen'; rest of libretto original.
17	c. 1737. Fourteenth S. after Trinity.	Wer Dank opfert, der preiset mich (Psalm l. 23).	? Bach. Schweitzer (ii. 343) attributes the text to Picander.	Part I.: Psalm l. 23; Part II.: St. Luke xvii. 15, 16; Stanza iii. of Johann Graumann's hymn, 'Nun lob', mein' Seel', den Herren'; rest original.
118	c. 1737. ? For a Funeral.	O Jesu Christ, mein's Lebens Licht.	Martin Behm.	Stanza i. of Martin Behm's hymn, 'O Jesu Christ, mein's Lebens Licht.' A Motet; cf. No. 50 (c. 1740).
197	? 1737. For a Wedding. Contains older material (? 1728).	Gott ist uns're Zuversicht.	? Bach. Pt. II.'s Arias are based on the Christmas Cantata 'Ehre sei Gott' (? 1728).	Stanza iii. of Luther's hymn, 'Nun bitten wir den heiligen Geist'; Stanza vii. (partly re-written) of Georg Neumark's hymn, 'Wer nur den lieben Gott lässt walten'; rest original. S. A. B. Soli.
30	1738. Feast of St. John Baptist (Midsummer Day).	Freue dich, erlöste Schaar.	Reconstruction, by ? Picander, of his 'Angenehmes Wiederau,' 1737, from which the music also is in part borrowed.	Part I.: Stanza iii. of Johannes Olearius' hymn, 'Tröstet, tröstet, meine Lieben'; rest of libretto original.

No.	Date / Occasion	Hymn	Author	Description
123	c. 1740. Feast of the Epiphany.	Liebster Immanuel, Herzog der Frommen.	Ahasuerus Fritsch (arranged by ? Christian Weiss, junr.).	Choral Cantata. Stanzas i. and v. of the hymn are set in their original form. Stanzas ii., iii., iv. are paraphrased in the intervening Arias and Recitativi. A. T. B. Soli.
†32	c. 1740. First S. after the Epiphany.	Leibster Jesu, mein Verlangen.	? Picander.	St. Luke ii. 49; Stanza xii. of Paul Gerhardt's hymn, 'Weg, mein Herz, mit den Gedanken'; rest of libretto original. S. B. Soli.
124	c. 1740. First S. after the Epiphany.	Meinen Jesum lass' ich nicht.	Christian Keimann (arranged by ? Picander).	Choral Cantata. Stanzas i. and vi. of the hymn are set in their original form. Stanzas ii.-v. are paraphrased in the intervening Arias and Recitativi.
3	c. 1740. Second S. after the Epiphany.	Ach Gott, wie manches Herzeleid.	Martin Moller (arranged by ? Christian Weiss, junr.).	Choral Cantata. Stanzas i., ii., xii. of the hymn are set in their original form. Stanzas iv.-vi., ix., x. are paraphrased in the Arias and Recitativo.
111	c. 1740. Third S. after the Epiphany.	Was mein Gott will, das g'scheh' allzeit.	Albrecht, Margrave of Brandenburg-Culmbach (arranged).	Choral Cantata. Stanzas i. and iv. of the hymn are set in their original form. Stanzas ii. and iii. are paraphrased in the Arias and Recitativi.
92	c. 1740. Septuagesima.	Ich hab' in Gottes Herz und Sinn.	Paul Gerhardt (arranged by ? Picander).	Choral Cantata. Stanzas i., ii., v., x., xii. of the hymn are set in their original form. Stanzas iii., iv., vi.-viii., ix. are paraphrased in the Arias and Recitativo.

No.	Date.	Title.	Author of Libretto.	Composition of the Text.
125	c. 1740. Feast of the Purification.	Mit Fried' und Freud' ich fahr' dahin.	Luther (arranged).	Choral Cantata. Stanzas i., ii., iv. are set in their original form. Stanza iii. is paraphrased in the second Aria and Recitativo. A. T. B. Soli.
126	c. 1740. Sexagesima.	Erhalt' uns, Herr, bei deinem Wort.	Luther (arranged).	Choral Cantata. Stanzas i., iii., and Luther's 'Verleih' uns Frieden gnädiglich' are set in their original form. The other stanzas are paraphrased in the Arias and second Recit. A. T. B. Soli.
127	c. 1740. Quinquagesima ('Estomihi').	Herr Jesu Christ, wahr'r Mensch und Gott.	Paul Eber (arranged by ? Picander).	Choral Cantata. Stanzas i. and viii. of the hymn are set in their original form. The intervening stanzas are paraphrased in the Recitativi and Arias. S. T. B. Soli.
1	c. 1740. Feast of the Annunciation.	Wie schön leuchtet der Morgenstern.	Philipp Nicolai (arranged by ? Picander).	Choral Cantata. Stanzas i. and vii. of the hymn are set in their original form. Stanzas ii.-vi. are paraphrased in the intervening Recitativi and Arias. S. T. B. Soli.
146	c. 1740. Third S. after Easter ('Jubilate'). Incorporates older instrumental material.	Wir müssen durch viel Trübsal in das Reich Gottes eingehen (Acts xiv. 22).	Author unknown. Schweitzer (ii. 343) names Picander.	Acts xiv. 22; excepting the concluding Choral (words wanting in the score) the rest of the libretto is original.

34	c. 1740 (or 1741). Whit Sunday ('Am Pfingst-feste'). Incorporates (modified) parts of the Wedding Cantata (c. 1730) bearing the same title.	O ewiges Feuer, O Ursprung der Liebe.	? by Bach.	Original throughout. Movements 1, 3, 5, follow the Wedding Cantata, words and music. A. T. B. Soli.
2	c. 1740. Second S. after Trinity.	Ach Gott, vom Himmel sieh darein.	Luther (arranged by ? Picander).	Choral Cantata. Stanzas i. and vi. of the hymn are set in their original form. The intervening stanzas are paraphrased in the Arias and Recitativi. A. T. B. Soli.
135	c. 1740. Third S. after Trinity.	Ach Herr, mich armen Sünder.	Cyriacus Schneegass. Also attributed to Christoph Demantius (arranged by ?Christian Weiss, junr.).	Choral Cantata. Stanzas i. and vi. of the hymn (see Psalm vi.) are set in their original form. The intervening stanzas are paraphrased in the Arias and Recitativi. A. T. B. Soli.
7	c. 1740. Feast of St. John Baptist (Midsummer Day).	Christ unser Herr zum Jordan kam.	Luther (arranged).	Choral Cantata. Stanzas i. and vii. of the hymn are set in their original form. The intervening stanzas are paraphrased in the Arias and Recitativi. A. T. B. Soli.
10	c. 1740. Feast of the Visitation.	Meine Seel' erhebt den Herren. (St. Luke, i. 46).	St. Luke, i. 46-55 (arranged).	Choral Cantata. Verses 46-48, 54, and the Doxology, are set in their original form. The other verses are paraphrased in the Arias and Recitativi.

No.	Date.	Title.	Author of Libretto.	Composition of the Text.
45	c. 1740. Eighth S. after Trinity.	Est ist dir gesagt, Mensch, was gut ist (Micah vi. 8).	? Christian Weiss, senr. Schweitzer (ii. 343) attributes the text to Picander.	*Part I.*: Micah vi. 8; *Part II.*: St. Matthew vii. 22, 23; Stanza ii. of Johann Heermann's hymn, 'O Gott, du frommer Gott'; rest original. A. T. B. Soli.
178	c. 1740. Eighth S. after Trinity.	Wo Gott der Herr nicht bei uns hält (Psalm cxxiv.).	Justus Jonas (arranged).	Choral Cantata. Stanzas i., ii., iv., v., vii., viii., of the hymn are set in their original form. The other stanzas are paraphrased. A. T. B. Soli.
101	c. 1740. Tenth S. after Trinity.	Nimm von uns, Herr, du treuer Gott.	Martin Moller (arranged). Schweitzer (ii. 375) names Picander.	Choral Cantata. Stanzas i., iii., v., vii. are set in their original form. Stanzas ii., iv., vi. are paraphrased in the Arias.
113	c. 1740. Eleventh S. after Trinity.	Herr Jesu Christ, du höchstes Gut.	Bartholomäus Ringwaldt (arranged).	Choral Cantata. Stanzas i., ii., iv., viii. of the hymn are set in their original form. Stanzas iii., v.-vii. are paraphrased in the Arias and Recitativo.
193	c. 1740. Inauguration of the Town Council (c. August 24). Incomplete.	Ihr Pforten [Tore] zu Zion	Author unknown.	Original throughout. S. A. T. (or B.) Soli.
33	c. 1740. Thirteenth S. after Trinity.	Allein zu dir, Herr Jesu Christ.	Johannes Schneesing. Attributed also to Conrad Hubert. Arranged.	Choral Cantata. Stanzas i. and iv. of the hymn are set in their original form. The intervening stanzas are paraphrased. A. T. B. Soli.

78	c. 1740 (or after 1734) Fourteenth S. after Trinity.	Jesu, der du meine Seele.	Johann Rist (arranged by ? Picander).	Choral Cantata. Stanzas i. and xii. of the hymn are set in their original form. Four lines of Stanza x. are inserted into the last Recitativo.
138	c. 1740 (or earlier). Fifteenth S. after Trinity.	Warum betrübst du dich, mein Herz.	? Hans Sachs and ? Picander.	Choral Cantata. Stanzas i., ii., iii. of the hymn are set in their original form. Rest of libretto original. A. T. B. Soli.
114	c. 1740. Seventeenth S. after Trinity.	Ach, lieben Christen, seid getrost.	Johannes Gigas (arranged).	Choral Cantata. Stanzas i., iii., vi. of the hymn are set in their original form. The other stanzas are paraphrased in the remaining movements.
96	c. 1740. Eighteenth S. after Trinity.	Herr Christ, der ein'ge Gottes-Sohn.	Elisabethe Cruciger (arranged by ? Picander).	Choral Cantata. Stanzas i. and v. of the hymn are set in their original form. The intervening stanzas are paraphrased in the Recitativi and Arias.
130	c. 1740. Feast of St. Michael the Archangel.	Herr Gott, dich loben alle wir.	Paul Eber (arranged).	Choral Cantata. Stanzas i., xi., xii. (in score only) of the hymn are set in their original form. The remaining stanzas are paraphrased.
50	c. 1740. Feast of St. Michael the Archangel.	Nun ist das Heil und die Kraft.	Revelation xii. 10.	Rev. xii. 10; a single Bible passage. A Motet. Cf. No. 118 (c. 1737).

No.	Date.	Title.	Author of Libretto.	Composition of the Text.
48	c. 1740. Nineteenth S. after Trinity.	Ich elender Mensch, wer wird mich erlösen (Rom. vii. 24).	? Picander.	Romans vii. 24; Stanza iv. of the anonymous hymn, 'Ach Gott und Herr'; Stanza xii. of the anonymous hymn, 'Herr Jesu Christ, ich schrei zu dir'; rest original. A. T. Soli.
180	c. 1740. Twentieth S. after Trinity.	Schmücke dich, O liebe Seele.	Johann Franck (arranged).	Choral Cantata. Stanzas i., iv., ix. of the hymn are set in their original form. The remaining stanzas are paraphrased.
38	c. 1740. Twenty-first S. after Trinity.	Aus tiefer Noth schrei ich zu dir (Psalm cxxx.).	Luther (arranged by ? Christian Weiss, junr.).	Choral Cantata. Stanzas i. and v. of the hymn are set in their original form. The intervening stanzas are paraphrased.
115	c. 1740. Twenty-second S. after Trinity.	Mache dich, mein Geist, bereit.	Johann Burchard Freystein (arranged by ? Picander.	Choral Cantata. Stanzas i. and x. of the hymn are set in their original form. The intervening ones are paraphrased.
139	c. 1740. Twenty-third S. after Trinity.	Wohl dem, der sich auf seinen Gott.	Johann Christoph Rube (arranged).	Choral Cantata. Stanzas i. and v. are set in their original form. The intervening ones are paraphrased.
26	c. 1740. Twenty-fourth S. after Trinity.	Ach wie flüchtig.	Michael Franck (arranged by ? Picander).	Choral Cantata. Stanzas i. and xiii. of the hymn are set in their original form. Stanzas ii.-xii. are paraphrased.

†90	c. 1740. Twenty-fifth S. after Trinity.	Es reifet euch ein schreck-lich Ende.	? Picander.	Stanza vii. of Martin Moller's hymn, 'Nimm von uns, Herr, du treuer Gott'; rest of libretto original. A. T. B. Soli.
62	c. 1740 (after 1734). First S. in Advent.	Nun komm, der Heiden Heiland.	Luther (arranged by ? Picander).	Choral Cantata. Stanzas i. and viii. are set in their original form. The intervening stanzas are paraphrased.
91	c. 1740. Christmas Day.	Gelobet seist du, Jesu Christ.	Luther (arranged by ? Picander).	Choral Cantata. Stanzas i., ii., vii. of the hymn are set in their original form. The remaining stanzas are paraphrased.
110	After 1734. Christmas Day. Has older instrumental material.	Unser Mund sei voll Lachens (Psalm cxxvi. 2).	? Christian Weiss, senr. Schweitzer (ii. 343) suggests Picander.	Psalm cxxvi. 2, 3; Jeremiah x. 6; St. Luke ii. 14; Stanza v. of Caspar Fuger's hymn, 'Wir Christenleut'; rest of libretto original.
†57	c. 1740. Feast of St. Stephen.	Selig ist der Mann (St. James i. 12).	? Picander.	St. James i. 12; Stanza vi. of Ahasuerus Fritsch's hymn, 'Hast du, denn, Jesu, dein Angesicht gantzlich verborgen'; rest of libretto original. S. B. Soli.
121	c. 1740. Feast of St. Stephen.	Christum wir sollen loben schon.	Luther (arranged by ? Picander).	Choral Cantata. Stanzas i. and viii. of the hymn are set in their original form. Stanzas ii.-vi. are paraphrased. A. T. B. Soli.

No.	Date.	Title.	Author of Libretto.	Composition of the Text.
†151	c. 1740. Feast of St. John the Evangelist.	Süsser Trost, mein Jesus kommt.	? Bach.	Stanza viii. of Nikolaus Herman's hymn, 'Lobt Gott, ihr Christen alle gleich'; rest of libretto original.
Incomplete	c. 1740 (after 1734). For a Wedding.	Herr Gott, Beherrscher aller Dinge.	? Bach.	Stanzas iv. and v. of Joachim Neander's hymn, 'Lobe den Herren'; rest original. S. B. Soli.
122	c. 1742. Sunday after Christmas Day.	Das neugebor'ne Kindelein.	Cyriacus Schneegass and ? Bach.	Choral Cantata. Stanzas i., iii., iv. of the hymn are set in their original form. Stanza ii. is paraphrased in the first Aria. The two Recitativi are original.
116	1744 (Nov. 15). Twenty-fifth S. after Trinity.	Du Friedefürst, Herr Jesu Christ.	Jakob Ebert. Also attributed to Ludwig Helmbold (arranged).	Choral Cantata. Stanzas i. and vii. of the hymn are set in their original form. The intervening stanzas are paraphrased.

APPENDIX III

THE BACHGESELLSCHAFT EDITIONS OF BACH'S WORKS

THE Bachgesellschaft was founded on December 15, 1850, issued its first volume in 1851, and was dissolved on January 27, 1900, upon the publication of its sixtieth and concluding volume. The Society had fulfilled its fundamental purpose—the publication of Bach's works—and on the very date of its dissolution the Neue Bachgesellschaft was founded with the object of popularising Bach's music by publishing it in practicable form and by holding Bach Festivals. A secondary object, the foundation of a Bach Museum at Eisenach, in the house in which Bach was born, already has been achieved. Bach Festivals have been held at regular intervals—at Berlin in 1901, Leipzig in 1904, Eisenach—in connection with the opening of the Museum—in 1907, at Chemnitz in 1908, Duisburg in 1910, Breslau in 1912, Vienna in 1914. The publications of the new Society necessarily are unimportant by the side of those of its predecessor. It has, however, brought to light and published a Cantata overlooked by the old Bachgesellschaft. (See New B.G. xiii. (2).)

The publications of both Societies are quoted here by their year of issue—i., ii., iii., and so forth. When more than one volume has been published in a single year they are differentiated thus : xv.(1), xv.(2). When a volume appeared upon a date subsequent to the Vereinsjahr it bears, the date of the Preface is indicated in a bracket, *e.g.* 1872[1876].

The editorial work of the original Bachgesellschaft was undertaken, in unequal proportions, by ten editors during fifty years. Of the Society's sixty volumes three were edited by Moritz Hauptmann (1851-58), one by Carl F. Becker (1853), two by Julius Rietz (1854-56), twenty-seven by Wilhelm Rust (1855-81), one by Franz Kroll (1866), eleven by Alfred Dörffel (1876-98), six by Paul Graf Waldersee (1881-94), five by Ernst Naumann (1886-94), two by Franz Wüllner (1887-92), and two by Hermann Kretzschmar (1895-1900).

(A) PUBLICATIONS OF THE BACHGESELLSCHAFT

I. 1851.   **Kirchencantaten.   Erster Band.   Ed. Moritz Hauptmann.**[1]

No. *1. Wie schön leuchtet der Morgenstern.
   *2. Ach Gott, vom Himmel sieh darein.
   *3. Ach Gott, wie manches Herzeleid (*c.* 1740).
   *4. Christ lag in Todesbanden.
    5. Wo soll ich fliehen hin.
   *6. Bleib' bei uns, denn es will Abend werden.
    7. Christ unser Herr zum Jordan kam.
   *8. Liebster Gott, wann werd' ich sterben ?
    9. Es ist das Heil uns kommen her.
   *10. Meine Seel' erhebt den Herren !
Frontispiece : G. Haussmann's portrait of Bach, in the possession of St. Thomas' School, Leipzig.

---

[1] The Church Cantatas are published by Peters and also by Breitkopf and Haertel.   A prefixed asterisk indicates that an English edition of the Cantata or Oratorio is published by Novello or Breitkopf and Haertel.

The Organ music is published by Novello, to whose edition references are given (N.), Peters, and Breitkopf and Haertel.   A collation of the Peters and Novello editions is given in Appendix V.

The Clavier and Instrumental music is published by Peters, to whose edition references are given (P.).

II. 1852.   Kirchencantaten.   Zweiter Band.   Ed. Moritz
Hauptmann.

*No. 11. Lobet Gott in seinen Reichen.
 *12. Weinen, Klagen, Sorgen, Zagen.
  13. Meine Seufzer, meine Thränen.
  14. Wär' Gott nicht mit uns diese Zeit.
  15. Denn du wirst meine Seele nicht in der Hölle lassen.
  16. Herr Gott dich loben wir.
  17. Wer Dank opfert, der preiset mich.
  18. Gleich wie der Regen und Schnee vom Himmel fällt.
  19. Es erhub sich ein Streit.
  20. O Ewigkeit, du Donnerwort (*c.* 1725).

III. 1853.   Clavierwerke.   Erster Band.   Ed. Carl F. Becker.

(1) Fifteen Inventions and Fifteen Symphonies (Sinfonie)
    (P. bk. 201).[1]
(2) Clavierübung, Part I. :—
    Partiten 1-6 (P. bks. 205, 206).
(3) Clavierübung, Part II. :—
    Concerto, in F major, in the Italian style (P bk. 207).
    Partita (Overture) in B minor (P. bk. 208).
(4) Clavierübung, Part III. :—
    Organ Prelude and Fugue in E flat major (N. bk. 16
    pp. 19, 83).
    Four Duetti (P. bk. 208 p. 78).
    Catechism Choral Preludes (Organ) :—
        1. Kyrie, Gott Vater in Ewigkeit (N. bk. 16 p. 28).
           Christe, aller Welt Trost (*ib.* p. 30).
           Kyrie, Gott heiliger Geist (*ib.* p. 33).
        2. Kyrie, Gott Vater in Ewigkeit (alio modo) (*ib.*
           p. 36).
           Christe, aller Welt Trost (*ib.* p. 37).
           Kyrie, Gott heiliger Geist (*ib.* p. 38).
        3. Allein Gott in der Höh' sei Ehr' (*ib.* p. 39).
        4.   Ditto (*ib.* p. 40*).[2]

---

[1] A Variant of the first Invention is on p. 342 of the volume. A
Variant of Sinfonia ix. is on p. vi. of the Nachtrag.
[2] A Variant is in B.G. XL.

5. Allein Gott in der Höh' sei Ehr' (Fughetta) (N. bk. 16 p. 41).
6. Dies sind die heil'gen zehn Gebot' (*ib.* p. 42).
7.   Ditto (Fughetta) (*ib.* p. 47).
8. Wir glauben all' an einen Gott (*ib.* p. 49).
9.   Ditto (Fughetta) (*ib.* p. 52).
10. Vater unser im Himmelreich (*ib.* p. 53).
11.   Ditto (*ib.* p. 61).[1]
12. Christ unser Herr zum Jordan kam (*ib.* p. 62).
13.   Ditto (*ib.* p. 67).
14. Aus tiefer Noth schrei ich zu dir (*ib.* p. 68).
15.   Ditto (*ib.* p. 72).
16. Jesus Christus unser Heiland (*ib.* p. 74).
17.   Ditto (Fugue) (*ib.* p. 80).
(5) Clavierübung, Part IV. :—
    Aria and thirty Variations (Goldberg) (P. bk. 209).
(6) Toccata in F sharp minor (P. bk. 210 p. 30).
    Ditto. C minor (P. bk. 210 p. 40).
    Fugue (with Fantasia) in A minor (P. bk. 207 p. 16).

IV. 1854. ***Passionsmusik nach dem Evangelisten Matthäus. Ed. Julius Rietz.**

V (1). 1855. **Kirchencantaten. Dritter Band. Ed. Wilhelm Rust.**

No. *21. Ich hatte viel Bekümmerniss.
    22. Jesus nahm zu sich die Zwölfe.
  *23. Du wahrer Gott und Davids Sohn.
    24. Ein ungefärbt Gemüthe.
  *25. Es ist nichts Gesundes an meinem Leibe.
    26. Ach wie flüchtig, ach wie nichtig.
  *27. Wer weiss, wie nahe mir mein Ende.
  *28. Gottlob ! nun geht das Jahr zu Ende.
    29. Wir danken dir, Gott, wir danken dir.
  *30. Freue dich, erlöste Schaar.

V (2). 1855 [1856]. ***Weihnachts-Oratorium. Ed. Wilhelm Rust.**

---

[1] A Variant is in P. bk. 244 p. 109.

VI. 1856. *Messe. H moll. Ed. Julius Rietz.

VII. 1857. Kirchencantaten. Vierter Band. Ed. Wilhelm Rust.

No. 31. Der Himmel lacht, die Erde jubiliret.
*32. Liebster Jesu, mein Verlangen.
33. Allein zu dir, Herr Jesu Christ.
*34. O ewiges Feuer, O Ursprung der Liebe.
35. Geist und Seele wird verwirrt.
36. Schwingt freudig euch empor.
37. Wer da glaubet und getauft wird.
*38. Aus tiefer Noth schrei ich zu dir.
*39. Brich dem Hungrigen dein Brod.
*40. Dazu ist erschienen der Sohn Gottes.

VIII. 1858. Vier Messen. F dur, *A dur, G moll, G dur. Ed. Moritz Hauptmann.

IX. 1859 [1860]. Kammermusik. Erster Band. Ed. Wilhelm Rust.

Three Sonatas, in B minor, E flat major, A minor (and Variant), for Clavier and Flute (P. bk. 234).
Suite in A major, for Clavier and Violin (P. bk. 236).
Six Sonatas, in B minor, A major, E major, C minor, F minor (and Variant), G major (and Variants), for Clavier and Violin (P. bks. 232, 233).
Three Sonatas, in G major (or 2 Flutes), D major, G minor for Clavier and Viola da Gamba (P. bk. 239).
Sonata in G major, for Flute, Violin, and Clavier (P. bk. 237).
Sonata in C major, for two Violins and Clavier (P. bk. 237).
Sonata in G minor, for Clavier and Violin (not in P.).[1]

X. 1860. Kirchencantaten. Fünfter Band. Ed. Wilhelm Rust.

No. *41. Jesu, nun sei gepreiset.
42. Am Abend aber desselbigen Sabbaths.
*43. Gott fähret auf mit Jauchzen.
*44. Sie werden euch in den Bann thun (c. 1725).

---

[1] 'If genuine, the Sonata is a youthful work,' remarks Schweitzer, i. 401 n.

45. Es ist dir gesagt, Mensch, was gut ist.
46. Schauet doch und sehet, etc.
47. Wer sich selbst erhöhet, der soll erniedriget werden·
48. Ich elender Mensch, wer wird mich erlösen ?
49. Ich geh' und suche mit Verlangen.
*50. Nun ist das Heil und die Kraft.

XI (1). 1861 [1862]. *Magnificat, D dur, und vier Sanctus,
C dur, D dur, D moll, G dur. Ed. Wilhelm Rust.

The Appendix contains four additional numbers which
are found in one of the two Autograph scores of the
Magnificat.

XI (2). 1861 [1862]. Kammermusik für Gesang. Erster
Band. Ed. Wilhelm Rust.

Secular Cantata : *Phoebus und Pan.
Do.   Weichet nur, betrübte Schatten.
Do.   Amore traditore.
Do.   Von der Vergnügsamkeit, or, Ich bin in
         mir vergnügt.
Do.   Der zufriedengestellte Aeolus, or, Zer-
         reisset, zersprenget, zertrümmert die
         Gruft.

XII (1). 1862 [1863]. *Passionsmusik nach dem Evangelisten
Johannes. Ed. Wilhelm Rust.

XII (2). 1862 [1863]. Kirchencantaten. Sechster Band. Ed.
Wilhelm Rust.

No. 51. Jauchzet Gott in allen Landen.
52. Falsche Welt, dir trau ich nicht.
*53. Schlage doch, gewünschte Stunde.
*54. Widerstehe doch der Sünde.
55. Ich armer Mensch, ich Sündenknecht.
*56. Ich will den Kreuzstab gerne tragen.
57. Selig ist der Mann.
58. Ach Gott, wie manches Herzeleid (1733).
59. Wer mich liebet, der wird mein Wort halten (1716).
60. O Ewigkeit, du Donnerwort (1732).

XIII (1). 1863 [1864]. Trauungs-Cantaten.   Ed. Wilhelm Rust.

> No. *195. Dem Gerechten muss das Licht.
> 196. Der Herr denket an uns.
> 197. Gott ist uns're Zuversicht.
> Drei Choräle zu Trauungen : (1) Was Gott thut, (2) Sei Lob und Ehr', (3) Nun danket alle Gott.

XIII (2). 1863. Clavierwerke.   Zweiter Band.   Ed. Wilhelm Rust.

Six Great Suites, in A major, A minor, G minor, F major, E minor, D minor, known as the ' English Suites ' (P. bks. 203, 204).

Six Small Suites, in D minor, C minor, B minor, E flat major, G major, E major, known as the ' French Suites ' (P. bk. 202).[1]

XIII (3). 1863 [1865]. *Trauer-Ode.   Ed. Wilhelm Rust.

XIV. 1864 [1866]. Clavierwerke. Dritter Band. Das wohl-temperirte Clavier (P. bks. 2790 a-b.).   Ed. Franz Kroll.[2]

Erster Theil, 1722.
Zweiter Theil, 1744.

XV. 1865 [1867]. Orgelwerke.   Erster Band.   Ed. Wilhelm Rust.

Six Sonatas, in E flat major, C minor, D minor, E minor, C major, G major (N. bks. 4, 5), for 2 Claviers and Pedal.

Eighteen Preludes and Fugues :—

Prelude and Fugue in C major (N. bk. 7 p. 74).
Do.   do.   D major (N. bk. 6 p. 10).
Do.   do.   E minor (N. bk. 2 p. 44).

---

[1] Additional movements of the second, third, and fourth Suites are in Appendix II. of B.G. xxxvi.

[2] The volume contains an Appendix of Variants, etc. See also B.G. xlv. (1) Appendix. Variants of Nos. 1, 3, 6 of Part II. are in Appendix I. of B.G. xxxvi.

Prelude and Fugue in F minor (N. bk. 6 p. 21).
Do.   do.   G minor (N. bk. 8 p. 120).
Do.   do.   A major (N. bk. 3 p. 64).
Do. (Fantasia) do. C minor (N. bk. 3 p. 76).
Do. (Toccata)   D minor (N. bk. 10 p. 196).
Do.   do.   D minor (N. bk. 9 p. 150).
Do. (Toccata) do. F major (N. bk. 9 p. 176).
Do. do. the Great, G major (N. bk. 8 p. 112).
Do. (Fantasia) do. do. G minor (N. bk. 8 p. 127).[1]
Do.   do. do. A minor (N. bk. 7 p. 42).[2]
Do.   do. do. B minor (N. bk. 7 p. 52).
Do.   do. do. C minor (N. bk. 7 p. 64).
Do.   do. do. C major (N. bk. 9 p. 156).
Do.   do. do. E minor (N. bk. 8 p. 98).
Do.   do. C major (N. bk. 3 p. 70).
Three Toccatas and Fugues, in C major, the ' Great ' (N.
bk. 9 p. 137).
Do.   do.   D minor (N. bk. 6 p. 2).
Do.   do.   E major (N. bk. 8 p. 88,
as Prelude and Fugue
in C major).
Passacaglia, in C minor (N. bk. 10 p. 214).

XVI. 1866 [1868].   Kirchencantaten.   Siebenter Band.   Ed. Wilhelm Rust.

No. *61. Nun komm, der Heiden Heiland (1714).
    62. Nun komm, der Heiden Heiland (c. 1740).
    63. Christen, ätzet diesen Tag.
    64. Sehet, welch' eine Liebe.
   *65. Sie werden aus Saba Alle kommen.
    66. Erfreut euch, ihr Herzen.
   *67. Halt' im Gedächtniss Jesum Christ.
   *68. Also hat Gott die Welt geliebt.
    69. Lobe den Herren, meine Seele.
   *70. Wachet, betet, seid bereit allezeit.

---

[1] See publications of the N.B.G. xiv. (2) no. 5.
[2] See publications of the N.B.G. vii. (3) no. 3.

XVII. 1867 [1869]. **Kammermusik. Zweiter Band. Ed. Wilhelm Rust.**

Seven Concertos, in D minor (and Variant),[1] E major (and Variant), D major (and Variant), A major (and Variant), F minor, F major, G minor, for Clavier and Orchestra (Strings ; two flutes added in Concerto VI. (P. bks. 248-254).[2]

Triple Concerto in A minor, for Flute, Violin, Clavier, and Orchestra (Strings). (P. bk. 255).

XVIII. 1868 [1870]. **Kirchencantaten. Achter Band. Ed. Wilhelm Rust.**

No. 71. Gott ist mein König.
   72. Alles nur nach Gottes Willen.
   73. Herr, wie du willt, so schick's mit mir.
   74. Wer mich liebet, der wird mein Wort halten (? 1735).
   75. Die Elenden sollen essen.
   76. Die Himmel erzählen die Ehre Gottes.
   77. Du sollst Gott, deinen Herren, lieben.
   78. Jesu, der du meine Seele.
  *79. Gott, der Herr, ist Sonn' und Schild.
  *80. Ein' feste Burg ist unser Gott.

XIX. 1869 [1871]. **Kammermusik. Dritter Band. Ed. Wilhelm Rust.**

Six Concertos (' Brandenburg ') for Orchestra and Continuo :—
   No. I. in F major (Strings, 3 Ob., Fag., 2 Cor. (P. bk. 261).[3]
   No. II. in F major (Strings, Flute, Oboe, Tromba) (P. bk. 262).

---

[1] For this work, in its original form as a Violin Concerto, see N.B.G. XVIII. (1 and 2).

[2] The D major (No. 3) and G minor (No. 7) Concertos are identical with the Violin Concertos in E major and A minor. See B.G. XXI. (1). No. 6 (F. major) is the fourth Brandenburg Concerto (in G.). See B.G. XIX. no. 4.

[3] In a shortened form this work appears also as a Sinfonia in F major. See B.G. XXXI. (1) no. 5, and N.B.G. X. (2).

No. III. in G major (Strings) (P. bk. 263). [N.B.G. ix. (3)].
No. IV. in G major (Strings and 2 Flutes) (P. bk. 264).
No. V. in D major (Strings, Flute, Clavier) (P. bk. 265).
No. VI. in B flat major (2 Violas, 2 Violas da Gamba, Violoncello, Contrabasso) (P. bk. 266).

XX (1). 1870 [1872]. **Kirchencantaten. Neunter Band. Ed. Wilhelm Rust.**

No. *81. Jesus schläft, was soll ich hoffen ?
  *82. Ich habe genug.
   83. Erfreute Zeit im neuen Bunde.
   84. Ich bin vergnügt mit meinem Glücke.
   85. Ich bin ein guter Hirt. [Score, N.B.G. ix. (1)].
   86. Wahrlich, wahrlich, ich sage euch.
   87. Bisher habt ihr nichts gebeten in meinem Namen.
   88. Siehe, ich will viel Fischer aussenden. [Score, N.B.G. vii. (1)].
   89. Was soll ich aus dir machen, Ephraim ?
   90. Es reifet euch ein schrecklich Ende.

XX (2). 1870 [1873]. **Kammermusik für Gesang. Zweiter Band. Ed. Wilhelm Rust.**

Secular Cantata : Schleicht, spielende Wellen.
  Do.   Vereinigte Zwietracht der wechselnden Saiten.
  Do.   Auf, schmetternde Töne der muntern Trompeten. [See B.G. xxxiv].

XXI (1). 1871 [1874]. **Kammermusik. Vierter Band. Ed. Wilhelm Rust.**

Three Concertos for Violin and Orchestra (Strings) :—
  No. I. in A minor (P. bk. 229).[1]
  No. II. in E major (P. bk. 230).[2]

---

[1] Identical with the G minor Clavier Concerto. See B.G. xvii. no. 7, and also B.G. xlv. (1), Appendix, p. 233.
[2] Identical with the D major Clavier Concerto. See B.G. xvii. no. 3, and N.B.G. viii. (1)

No. III. in D minor (two Violins) (P. bk. 231).¹
Symphonic movement, in D major, for Violin and Orchestra
(Strings, 2 Ob., 3 Trombe, Timp.).²

**XXI (2). 1871 [1874]. Kammermusik. Fünfter Band. Ed.
Wilhelm Rust.**

Three Concertos for two Claviers and Orchestra (Strings) :—
No. I. in C minor (P. bk. 257).
No. II. in C major (P. bk. 256).
No. III. in C minor (P. bk. 257b).³

**XXI (3). 1871 [1874]. *Oster-Oratorium : ' Kommt, eilet und
laufet.' Ed. Wilhelm Rust.**

**XXII. 1872 [1875]. Kirchencantaten. Zehnter Band. Ed.
Wilhelm Rust.**

No. 91. Gelobet seist du, Jesu Christ.
    92. Ich hab' in Gottes Herz und Sinn.
  *93. Wer nur den lieben Gott lässt walten.
    94. Was frag ich nach der Welt.
    95. Christus, der ist mein Leben.
    96. Herr Christ, der ein'ge Gottes-Sohn.
    97. In allen meinen Thaten.
    98. Was Gott thut, das ist wohlgethan, in B major
       (c. 1732).
    99. Was Gott thut, das ist wohlgethan, in G major
       (c. 1733).
  100. Was Gott thut, das ist wohlgethan, in G major
       (c. 1735).

¹ Identical with the Concerto for two Claviers in C minor. See
B.G. XXI. (2) no. 3.
² The movement is described as being from ' einer unbekannten
Kirchencantate ' for four voices and Orchestra. The Autograph is
incomplete. The movement is not published elsewhere than in the
B.G. edition.
³ Identical with the Concerto for 2 Violins, in D minor. See
B.G. XXI. (1) no. 3. Also pp. 131, 158, 160, *supra*.

XXIII. 1873 [1876].   Kirchencantaten.   Elfter Band.   Ed. Wilhelm Rust.

   No. 101. Nimm von uns, Herr, du treuer Gott.
       102. Herr, deine Augen sehen nach dem Glauben.
       103. Ihr werdet weinen und heulen.
    *104. Du Hirte Israel, höre.
       105. Herr, gehe nicht in's Gericht.
    *106. Gottes Zeit ist die allerbeste Zeit (Actus tragicus).
       107. Was willst du dich betrüben.
       108. Es ist euch gut, dass ich hingehe.
       109. Ich glaube, lieber Herre.
       110. Unser Mund sei voll Lachens.

XXIV. 1874 [1876].   Kirchencantaten.   Zwölfter Band.   Ed. Alfred Dörffel.

   No. 111. Was mein Gott will, das g'scheh' allzeit.
    *112. Der Herr ist mein getreuer Hirt.
       113. Herr Jesu Christ, du höchstes Gut.
       114. Ach, lieben Christen, seid getrost.
    *115. Mache dich, mein Geist, bereit.
    *116. Du Friedefürst, Herr Jesu Christ.
       117. Sei Lob und Ehr' dem höchsten Gut.
       118. O Jesu Christ, mein's Lebens Licht.[1]
    *119. Preise, Jerusalem, den Herrn.
       120. Gott, man lobet dich in der Stille.

XXV (1). 1875 [1878].   Die Kunst der Fuge : 1749-1750 Ed. Wilhelm Rust.

Contrapunctus 1-14
Four Canons
Two Fugues for two Claviers } (P. bk. 218).
Fugue on three subjects

---

[1] Also in N.B.G. xvii. (1 and 2).

XXV (2) 1875 [1878]. **Orgelwerke. Zweiter Band. Ed. Wilhelm Rust.**

(1) Orgelbüchlein (N. bk. 15), containing Preludes on the following melodies : [1]

Advent—

1. Nun komm der Heiden Heiland.
2. Gott, durch deine Güte, *or*, Gottes Sohn ist kommen.
3. Herr Christ, der ein'ge Gottes-Sohn, *or*, Herr Gott, nun sei gepreiset.
4. Lob sei dem allmächtigen Gott.

Christmas—

5. Puer natus in Bethlehem.
6. Gelobet seist du, Jesu Christ.
7. Der Tag, der ist so freudenreich.
8. Vom Himmel hoch, da komm' ich her.
9. Vom Himmel kam der Engel Schaar.
10. In dulci jubilo.
11. Lobt Gott, ihr Christen, allzugleich.
12. Jesu, meine Freude.
13. Christum wir sollen loben schon.
14. Wir Christenleut'.

New Year—

15. Helft mir Gottes Güte preisen.
16. Das alte Jahr vergangen ist.
17. In dir ist Freude.

Feast of the Purification of the B.V.M.—

18. Mit Fried' und Freud' ich fahr' dahin.
19. Herr Gott, nun schleuss den Himmel auf.

Passiontide—

20. O Lamm Gottes, unschuldig.
21. Christe, du Lamm Gottes.
22. Christus, der uns selig macht.
23. Da Jesus an dem Kreuze stund.

---

[1] For an exposition of Bach's design in the 'Orgelbüchlein,' see the present writer's articles in 'The Musical Times' for January–March 1917, and 'Bach's Chorals,' Part III. See N.B.G. II. (1) for an arrangement of the Preludes for two pianofortes.

24. O Mensch, bewein' dein' Sünde gross.
25. Wir danken dir, Herr Jesu Christ.
26. Hilf Gott, dass mir's gelinge.

Easter—

27. Christ lag in Todesbanden.
28. Jesus Christus, unser Heiland, der den Tod.
29. Christ ist erstanden (three verses).
30. Erstanden ist der heil'ge Christ.
31. Erschienen ist der herrliche Tag.
32. Heut' triumphiret Gottes Sohn.

Whitsunday—

33. Komm, Gott, Schöpfer, heiliger Geist.

Trinity Sunday—

34. Herr Jesu Christ, dich zu uns wend'.
35-6. Liebster Jesu, wir sind hier (two settings).

The Catechism—

37. Dies sind die heil'gen zehn Gebot.
38. Vater unser im Himmelreich.

Penitence and Amendment—

39. Durch Adam's Fall ist ganz verderbt.
40. Es ist das Heil uns kommen her.

Christian Conduct and Experience—

41. Ich ruf' zu dir, Herr Jesu Christ.

In Time of Trouble—

42. In dich hab' ich gehoffet, Herr.
43. Wenn wir in höchsten Nöthen sein.
44. Wer nur den lieben Gott lässt walten.

Death and the Grave—

45. Alle Menschen müssen sterben.

The Life Eternal—

46. Ach wie nichtig, ach wie flüchtig.

(2) Six Chorals (Schübler) (N. bk. 16) on the following melodies :

Wachet auf, ruft uns die Stimme.
Wo soll ich fliehen hin, *or*, Auf meinen lieben Gott.
Wer nur den lieben Gott lässt walten.
Meine Seele erhebt den Herren.
Ach bleib bei uns, Herr Jesu Christ.
Kommst du nun, Jesu, vom Himmel herunter.

(3) Eighteen Chorals (N. bk. 17) on the following melodies :
- 1, 2. Komm, heiliger Geist, Herre Gott (two settings).
- 3. An Wasserflüssen Babylon.
- 4. Schmücke dich, O liebe Seele.
- 5. Herr Jesu Christ, dich zu uns wend'.
- 6. O Lamm Gottes unschuldig (three verses).
- 7. Nun danket Alle Gott.
- 8. Von Gott will ich nicht lassen.
- 9, 10, 11. Nun komm der Heiden Heiland (three settings).
- 12, 13, 14. Allein Gott in der Höh' sei Ehr' (three settings).
- 15, 16. Jesus Christus, unser Heiland, der von uns (two settings).
- 17. Komm, Gott, Schöpfer, heiliger Geist.
- 18. Vor deinen Thron tret' ich, or, Wenn wir in höchsten Nöthen sein.

(4) Older texts of the ' Orgelbüchlein ' and ' Eighteen ' Chorals :
- 1. Christus, der uns selig macht (Orgelbüchlein No. 22) (P. bk. 244 p. 108).
- 2. Komm, Gott, Schöpfer, heiliger Geist (Orgelbüchlein No. 33) (P. bk. 246 p. 86A).
- 3. Komm, heiliger Geist, Herre Gott (Eighteen No. 1) (P. bk. 246 p. 86).
- 4. Ditto (Eighteen No. 2) (P. bk. 246 p. 88).
- 5. An Wasserflüssen Babylon (Eighteen No. 3) (P. bk. 245 p. 103).
- 6. Herr Jesu Christ, dich zu uns wend' (Eighteen No. 5) (P. bk. 245 pp. 107, 108 prints two of the three Variants).
- 9. O Lamm Gottes unschuldig (Eighteen No. 6) (P. bk. 246 p. 97).
- 10. Von Gott will ich nicht lassen (Eighteen No. 8) (P. bk. 246 p. 102).
- 11. Nun komm der Heiden Heiland (Eighteen No. 9) (P. bk. 246 p. 92).
- 12. Ditto (Eighteen No. 10) (P. bk. 246 pp. 93, 94).
- 14. Ditto (Eighteen No. 11) (P. bk. 246 p. 96).
- 15. Allein Gott in der Höh' sei Ehr' (Eighteen No. 13) (P. bk. 245 p. 100).

16. Allein Gott in der Höh' sei Ehr' (Eighteen No. 14)
   (P. bk. 245 p. 97).
17. Jesus Christus unser Heiland (Eighteen No. 15) (P.
   bk. 245 p. 112).

**XXVI. 1876 [1878]. Kirchencantaten. Dreizehnter Band.
Ed. Alfred Dörffel.**

No. 121. Christum wir sollen loben schon.
   122. Das neugebor'ne Kindelein.
   123. Liebster Immanuel, Herzog der Frommen.
   124. Meinen Jesum lass' ich nicht.
   125. Mit Fried' und Freud' ich fahr' dahin.
   126. Erhalt' uns, Herr, bei deinem Wort.
   127. Herr Jesu Christ, wahr'r Mensch und Gott.
   128. Auf Christi Himmelfahrt allein.
   129. Gelobet sei der Herr.
   130. Herr Gott, dich loben alle wir.

**XXVII (1). 1877 [1879]. Kammermusik. Sechster Band.
Ed. Alfred Dörffel.**

Three Sonatas (Suites), in G minor, A minor,[1] C major,[1] for
   Violin Solo (Nos. 1, 3, 5 in P. bk. 228).
Three Partitas (Suites, Sonatas), in B minor, D minor, E
   major,[1] for Violin Solo (Nos. 2, 4, 6 in P. bk. 228).
Six Suites (Sonatas), in G major, D minor, C major, E flat
   major, C minor, D major, for Violoncello Solo (P. bks.
   238a, 238).

**XXVII (2). 1877 [1878]. Thematisches Verzeichniss der
Kirchencantaten No. 1-120. Ed. Alfred Dörffel.**

[*Note.*—The Thematic Catalogue is completed in B.G. XLVI.
(P. bk. 270b).]

**XXVIII. 1878 [1881]. Kirchencantaten. Vierzehnter Band
Ed. Wilhelm Rust.**

No. 131. Aus der Tiefe rufe ich, Herr, zu dir.
   132. Bereitet die Wege, bereitet die Bahn.
   133. Ich freue mich in dir.

[1] See B.G. XLII. for a Clavier version.

134. Ein Herz, das seinen Jesum lebend weiss [and Variant].
135. Ach Herr, mich armen Sünder.
136. Erforsche mich, Gott.
137. Lobe den Herren, den mächtigen König.
138. Warum betrübst du dich, mein Herz ?
139. Wohl dem, der sich auf seinen Gott.
*140. Wachet auf, ruft uns die Stimme.[1]
Mit Gnaden bekröne der Himmel die Zeiten (No. 134 adapted).

XXIX. 1879 [1881]. **Kammermusik für Gesang. Dritter Band. Ed. Paul Graf Waldersee.**

Secular Cantata : Was mir behagt, ist nur die muntre Jagd.
Do.   Non sa che sia dolore.
Do.   O holder Tag, erwünschte Zeit (Wedding).
Church Cantata No. 194 : Höchsterwünschtes Freudenfest.
Secular Cantata : Schweigt stille, plaudert nicht.
Do.   Mer hahn en neue Oberkeet.
Do.   Mit Gnaden bekröne der Himmel die Zeiten.
Do.   O angenehme Melodei.
Instrumental Piece for Violin, Flute, and Continuo. (Not in P.).

XXX. 1880 [1884]. **Kirchencantaten. Fünfzehnter Band. Ed. Paul Graf Waldersee.**

No. 141. Das ist je gewisslich wahr.
142. Uns ist ein Kind geboren.
143. Lobe den Herren, meine Seele.
144. Nimm, was dein ist, und gehe hin.
145. So du mit deinem Munde bekennest Jesum.
146. Wir müssen durch viel Trübsal in das Reich Gottes eingehen.
147. Herz und Mund und That und Leben.
148. Bringet dem Herrn Ehre seines Namens.
*149. Man singet mit Freuden vom Sieg.
150. Nach dir, Herr, verlanget mich.

[1] Boosey and Co. also publish an English edition.

XXXI (1). 1881 [1885]   Orchesterwerke.   Ed. Alfred Dörffel.

Overture in C major (Strings, Ob. 1 and 2, Fagotto) (P. bk. 267).
Do.   B minor (Strings, Flauto traverso) (P. bk. 268).
Do.   D major (Strings, Ob. 1 and 2, Trombe 1, 2, 3, Timpani) (P. bk. 269).
Do.   D major (Strings, Ob. 1, 2, 3, Fagotto, Trombe 1, 2, 3, Timpani) (P. bk. 2068).
Sinfonia in F major (Strings, Ob. 1, 2, 3, Fagotto, Corno da caccia 1 and 2).[1]

XXXI (2). 1881 [1885]. Musikalisches Opfer. 1747. Ed. Alfred Dörffel.

Ricercare a tre voci.
Canon perpetuus super thema regium.
Canones diversi 1-5.
Fuga canonica in Epidiapente.
Ricercare a sei voci.
Two Canons.
Sonata in C minor, for Flute, Violin, Clavier.
Canone perpetuo (Flute, Violin, Clavier).[2]

(P. bk. 219)

XXXI (3). 1881 [1885]. Kammermusik. Siebenter Band. Ed. Paul Graf Waldersee.

Two Concertos for three Claviers and Orchestra (Strings) :
No. 1 in D minor (P. bk. 258).[3]
No. 2 in C major (P. bk. 259).[3]

[1] This is a shortened form of the first Brandenburg Concerto (see B.G. xix. no. 1). It consists of the Allegro, Adagio, Minuet, Trio I. and Trio II. of the latter, and omits its second Allegro and Polacca.

[2] The Appendix contains Joh. Philipp Kirnberger's solutions of the Canons and his expansion of the figured bass of the Clavier part of the Sonata.

[3] See publications of the N.B.G. xiv. (2) no. 2.

XXXII. 1882 [1886]. Kirchencantaten. Sechzehnter Band. Ed. Ernst Naumann.

No. 151. Süsser Trost, mein Jesus kommt.
*152. Tritt auf die Glaubensbahn.
153. Schau', lieber Gott, wie meine Feind'.
154. Mein liebster Jesus ist verloren.
155. Mein Gott, wie lang', ach lange.
156. Ich steh' mit einem Fuss im Grabe.
157. Ich lasse dich nicht.
158. Der Friede sei mit dir.
159. Sehet, wir geh'n hinauf gen Jerusalem.
160. Ich weiss, das mein Erlöser lebt.

XXXIII. 1883 [1887]. Kirchencantaten. Siebzehnter Band: Ed. Franz Wüllner.

No. 161. Komm, du süsse Todesstunde.
162. Ach, ich sehe, jetzt da ich zur Hochzeit gehe.
163. Nur Jedem das Seine.
164. Ihr, die ihr euch von Christo nennet.
165. O heil'ges Geist- und Wasserbad.
166. Wo gehest du hin ?
*167. Ihr Menschen, rühmet Gottes Liebe.
168. Thue Rechnung ! Donnerwort.
169. Gott soll allein mein Herze haben.
170. Vergnügte Ruh', beliebte Seelenlust.

XXXIV. 1884 [1887]. Kammermusik für Gesang. Vierter Band. Ed. Paul Graf Waldersee.

Secular Cantata : Durchlaucht'ster Leopold.
Do.　　Schwingt freudig euch empor, *or,* Die Freude reget sich.
Do.　　Hercules auf dem Scheidewege, *or,* Lasst uns sorgen, lasst uns wachen.
Do.　　Tönet, ihr Pauken ! Erschallet, Trompeten.
Do.　　Preise dein Glücke, gesegnetes Sachsen.

Secular Cantata : Angenehmes Wiederau.
Do.   Auf, schmetternde Töne der muntern Trompeten.[1]

XXXV. 1885 [1888]. Kirchencantaten. Achtzehnter Band. Ed. Alfred Dörffel.

No. 171. Gott, wie dein Name, so ist auch dein Ruhm.
172. Erschallet, ihr Lieder.
173. Erhötes Fleisch und Blut.
174. Ich liebe den Höchsten von ganzem Gemüthe.
175. Er rufet seinen Schafen mit Namen.
176. Es ist ein trotzig und verzagt Ding.
177. Ich ruf' zu dir, Herr Jesu Christ.
178. Wo Gott der Herr nicht bei uns hält.
179. Siehe zu, dass deine Gottesfurcht nicht Heuchelei sei.
*180. Schmücke dich, O liebe Seele.

XXXVI. 1886 [1890]. Clavierwerke. Vierter Band. Ed. Ernst Naumann.

1. Suite in A minor (Appendix version in P. bk. 214).
2.   Do.   E flat major (P. bk. 214).[2]
3. Suite (Overture), in F major (P. bk. 215).
4. Sonata in D major (P. bk. 215).
5. Toccata in D major (P. bk. 211).
6.   Do.   D minor (P. bk. 210).
7.   Do.   E minor (P. bk. 210).
8.   Do.   G minor (P. bk. 211).
9.   Do.   G major (P. bk. 215).
10. Chromatic Fantasia and Fugue in D minor (P. bk. 207).
11. Fantasia and Fugue in A minor (P. bk. 208).
12. Prelude and Fugue in E flat major (not in P.).
13.   Do.   do.   A minor (P. bk. 211).
14.   Do.   do.   A minor (P. bk. 200).
15. Prelude and Fughetta in D minor (P. bk. 200).
16.   Do.   do.   E minor (P. bk. 200).

[1] Text and music are identical with the version in B.G. xx. (2).
[2] Another Allemande to the Suite is in B.G. xxxvi. 217 (also in P.).

17. Prelude and Fughetta in F major (P. bk. 214).[1]
18. Do.   do.   G major (P. bk. 214).[2]
19. Twelve Preludes for Beginners (P. bk. 200).
20. Six Little Preludes (P. bk. 200).
21. Prelude in C major (for Organ, N. bk. 12 p. 94).
22. Do.   (Fantasia) in C minor (not in P.).
23. Do.   do.   in A minor (P. bk. 215).
24. Fantasia in G minor (P. bk. 215).
25. Do.   C minor (P. bk. 207).
26. Do.   (on a Rondo), in C minor (not in P.).
27. Do.   C minor (P. bk. 212).
28. Fughetta in C minor (two-parts) (P. bk. 200).
29. Fugue in E minor (P. bk. 212).
30. Do.   A major (P. bk. 212).
31. Do.   C major (for Organ, N. bk. 12 p. 100).
32. Do.   A minor (P. bk. 212).
33. Do.   D minor (P. bk. 212 p. 61).
34. Do.   A major (P. bk. 215 p. 52).
35. Do.   A major (P. bk. 215 p. 57).
36. Do.   B minor (Theme by Albinoni) (P. bk. 214).
37. Do.   C major (P. bk. 200 p. 54).
38. Do.   C major (P. bk. 200 p. 56).
39. Do.   D minor (P. bk. 212 p. 59).
40. Capriccio in B flat major, sopra la lontananza del suo
      fratello dilettissimo (P. bk. 208).
41. Do.   E major, in honorem J.C. Bach (P. bk. 215).
42. Aria variata in A minor (P. bk. 215).
43. Three Minuets, in G major, G minor, G major (P. bk.
      215).
44. Fragment of a Suite in F minor (P. bk. 212).
45. Do.   do.   A major (P. bk. 1959, p. 3).
46. Prelude, Gavotte II, and Minuet in E flat major.[3]

[1] The subject of the Fughetta is the same as that of Fugue No. 17 in the second part of the ' Well-tempered Clavier.'

[2] The Prelude is No. 11 in Peters (B.G. xxxvi. 220). The Fughetta is his No. 10. It is the same subject as that of Fugue 15 in the second part of the ' Well-tempered Clavier.' An alternative Prelude (P. 214 p. 78) is in the Appendix (p. 220).

[3] They are described as ' zur vierten französischen Suite.' The Prelude is in P. bk. 1959 p. 67.

47. Two Minuet-Trios, in C minor and B minor.[1]
48. 'Applicatio' in C major.[2]
49. Prelude in A minor (not in P.).
50. Do. (unfinished) in E minor (not in P.).
51. Fugue (unfinished) in C minor (P. bk. 212 p. 88).[3]

XXXVII. 1887 [1891]. Kirchencantaten. Neunzehnter Band. Ed. Alfred Dörffel.

No. 181. Leichtgesinnte Flattergeister.
182. Himmelskönig, sei willkommen.
183. Sie werden euch in den Bann thun (? 1735).
184. Erwünschtes Freudenlicht.
185. Barmherziges Herze der ewigen Liebe.
186. Aergre dich, O Seele, nicht.
187. Es wartet Alles auf dich.
188. Ich habe meine Zuversicht.[4]
189. Meine Seele rühmt und preist.
*190. Singet dem Herrn ein neues Lied.

XXXVIII. 1888 [1891]. Orgelwerke. Dritter Band. Ed. Ernst Naumann.

1. Prelude and Fugue in C minor (N. bk. 2 p. 48).
2. Do.   do.   G major (N. bk. 7 p. 80).
3. Do.   do.   A minor (N. bk. 10 p. 208).
4. Eight Short Preludes and Fugues in C major, D minor, E minor, F major, G major, G minor, A minor, B flat major (N. bk. 1).
5. Fantasia and Fugue in A minor (N. bk. 12 p. 60).
6. Fantasia con Imitazione in B minor (N. bk. 12 p. 71).

---

[1] Written respectively for the second and third French Suites (not in P.).
[2] A fingered exercise.
[3] The Appendices of the volume contain variant readings of movements elsewhere contained in it, and of the first, third, and sixth Preludes and Fugues in the second part of the 'Well-tempered Clavier.'
[4] See B.G. xlv. (1) Appendix.

7. Fantasia in C major (N. bk. 12 p. 92).
8.   Do.   C minor (N. bk. 3 p. 57).
9.   Do.   G major (N. bk. 12 p. 75).
10.   Do.   G major (N. bk. 9 p. 168).
11. Prelude in C major (N. bk. 12 p. 91).
12.   Do.   G major (N. bk. 2 p. 30).
13.   Do.   A minor (N. bk. 10 p. 238).
14. Fugue (Theme by Legrenzi) in C minor (and Variant)
    (N. bk. 10 p. 230).
15.   Do.   in C minor (N. bk. 12 p. 95).
16.   Do.   G major (N. bk. 12 p. 86).
17.   Do.   G major (N. bk. 12 p. 55).
18.   Do.   G minor (N. bk. 3 p. 84).
19.   Do.   B minor (Theme by Corelli) (N. bk. 3 p. 60).
20. Canzona in D minor (N. bk. 2 p. 34).
21. Allabreve in D major (N. bk. 2 p. 26).
22. Pastorale in F major (N. bk. 12 p. 102).
23. Trio in D minor (N. bk. 2 p. 54).
24. Four Concertos after Antonio Vivaldi :[1]
    No. 1, in G major (N. bk. 11 no. 1).[2]
        2, in A minor (N. bk. 11 no. 2).[3]
        3, in C major (N. bk. 11 no. 3).
        4, in C major (N. bk. 11 no. 4).
25. Fantasia (incomplete) in C major (not in N. or P.).[4]
26. Fugue (incomplete) in C minor (not in N. or P.).
27. Pedal Exercise in G minor (not in N. or P.).
28. Fugue (authenticity doubtful) in C major (not in N.
    or P.).
29.   Do.   do.   in D major (N. bk. 12 p. 83).[5]
30.   Do.   do.   in G minor (N. bk. 2 p. 41).
31. Trio in C minor (N. bk. 12 p. 108).
32. Aria in F major (N. bk. 12 p. 112).
33. Kleines harmonisches Labyrinth (authenticity doubtful)
    (P. bk. 2067 p. 16) (not in N.).

[1] Only nos. 2 and 3 are derived from Vivaldi.
[2] A variant text is in B.G. XLII. 282.
[3] Vivaldi's text of the first movement is in the Appendix
(p. 229).   [4] See B.G. XLIII. (2) sec. 1 no. 2.
[5] The fugal subject is taken from the Allabreve.

XXXIX. 1889 [1892]. Motetten, Choräle und Lieder. Ed. Franz Wüllner.

(1) Motet : *Singet dem Herrn ein neues Lied.

Do.   *Der Geist hilft unsrer Schwachheit auf.[1]

Do.   *Jesu, meine Freude.

Do.   *Fürchte dich nicht, ich bin bei dir.

Do.   *Komm, Jesu, komm.

Do.   *Lobet den Herrn, alle Heiden.

Do.   *Ich lasse dich nicht, du segnest mich denn (by Johann Christoph Bach).

Do.   *Sei Lob und Preis mit Ehren (the second number, Nun lob' mein' Seel' den Herrn, of Cantata 28).

(2) 185 Chorals harmonised by Bach, from the collection made by Carl Philipp Emmanuel Bach : [2]

1 (1).   Ach bleib' bei uns, Herr Jesu Christ.

2 (2).   Ach Gott, erhör' mein Seufzen und Wehklagen.

3 (3).   Ach Gott und Herr, wie gross und schwer.

4 (385).   Ach lieben Christen, seid getrost (Wo Gott der Herr nicht bei uns hält).[3]

5 (388).   Wär' Gott nicht mit uns diese Zeit (Wo Gott der Herr nicht bei uns hält).

6 (383).   Wo Gott der Herr nicht bei uns hält.

7 (10).   Ach, was soll ich Sünder machen.

8 (12).   Allein Gott in der Höh' sei Ehr.

9 (15).   Allein zu dir, Herr Jesu Christ.

10 (17).   Alle Menschen müssen sterben.

11 (19).   Alles ist an Gottes Segen.

---

[1] Bach's instrumental accompaniments are in the Appendix (p. 143).

[2] C. P. E. Bach's collection of his father's Choral settings was published by Immanuel Breitkopf in four volumes between the years 1784-87. They are all included in Breitkopf and Haertel's edition (1898) of Bach's ' Choralgesänge ' ; the numerals in brackets in the above list indicate the position of each Choral in that collection. The latter includes also the simple four-part Chorals from the Oratorios and Cantatas ; hence the numeration of that volume and B.G. xxxix. is not uniform.

[3] The bracket states the title by which the tune is better known.

12 (20). Als der gütige Gott.
13 (21). Als Jesus Christus in der Nacht.
14 (22). Als vierzig Tag' nach Ostern war'n.
15 (23). An Wasserflüssen Babylon.
16 (24). Auf, auf mein Herz.
17 (30). Aus meines Herzens Grunde.
18 (157). Befiehl du deine Wege (Herzlich thut mich verlangen).
19 (158). Ditto.
20 (32). Befiehl du deine Wege.
21 (33). Christ, der du bist der helle Tag.
22 (34). Christe, der du bist Tag und Licht.
23 (35). Christe, du Beistand deiner Kreuzgemeinde.
24 (36). Christ ist erstanden.
25 (38). Christ lag in Todesbanden.
26 (39). Ditto.
27 (43). Christ, unser Herr, zum Jordan kam.
28 (46). Christus, der ist mein Leben.
29 (47). Ditto.
30 (48). Christus, der uns selig macht.
31 (51). Christus ist erstanden.
32 (52). Da der Herr zu Tische sass.
33 (53). Danket dem Herren, denn er ist sehr freundlich.
34 (54). Dank sei Gott in der Höhe.
35 (55). Das alte Jahr vergangen ist.
36 (56). Ditto.
37 (58). Das walt' Gott Vater und Gott Sohn.
38 (59). Das walt' mein Gott, Vater, Sohn.
39 (60). Den Vater dort oben.
40 (61). Der du bist drei in Einigkeit.
41 (62). Der Tag, der ist so freudenreich.
42 (63). Des heil'gen Geistes reiche Gnad'.
43 (64). Die Nacht ist kommen.
44 (65). Die Sohn' hat sich mit ihrem Glanz.
45 (66). Dies sind die heil'gen zehn Gebot.
46 (67). Dir, dir, Jehovah, will ich singen (Bach's melody).
47 (70). Du grosser Schmerzensmann.

48 (71). Du, O schönes Weltgebäude.
49 (74). Ein' feste Burg ist unser Gott.
50 (75). Ditto.
51 (77). Eins ist noth, ach Herr, dies Eine.
52 (78). Erbarm' dich mein, O Herre Gott.
53 (85). Erstanden ist der heil'ge Christ.
54 (262). Est ist gewisslich an der Zeit (Nun freut euch,
lieben Christen g'mein).
55 (92). Es spricht der Unweisen Mund wohl.
56 (93). Es steh'n vor Gottes Throne.
57 (94). Es wird schier der letzte Tag herkommen.
58 (95). Es woll' uns Gott genädig sein.
59 (96). Ditto.
60 (106). Für Freuden lasst uns springen.
61 (107). Gelobet seist du, Jesu Christ.
62 (111). Gieb dich zufrieden und sei stille (Bach's
melody).
63 (112). Gott, der du selber bist das Licht.
64 (113). Gott der Vater wohn' uns bei.
65 (115). Gottes Sohn ist kommen.
66 (116). Gott hat das Evangelium.
67 (117). Gott lebet noch.
68 (118). Gottlob, es geht nunmehr zum Ende.
69 (119). Gott sei gelobet und gebenedeiet.
70 (120). Gott sei uns gnädig und barmherzig.
71 (121). Meine Seele erhebet den Herrn.
72 (123a). Heilig, Heilig, Heilig !
73 (129). Herr Gott, dich loben alle wir.
74 (132). Für deinen Thron tret' ich hiermit (Herr
Gott dich loben alle wir).
75 (133). Herr Gott dich loben wir.
76 (136). Herr, ich denk' an jene Zeit.
77 (137). Herr, ich habe missgehandelt.
78 (138). Ditto.
79 (139). Herr Jesu Christ, dich zu uns wend'.
80 (140). Herr Jesu Christ, du hast bereit't.
81 (141). Herr Jesu Christ, du höchstes Gut.
82 (145). Herr Jesu Christ, mein's Lebens Licht.
83 (146). Herr Jesu Christ, wahr' Mensch und Gott.

84 (148). Herr, nun lass in Friede.

85 (149). Herr, straf' mich nicht in deinem Zorn.

86 (151). Herr, wie du willst, so schick's mit mir.

87 (152). Herzlich lieb hab' ich dich, O Herr.

88 (170). Heut' ist, O Mensch, ein grosser Trauertag.

89 (171). Heut' triumphiret Gottes Sohn.

90 (172). Hilf, Gott, dass mir's gelinge.

91 (173). Hilf, Herr Jesu, lass gelingen.

92 (174). Ich bin ja, Herr, in deiner Macht (Bach's melody).

93 (175). Ich dank' dir, Gott, für all' Wohlthat.

94 (176). Ich dank' dir, lieber Herre.

95 (177).   Ditto.

96 (179). Ich dank' dir schon durch deinen Sohn.

97 (180). Ich danke dir, O Gott, in deinem Throne.

98 (182). Ich hab' mein' Sach' Gott heimgestellt.

99 (185). Jesu, der du meine Seele.

100 (186).   Ditto.

101 (187).   Ditto.

102 (189). Jesu, der du selbst so wohl.

103 (190). Jesu, du mein liebstes Leben.

104 (191). Jesu, Jesu, du bist mein (Bach's melody).

105 (195). Jesu, meine Freude.

106 (363). Jesu, meiner Seelen Wonne (Werde munter, mein Gemüthe).

107 (364).   Ditto.

108 (202). Jesu, meines Herzens Freud'.

109 (203). Jesu, nun sei gepreiset.

110 (206). Jesus Christus, unser Heiland, der von uns.

111 (207). Jesus Christus, unser Heiland, der den Tod.

112 (208). Jesus, meine Zuversicht.

113 (210). Ihr Gestirn', ihr hohlen Lüfte.

114 (211). In allen meinen Thaten.

115 (215). In dulci jubilo.

116 (217). Keinen hat Gott verlassen.

117 (218). Komm, Gott, Schöpfer, heiliger Geist.

118 (225). Kyrie ! Gott Vater in Ewigkeit.

119 (226). Lass, O Herr, dein Ohr sich neigen.

120 (228). Liebster Jesu, wir sind hier.

121 (232). Lobet den Herren, denn er ist sehr freundlich.

122 (233). Lobt Gott, ihr Christen allzugleich.

123 (234). Ditto.

124 (237). Mach's mit mir, Gott, nach deiner Güt.'

125 (240). Mein' Augen schliess' ich jetzt.

126 (241). Meinen Jesum lass' ich nicht, Jesus.

127 (242). Meinen Jesum lass' ich nicht, weil.

128 (248). Meines Lebens letzte Zeit.

129 (249). Mit Fried' und Freud' ich fahr' dahin.

130 (252). Mitten wir im Leben sind.

131 (253). Nicht so traurig, nicht so sehr (Bach's melody).

132 (254). Nun bitten wir den heiligen Geist.

133 (257). Nun danket Alle Gott.

134 (260). Nun freut euch, Gottes Kinder all.

135 (261). Nun freut euch, lieben Christen g'mein.

136 (269). Nun lob', mein' Seel', den Herren.

137 (270). Ditto.

138 (273). Nun preiset alle Gottes Barmherzigkeit.

139 (298). Nun ruhen alle Wälder (O Welt, ich muss dich lassen).

140 (289). O Welt, sieh' hier dein Leben (O Welt, ich muss dich lassen).

141 (290). Ditto.

142 (291). Ditto.

143 (274). Nun sich der Tag geendet hat.

144 (275). O Ewigkeit, du Donnerwort.

145 (277). O Gott, du frommer Gott (1679 tune).

146 (282). Ditto (1693 tune).

147 (284). O Herzensangst, O Bangigkeit und Zagen (Bach's melody).

148 (285). O Lamm Gottes, unschuldig.

149 (286). O Mensch, bewein' dein Sünde gross.

150 (287). O Mensch, schau' Jesum Christum an.

151 (288). O Traurigkeit, O Herzeleid.

152 (299). O wie selig seid ihr doch, ihr Frommen (1649).

153 (300). Ditto (1566).

154 (301). O wir armen Sünder.

155 (303). Schaut, ihr Sünder.

156 (306). Seelenbräutigam, Jesu, Gottes Lamm.
157 (307). Sei gegrüsset, Jesu gütig.
158 (309). Singt dem Herrn ein neues Lied.
159 (310). So giebst du nun, mein Jesu, gute Nacht.
160 (311). Sollt' ich meinem Gott nicht singen.
161 (313). Uns ist ein Kindlein heut' gebor'n.
162 (314). Valet will ich dir geben.
163 (316). Vater unser im Himmelreich.
164 (324). Von Gott will ich nicht lassen.
165 (325).   Ditto.
166 (326).   Ditto.
167 (331). Warum betrübst du dich, mein Herz.
168 (332).   Ditto.
169 (334). Warum sollt' ich mich denn grämen.
170 (336). Was betrübst du dich, mein Herze (Bach's
        melody).
171 (337). Was bist du doch, O Seele, so betrübet.
172 (349). Was willst du dich, O meine Seele.
173 (351). Weltlich Ehr' und zeitlich Gut.
174 (352). Wenn ich in Angst und Noth.
175 (353). Wenn mein Stündlein vorhanden ist.
176 (354).   Ditto.
177 (355).   Ditto.
178 (358). Wenn wir in höchsten Nöthen sein.
179 (359).   Ditto.
180 (366). Wer Gott vertraut, hat wohlgebaut.
181 (367). Wer nur den lieben Gott lässt walten.
182 (374). Wie bist du, Seele, in mir so gar betrübt.
183 (375). Wie schön leuchtet der Morgenstern.
184 (382). Wir glauben all' an einen Gott, Schöpfer.
185 (389). Wo Gott zum Haus nicht gibt sein'
        Gunst.
(3) Seventy-five Chorals harmonised by Bach : [1]
    *1 (S). Ach, dass ich nicht die letzte Stunde.
    2 (S). Auf, auf ! die rechte Zeit ist hier.
    3 (S). Auf, auf ! mein Herz, mit Freuden.
    4 (S). Beglückter Stand getreuer Seelen.

[1] The Chorals are taken from two sources, Anna Magdalena Bach's
'Notenbuch' (1725 ; see B.G. XLIII. (2)), and Schemelli's 'Musical-

*5 (S). Beschränkt, ihr Weisen dieser Welt.

6 (S). Brich entzwei, mein armes Herze.

7 (S). Brunnquell aller Güter.

8 (S). Der lieben Sonne Licht und Pracht.

9 (S). Der Tag ist hin, die Sonne gehet nieder.

10 (S). Der Tag mit seinem Lichte.

*11 (S). Dich bet' ich an, mein höchster Gott.

12 (S). Die bitt're Leidenszeit beginnet.

13 (S). Die gold'ne Sonne, voll Freud' und Wonne.

*14 (S). Dir, dir, Jehova, will ich singen.

*15 (S). Eins ist noth, ach Herr, dies Eine.

16 (S). Ermuntre dich, mein schwacher Geist.

17 (S). Erwürgtes Lamm, das die verwahrten Siegel.

18 (S). Es glänzet der Christen inwendiges Leben.

19 (S). Es ist nun aus mit meinem Leben.

20 (S). Es ist vollbracht ! Vergiss ja nicht dies Wort.

21 (S). Es kostet viel, ein Christ zu sein.

*22.   Gieb dich zufrieden und sei stille (erste Composition).

*23.   Ditto.   (zweite Composition).[1]

24 (S).   Ditto.   (dritte Composition).

25 (S). Gott lebet noch ! Seele, was verzagst du doch ?

*26 (S). Gott, wie gross ist deine Güte.

27 (S). Herr, nicht schricke deine Rache.

*28 (S). Ich bin ja, Herr, in deiner Macht.

29 (S). Ich freue mich in dir.

*30 (S). Ich halte treulich still.

31 (S). Ich lass' dich nicht.

32 (S). Ich liebe Jesum alle Stund'.

isches Gesang-Buch ' (1736), of which Bach was the musical editor. The latter contains sixty-nine melodies (with figured bass), the former seven : one melody (No. 14) is in both collections. The Schemelli tunes are indicated by an S within a bracket after the numeral. One melody (No. 71) is indubitably by Bach himself. It and others, which may be attributed to him on good evidence, are marked by an asterisk. The seventy-five settings are published in practicable form by the N.B.G. I. (1) and I. (2).

[1] Nos. 22 and 23 are the same tune.

*33 (S). Ich steh' an deiner Krippen hier.

*34 (S). Jesu, Jesu, du bist mein.

35 (S). Jesu, deine Liebeswunden.

36 (S). Jesu, meines Glaubens Zier.

37 (S). Jesu, meines Herzens Freud'.

38 (S). Jesus ist das schönste Licht.

39 (S). Jesus, unser Trost und Leben.

40 (S). Ihr Gestirn', ihr hohlen Lüfte.

41 (S). Kein Stündlein geht dahin.

*42 (S). Komm, süsser Tod, komm, sel'ge Ruh'!

*43 (S). Kommt, Seelen, dieser Tag.

*44 (S). Kommt wieder aus der finst'ren Gruft.

45 (S). Lasset uns mit Jesu ziehen.

46 (S). Liebes Herz, bedenke doch.

47 (S). Liebster Gott, wann werd' ich sterben.

*48 (S). Liebster Herr Jesu, wo bleibst du so lange.

49 (S). Liebster Immanuel.

50 (S). Mein Jesu, dem die Seraphinen.

*51 (S). Mein Jesu, was für Seelenweh.

52 (S). Meines Lebens letzte Zeit.

*53 (S). Nicht so traurig, nicht so sehr.

54 (S). Nur mein Jesus ist mein Leben.

55 (S). O du Liebe, meiner Liebe.

56. O Ewigkeit, du Donnerwort.

*57 (S). O finst're Nacht, wann wirst du doch vergehen.

58 (S). O Jesulein süss, O Jesulein mild.

*59 (S). O liebe Seele, zieh' die Sinnen.

60 (S). O wie selig seid ihr doch.

*61. Schaff's mit mir, Gott, nach deinem Willen.

62 (S). Seelenbräutigam, Jesu, Gottes Lamm.

63 (S). Seelenweide, meine Freude.

64 (S). Selig, wer an Jesum denkt.

65 (S). Sei gegrüsset, Jesu gütig.

66 (S). So gehest du nun, mein Jesu, hin.

67 (S). So giebst du nun, mein Jesu, gute Nacht.

68 (S). So wünsch' ich mir zu guter Letzt.

69 (S). Steh' ich bei meinem Gott.

70 (S). Vergiss mein nicht, dass ich dein nicht vergesse.

    *71 (S). Vergiss mein nicht, mein allerliebster Gott.
    *72.   Warum betrübst du dich und beugest.
    73 (S). Was bist du doch, O Seele, so betrübet.
    *74.   Wie wohl ist mir, O Freund der Seelen.
    75 (S). Wo ist mein Schäflein, das ich liebe.[1]

(4) Five Arias from Anna Magdalena Bach's 'Notenbuch' (1725) : [2]
    *1. So oft ich meine Tabakspfeife.
    *2. Bist bu bei mir.
    *3. Gedenke doch, mein Geist, zurücke.
    4. Gieb dich zufrieden und sei stille.
    5. Willst du dein Herz mir schenken (Aria di
       Giovannini).

XL. 1890 [1893]. Orgelwerke. Vierter Band. Ed. Ernst Naumann.

(1) Choral Preludes, from Kirnberger's collection.[3]
    1. Wer nur den lieben Gott lässt walten (N. bk. 19
                              p. 21).
    2.   Ditto   (N. bk. 19 p. 22).
    3. Ach Gott und Herr (N. bk. 18 p. 1).
    4.   Ditto   (N. bk. 18 p. 2).
    5. Wo soll ich fliehen hin (N. bk. 19 p. 32).
    6. Christ lag in Todesbanden (Fantasia) (N. bk. 18
       p. 16).
    7. Christum wir sollen loben schon, *or*, Was fürcht'st
       du, Feind Herodes, sehr (N. bk. 18 p. 23).
    8. Gelobet seist du, Jesu Christ (Fughetta) (N. bk. 18
       p. 38).
    9. Herr Christ, der ein'ge Gottes-Sohn (Fughetta)
       (N. bk. 18 p. 43).

[1] For a discussion of Bach's original hymn-tunes see the present writer's 'Bach's Chorals,' Part II. Introduction, pp. 67 ff. Six more of Bach's original hymn-tunes are printed there.

[2] The first three Arias are published by Novello, and also by the N.B.G. i. (1).

[3] In the Royal Library, Berlin. Kirnberger was a pupil of Bach. See section on Variants *infra.*

10. Nun komm der Heiden Heiland (Fughetta) (N. bk. 18 p. 83).

11. Vom Himmel hoch da komm ich her (N. bk. 19 p. 16).

12.   Ditto.   (Fughetta) (N. bk. 19 p. 14).

13. Das Jesulein soll doch mein Trost (Fughetta) (N. bk. 18 p. 24).

14. Gottes Sohn ist kommen (Fughetta) (N. bk. 18 p. 41).

15. Lob sei dem allmächtigen Gott (Fughetta) (N. bk. 18 p. 73).

16. Durch Adams Fall ist ganz verderbt (N. bk. 18 p. 28).

17. Liebster Jesu wir sind hier (N. bk. 18 p. 72a).

18.   Ditto.   (N. bk. 18 p. 72b).

19. Ich hab' mein' Sach' Gott heimgestellt (N. bk. 18 p. 54).[1]

20.   Ditto.   (N. bk. 18 p. 58A).

21. Herr Jesu Christ, dich zu uns wend' (N. bk. 18 p. 50).

22. Wir Christenleut' (N. bk. 19 p. 28b).[2]

23. Allein Gott in der Höh' sei Ehr (Bicinium) (N. bk. 18 p. 5).

24. In dich hab' ich gehoffet, Herr (N. bk. 18 p. 59).

25. Jesu, meine Freude (Fantasia) (N. bk. 18 p. 64).

(2) Twenty-eight other Choral Preludes : [3]

1. Ach Gott und Herr (Canon) (N. bk. 18 p. 3).

2. Allein Gott in der Höh' sei Ehr' (N. bk. 18 p. 4).

3.   Ditto.   (Fuga) (N. bk. 18 p. 7).

4.   Ditto.   (N. bk. 18 p. 11).

5. An Wasserflüssen Babylon (N. bk. 18 p. 13).

6. Christ lag in Todesbanden (N. bk. 18 p. 19).

7. Der Tag der ist so freudenreich (N. bk. 18 p. 26).

8. Ein' feste Burg ist unser Gott (N. bk. 18 p. 30).

9. Erbarm' dich mein, O Herre Gott (N. bk. 18 p. 35).

10. Gelobet seist du, Jesu Christ (N. bk. 18 p. 37).

[1] Novello omits the concluding four-part Choral.
[2] The Prelude is also attributed to J. L. Krebs, a pupil of Bach.
[3] See section on Variants *infra.*

11. Gelobet seist du, Jesu Christ (N. bk. 18 p. 39).
12. Gottes Sohn ist kommen (N. bk. 18 p. 42).
13. Herr Gott, dich loben wir (N. bk. 18 p. 44).
14. Herr Jesu Christ, dich zu uns wend' (N. bk. 18 p. 52).
15. Herzlich thut mich verlangen (N. bk. 18 p. 53).
16. Jesus, meine Zuversicht (N. bk. 18 p. 69).
17. In dulci jubilo (N. bk. 18 p. 61).
18. Liebster Jesu, wir sind hier (N. bk. 18 p. 70).
19.   Ditto.   (N. bk. 18 p. 71).
20. Lobt Gott, ihr Christen allzugleich (N. bk. 18 p. 74).
21. Meine Seele erhebt den Herren (Magnificat) (Fuga) (N. bk. 18 p. 75).
22. Nun freut euch, lieben Christen g'mein, *or*, Es ist gewisslich an der Zeit (N. bk. 18 p. 80).
23. Valet will ich dir geben (Fantasia) (N. bk. 19 p. 2).
24.   Ditto.   (N. bk. 19 p. 7).
25. Vater unser im Himmelreich (N. bk. 19 p. 12).
26. Vom Himmel hoch da komm ich her (N. bk. 19 p. 19).
27. Wie schön leuchtet der Morgenstern (N. bk. 19 p. 23).
28. Wir glauben all' an einen Gott (N. bk. 19 p. 30).

(3) Choral Variations :
1. Christ, der du bist der helle Tag (N. bk. 19 p. 36).
2. O Gott, du frommer Gott (N. bk. 19 p. 44).
3. Sei gegrüsset, Jesu gütig (N. bk. 19 p. 55).
4. Vom Himmel hoch da komm ich her (N. bk. 19 p. 73).

(4) Variant texts and fragments :
1. Variant of Kirnberger's No. 2 (P. bk. 244 p. 111).
2.   Do.   No. 3 (not in N. or P.).
3. Ich hab' mein' Sach' Gott heimgestellt (N. bk. 18 p. 58B).
4. Variant of Kirnberger's No. 6 (P. bk. 245 p. 104).
5.   Do.   No. 25 (P. bk. 245 p. 110).
6. Variant of No. 10 of the Twenty-eight *supra* (not in N. or P.).

7. Variant of No. 17 (not in N. or P.).

8.   Do.   No. 20 (not in N. or P.).

9.   Do.   No. 26 (not in N. or P.).

10.   Do.   No. 22 (P. bk. 246 p. 91).

11.   Do.   No. 23 (P. bk. 246 p. 100).

12. Jesu, meine Freude (fragment) (P. bk. 244 p. 112).

13. Wie schön leuchtet der Morgenstern (fragment) (not in N. or P.).

(5) Choral Preludes and Variations of faulty text or doubtful authenticity :

    1. Ach Gott vom Himmel sieh' darein (P. bk. 2067 p. 44).

    2. Auf meinen lieben Gott (P. bk. 2067 p. 39).

    3. Aus der Tiefe rufe ich (P. bk. 2067 p. 54).

    4. Christ ist erstanden (not in N. or P.).

    5. Christ lag in Todesbanden (P. bk. 2067 p. 56).

    6. Gott der Vater wohn' uns bei (P. bk. 245 p. 62) (by J. G. Walther).[1]

    7. O Vater, allmächtiger Gott (not in N. or P.).

    8. Schmücke dich, O liebe Seele (not in N. or P.) (also attributed to G. A. Homilius).

    9. Vater unser im Himmelreich (not in N. or P.) (also attributed to G. Böhm).

    10.   Ditto.

    11. Wir glauben all' an einen Gott, Schöpfer (P. bk. 2067 p. 40).[2]

    12. Variations on Ach, was soll ich Sünder machen (not in N. or P.).

    13.   Do.   Allein Gott in der Höh' sei Ehr' (not in N. or P.).

(6) Addendum to B.G. III. :

Allein Gott in der Höh' sei Ehr' (an early version of N. bk. 16 p. 40*) (P. bk. 245 p. 96).

---

[1] Variant, P. bk. 245 p. 106.

[2] Ernst Naumann remarks, 'Das Stück kann recht gut von Seb. Bach herrühren.' The text is complete, and the omission of the Prelude from the Novello edition is to be regretted.

XLI. 1891 [1894].   Kirchenmusikwerke.   Ergänzungsband.
Ed. Alfred Dörffel.

Cantata No. 191 : Gloria in excelsis (the B minor Mass
'Gloria ').
192 : Nun danket Alle Gott (incomplete).
193 : Ihr Pforten zu Zion (incomplete).
Ehre sei Gott in der Höhe (incomplete).
Wedding Cantata : O ewiges Feuer, O Ursprung der Liebe
(incomplete).
Do.   Herr Gott, Beherrscher aller Dinge
(incomplete).
Sanctus in D major.
Kyrie eleison (Christe, du Lamm Gottes).
Christe eleison (Johann Ludwig Bach).
Jesum lass' ich nicht von mir (the original concluding
Choral of the first Part of the ' St. Matthew Passion '
(Breitkopf and Haertel's ' Choralgesänge,' No. 247).
Four Cantatas of doubtful authenticity :
Gedenke, Herr, wie es uns gehet.
Gott der Hoffnung erfülle euch.
Siehe, es hat überwunden der Löwe.
Lobt ihn mit Herz und Munde.

XLII. 1892 [1894].   Clavierwerke.   Fünfter Band.   Ed.
Ernst Naumann.

Sonata in D minor (P. bk. 213 p. 24).[1]
Suite in E major (not in P.).[2]
Adagio in G major (P. bk. 213 p. 1).[3]
Sonata in A minor (P. bk. 213 p. 2).[4]
Do.   C major (P. bk. 213 p. 16).[4]
Fugue in B flat major (P. bk. 1959 p. 75).[5]

[1] A transcription of the second Sonata for Solo Violin, in A minor,
See B.G. xxvii. (1).
[2] A transcription of the third Partita, in E major, for Solo Violin.
See *ibid.*
[3] From the third Sonata for Solo Violin, in C major.   See *ibid.*
[4] Both Sonatas are arrangements of instrumental Sonatas in
J. A. Reinken's ' Hortus Musicus.'   See Spitta, i. 430.
[5] After a Sonata movement by J. A. Reinken.

Fugue in B flat major (P. bk. 1959 p. 90).[1]
Sixteen Concertos after Antonio Vivaldi (P. bk. 217).[2]
Fifteen Compositions of probable authenticity :

1. Prelude and Fugue in A minor (P. bk. 1959 p. 84).
2. Fantasia and Fugue in D minor (P. bk. 1959 p. 80).
3. Fantasia in G minor (P. bk. 1959 p. 94).
4. Concerto and Fugue in C minor (not in P.).
5. Fugato in E minor (P. bk. 1959 p. 24).
6. Fugue in E minor (P. bk. 1959 p. 72).
7. Do.   G major (P. bk. 1959 p. 68).
8. Do.   A minor (not in P.).
9.   Do.
10. Prelude in B minor (and Variant) (not in P.).
11. Suite in B flat major (P. bk. 1959 p. 54).
12. Andante in G minor (P. bk. 1959 p. 63).
13. Scherzo in D minor (and Variant) (P. bk. 1959 p. 62).
14. Sarabande con Partite in C major (P. bk. 1959 p. 26).
15. Passacaglia in D minor (P. bk. 1959 p. 40).

Ten Compositions of doubtful authenticity :

1. Fantasia in C minor (not in P.).
2. Toccata quasi Fantasia con Fuga in A major (not in P.).[3]
3. Partie in A major (not in P.).
4. Allemande in C minor (not in P.).
5. Gigue in F minor (not in P.).
6. Allemande and Courante in A major (not in P.).
7. Allemande in A minor (not in P.).
8. Fantasia and Fughetta in B flat major (P. bk. 212 p. 58).
9.   Do.   D major (P. bk. 212 p. 60).
10. Fugue (unfinished) in E minor (not in P.).

Concerto in G major by Antonio Vivaldi (original of the second Clavier Concerto *supra*).[4]

[1] After a Fugue by J. C. Erselius.   The original is given in Anhang II. of the volume.

[2] Only Nos. 1, 2, 4, 5, 7, 9, 14 are derived from Vivaldi.   The others are founded on Benedetto Marcello (No. 3), Duke Johann Ernst of Weimar (Nos. 11, 16, and perhaps 13).

[3] The Toccata is by Henry Purcell.   See Grove, vol. iii. p. 857.

[4] The volume also contains a Variant of the first Organ Concerto (B.G. XXXVIII.).

XLIII (1). 1893 [1894]. Kammermusik. Achter Band. Ed. Paul Graf Waldersee.

Three Sonatas for Flute and Clavier :
1. In C major (P. bk. 235 p. 33).
2. In E minor (*ib*. p. 39).
3. In E major (*ib*. p. 51).

Sonata in E minor, for Violin and Clavier (P. bk. 236).

Fugue in G minor for Violin and Clavier (P. bk. 236).

Sonata in F major for two Claviers (by Wilhelm Friedemann Bach).

Concerto in A minor for four Claviers and Orchestra (Strings) (P. bk. 260 p. 3).[1]

XLIII (2). 1893 [1894]. Musikstücke in den Notenbüchen der Anna Magdalena Bach. Ed. Paul Graf Waldersee.

(1) The Notebook of the year 1722 contains :
1. The French Suites (incomplete) (see B.G. XIII. (2)).
2. Fantasia in C major for the Organ (see B.G. XXXVIII. No. 25).
3. Air (unfinished) in C minor (not in P.).
4. Choral Prelude, ' Jesus, meine Zuversicht ' (see B.G. XL. sec. 2 No. 16).
5. Minuet in G major (see B.G. XXXVI. and P. bk. 215 p. 62).

(2) The Notebook of the year 1725 contains :[2]
1. Partita III. (A minor) from the ' Clavierübung,' Part I. (see B.G. III.).
2. Partita VI. (E minor) from the same (see B.G. III.).
3 (P). Minuet in F major.
4 (P).   Do.   G major.
5 (P).   Do.   G minor.

[1] The Concerto is an arrangement of one by Antonio Vivaldi for four Violins, the original of which (in B minor) is given in the Appendix to the volume.

[2] Omitting the vocal numbers, movements printed elsewhere, and the ' Menuet fait par Mons. Böhm,' Peters' Bk. 1959 contains the remaining twenty numbers of the Notebook. They are indicated in the above index by a P in a bracket.

6 (P). Rondeau in B flat major (by Couperin).

7 (P). Minuet in G major.

8 (P). Polonaise in F major (two versions).

9 (P). Minuet in B flat major.

10 (P). Polonaise in G minor.

11. Choral Prelude, ' Wer nur den lieben Gott lässt walten ' (see B.G. XL., Kirnberger's Collection, no. 2).

12. Choral, ' Gieb dich zufrieden und sei stille ' (see B.G. XXXIX. sec. 4 no. 4).

13. Aria, ' Gieb dich zufrieden un sei stille ' (see B.G. XXXIX. sec. 2 no. 62).

14 (P). Minuet in A minor.

15 (P).   Do.   C minor.

16 (P). March in D major.

17 (P). Polonaise in G minor.

18 (P). March in A major.

19 (P). Polonaise in G minor.

20. Aria, ' So oft ich meine Tabakspfeife ' (see B.G. XXXIX. sec. 4 no. 1).

21. Minuet in G major, ' fait par Mons. Böhm.'

22 (P). Musette in D major.

23 (P). March in E flat major.

24 (P). Polonaise in D minor.

25. Aria, ' Bist du bei mir ' (see B.G. XXXIX. sec. 4 no. 2).

26. Aria in G major (the Aria of the Goldberg Variations. See B.G. III.).

27 (P). Solo per il Cembalo in E flat major.

28 (P). Polonaise in G major.

29. Prelude in C major (Prelude I. of the first Part of the ' Well-tempered Clavier.' See B.G. XIV.).

30. Suite in D minor (the first of the French Suites. See B.G. XIII (2)).

31. Suite in C minor (the first three movements of the second French Suite. See B.G. XIII (2)).

32. Choral (wordless) in F. major.

33.   Aria, ' Warum betrübst du dich ' (see B.G.
       XXXIX. sec. 3 no. 72).
34.   Recitativo and Aria, ' Ich habe genug,' and
       ' Schlummert ein,' for Basso (from Can-
       tata 82, nos. 2 and 3), transposed.
35.   Aria, ' Schaff's mit mir, Gott, nach deinem
       Willen ' (see B.G. XXXIX. sec. 3 no. 61).
36 (P). Minuet in D minor.
37.   Aria, ' Willst du dein Herz mir schenken ' (di
       Giovannini) (see B.G. XXXIX. sec. 4 no. 5).
38.   Aria, No. 34 *supra*.
39.   Choral, ' Dir, dir Jehovah, will ich singen '
       (see B.G. XXXIX. sec. 2 no. 46).
40.   Aria, ' Wie wohl ist mir, O Freund der Seelen '
       (see B.G. XXXIX. sec. 3 no. 74).
41.   Aria, ' Gedenke doch, mein Geist, zurücke '
       (see B.G. XXXIX. sec. 4 no. 3).
42.   Choral, ' O Ewigkeit, du Donnerwort ' (see
       B.G. XXXIX. sec. 2 no. 144).

XLIV. 1894 [1895]. **Handschrift in zeitlich geordneten
Nachbildungen. Ed. Hermann Kretzschmar.** Con-
tains facsimiles of Bach's handwriting and autograph
MSS.

XLV (1). 1895 [1897]. **Clavierwerke. Zweiter Band (neue
berichtigte Ausgabe). Ed. Alfred Dörffel.**[1]

The Six English Suites (see B.G. XIII. (2)). (P. bks. 2794,
2795.)
The Six French Suites (see B.G. XIII. (2)). (P. bk. 2793.)
Five Canons in 4, 6, 7, 8 parts.
Prelude and Fugue in E flat major (P. bk. 214 p. 40).
Suite in E minor (P. bk. 214 p. 68).
Suite in C minor (not in P.).
Sonata (first movement) in A minor (not in P.).[2]

[1] A separate Preface to the reprinted Suites is by Ernst Naumann.
It is dated 1895.
[2] Perhaps an arrangement of an orchestral piece. See Schweitzer,
i. 342 n.

Four Inventions, in B minor, B flat major, C minor, D major, for Violin and Clavier (P. bk. 2957).

Overture in G minor for Strings and Clavier (not in P.).

The 'Clavier-Büchlein' of Wilhelm Friedemann Bach contains :

1. Applicatio in C major (see B.G. XXXVI. no. 48).
2. Prelude in C major (the first of the Twelve Little Preludes) (see B.G. XXXVI. no. 19).
3. Choral Prelude, 'Wer nur den lieben Gott lässt walten' (see B.G. XL., Kirnberger's Collection, no. 2).
4. Prelude in D minor (the fifth of the Little Preludes) (see B.G. XXXVI. no. 19).
5. Choral Prelude, 'Jesu meine Freude' (fragment) (see B.G. XL. sec. 4 no. 12).
6. Allemande in G minor (not in P.).
7. Allemande (fragment) in G minor (not in P.).
8. Prelude in F major (the eighth of the Little Preludes) (see B.G. XXXVI. no. 19).
9. Do.   G minor (the eleventh of the Little Preludes) (see B.G. XXXVI. no. 19).
10. Do.   F major (the ninth of the Little Preludes) (see B.G. XXXVI. no. 19).
11. Minuet in G major (the first of the three Minuets) (see B.G. XXXVI. no. 43).
12. Do.   G minor (the second of the three Minuets) (see B.G. XXXVI. no. 43).
13. Do.   G major (the third of the three Minuets) (see B.G. XXXVI. no. 43).
14. Prelude in C major (the first Prelude of the first Part of the 'Well-tempered Clavier.' See B.G. XIV.).
15. Do.   C minor (the second Prelude of the first Part of the same. See B.G. XIV.).
16. Do.   D minor (the sixth Prelude of the first Part of the same. See B.G. XIV.).
17. Do.   D major (the fifth Prelude of the first Part of the same. See B.G. XIV.).

18. Prelude in E minor (the tenth Prelude of the first
    Part of the same. See B.G. xiv.).
19. Do. E major (the ninth Prelude of the first
    Part of the same. See B.G. xiv.).
20. Do. F major (the eleventh Prelude of the first
    Part of the same. See B.G. xiv.).
21. Do. C sharp major (the third Prelude of the
    first Part of the same. See B.G. xiv.).
22. Do. C sharp minor (the fourth Prelude of the
    first Part of the same. See B.G. xiv.).
23. Do. E flat minor (the eighth Prelude of the
    first Part of the same. See B.G. xiv.).
24. Do. F minor (the twelfth Prelude of the first
    Part of the same. See B.G. xiv.).
25. Allemande and Courante in C major, by J. C. Richter.
26. Prelude in C major (first of the Little Preludes. See
    B.G. xxxvi. no. 19).
27. Do. D major (fourth of the Little Preludes.
    See B.G. xxxvi. no. 19).
28. Do. E minor (see B.G. xxxvi. no. 50).
29. Do. A minor (B.G. xxxvi. no. 49).
30. Do. G minor (not in P.).
31. Fugue in C major (see B.G. xxxvi. no. 38).
32. Prelude in C major (Invention i. See B.G. iii.).
33. Do. D minor (Invention iv. See B.G. iii.).
34. Do. E minor (Invention vii. See B.G. iii.).
35. Do. F major (Invention viii. See B.G. iii.).
36. Do. G major (Invention x. See B.G. iii.).
37. Do. A minor (Invention xiii. See B.G. iii.).
38. Do. B minor (Invention xv. See B.G. iii.).
39. Do. B flat major (Invention xiv. See
    B.G. iii.).
40. Do. A major (Invention xii. See B.G. iii.).
41. Do. G minor (Invention xi. See B.G. iii.).
42. Do. F minor (Invention ix. See B.G. iii.).
43. Do. E major (Invention vi. See B.G. iii.).
44. Do. E flat major (Invention v. See B.G. iii.).
45. Do. D major (Invention iii. See B.G. iii.).
46. Do. C minor (Invention ii. See B.G. iii.).

47. Suite in A major (fragment) (see B.G. xxxvi. no. 45).
48. Partita in G minor by Steltzel, including a Minuet-Trio by J. S. B. (Minuet in P. bk. 1959 p. 8).
49. Fantasia in C major (Sinfonia i. See B.G. iii.).

50.	Do.	D minor (Sinfonia iv. See B.G. iii.).
51.	Do.	E minor (Sinfonia vii. See B.G. iii.).
52.	Do.	F major (Sinfonia viii. See B.G. iii.).
53.	Do.	G major (Sinfonia x. See B.G. iii.).
54.	Do.	A minor (Sinfonia xiii. See B.G. iii.).
55.	Do.	B minor (Sinfonia xv. See B.G. iii.).
56.	Do.	B flat major (Sinfonia xiv. See B.G. iii.).
57.	Do.	A major (Sinfonia xii. See B.G. iii.).
58.	Do.	G minor (Sinfonia xi. See B.G. iii.).
59.	Do.	F minor (Sinfonia ix. See B.G. iii.).
60.	Do.	E major (Sinfonia vi. See B.G. iii.).
61.	Do.	E flat major (Sinfonia v. See B.G. iii.).
62.	Do.	D major (Sinfonia iii. See B.G. iii.).[1]

XLV (2). 1895 [1898]. **Passionsmusik nach dem Evangelisten Lucas. Ed. Alfred Dörffel.**

Though the Score is in Bach's autograph, the work is generally held not to be his.

XLVI. 1896 [1899].[2] **Schlussband. Bericht und Verzeichnisse. Ed. Hermann Kretzschmar.**

The volume contains :—

Historical retrospect of the Society and its activities.

Thematic Index to Cantatas 121-191 (see B.G. xxvii (2)), unfinished Cantatas, Cantatas of doubtful authenticity, Christmas Oratorio, Easter Oratorio, St. Matthew Passion, St. John Passion, St. Luke Passion, Mass in B minor, the four Masses in F major, A major, G minor, G major,

---

[1] The Appendix to the volume contains addenda to the Violin Concerto in A minor (see B.G. xxi. (1)) and Cantata 188 (see B.G. xxxvii.). Also the Zurich and London texts of the 'Well-tempered Clavier' (B.G. xiv.), with critical notes.

[2] The Preface is dated 1899. The volume was issued in 1900.

the four Sanctus in C major, D major, D minor, G major, Magnificat in D major, the 'Trauer-Ode' Wedding Cantatas and Chorals, Motets, Secular Cantatas (P. bk. 270b).

Alphabetical Index of the movements throughout the vocal works.

Thematic Index to the Clavier music.

Do.	Chamber music.	
Do.	Orchestral music.	(P. bk.
Do.	Organ music.	270a).
Do.	'Musikalisches Opfer.'	
Do.	'Die Kunst der Fuge.'	
Do.	W. F. Bach's and A. M. Bach's Notebooks.	

Index to the several movements throughout the instrumental works.

Index of names and places occurring in the Prefaces of the B.G. volumes.

Bach's vocal and instrumental works arranged (1) in the order of the yearly volumes, (2) in groups.

(B) PUBLICATIONS OF THE NEW BACHGESELLSCHAFT

I (1). 1901. Lieder und Arien. Für eine Singstimme mit Pianoforte (Orgel oder Harmonium). Ed. Ernst Naumann.

The seventy-eight Songs are those contained in B.G. xxxix. secs. 3 and 4 (first three only) *supra*.

I (2). 1901. Lieder und Arien. Für vierstimmigen gemischten Chor. Ed. Franz Wüllner.

The seventy-five Songs are those contained in I (1), omitting those in sec. 4 of B.G. xxxix. *supra*.

I (3). 1901. Erstes deutsches Bach-Fest in Berlin 21 bis 23 März 1901. Festschrift.

The frontispiece is Carl Seffner's bust of Bach.

II (1). 1902. Orgelbüchlein. 46 kürzere Choralbearbeitungen
für Klavier zu vier Händen. Ed. Bernhard Fr. Richter.

The original forty-six Organ Preludes, here arranged for
two pianofortes (see B.G. xxv (2), sec. 1).

II (2). 1902.   Kirchen-Kantaten.   Klavierauszug.   Erstes
Heft. Ed. Gustav Schreck and Ernst Naumann.

Contains Breitkopf and Haertel's vocal scores of—
Cantata 61 : Nun komm, der Heiden Heiland.
Do.   64 : Sehet, welch' eine Liebe.
Do.   28 : Gottlob ! nun geht das Jahr zu Ende.
Do.   65 : Sie werden aus Saba Alle kommen.
Do.   4 : Christ lag in Todesbanden.

III (1). 1903. Kirchen-Kantaten.   Klavierauszug.   Zweites
Heft. Ed. Ernst Naumann.

Contains Breitkopf and Haertel's vocal scores of—
Cantata 104 : Du Hirte Israel, höre.
Do.   11 : Lobet Gott in seinen Reichen.
Do.   34 : O ewiges Feuer.
Do.   45 : Es ist dir gesagt.
Do.   80 : Ein' feste Burg.

III (2). 1903. Drei Sonaten für Klavier und Violine. Ed.
Ernst Naumann.

Sonata i. in B minor.⎫
Do.   ii. in A major.⎬(See B.G. ix.)
Do.   iii. in E major.⎭

IV (1). 1904. Drei Sonaten für Klavier und Violine. Ed.
Ernst Naumann.

Sonata iv. in C minor.⎫
Do.   v. in F minor⎬(See B.G. ix.)
Do.   vi. in G major.⎭

IV (2). 1904.   Joh. Seb. Bach, Bildnis in Heliogravure.

A print of the portrait discovered by Dr. Fritz Volbach ; reproduced at p. 92 of this present volume.

IV (3). 1904.   Zweites deutsches Bach-Fest in Leipzig 1 bis 3 Oktober 1904.   Festschrift.

V (1). 1905.   Fest-Gottesdienst zum deutschen Bachfeste in der Thomaskirche zu Leipzig.   Ed. Georg Rietschel.

Contains the order of service and music sung on the occasion.

V (2). 1905.   Ausgewählte Arien und Duette mit einem obligaten Instrument und Klavier- oder Orgelbegleitung. I Abteilung : Arien für Sopran.   Ed. Eusebius Mandyczewski.

1. Auch mit gedämpften schwachen Stimmen (Cantata 36 : Violin).
2. Die Armen will der Herr unarmen (Cantata 186 : Violin).
3. Es halt' es mit der blinden Welt (Cantata 94 : Oboe d'amore).
4. Gerechter Gott, ach, rechnest du (Cantata 89 : Oboe).
5. Gott versorget alles Leben (Cantata 187 : Oboe).
6. Höchster, was ich habe, ist nur deine Gabe (Cantata 39 : Flauto).
7. Hört, ihr Augen, auf zu weinen (Cantata 98 : Oboe).
8. Ich bin vergnügt in meinem Leiden (Cantata 58 : Violin).
9. Ich ende behende mein irdisches Leben (Cantata 57 : Violin).
10. Ich nehme mein Leiden mit Freuden auf mich (Cantata 75 : Oboe d'amore).
11. Ich will auf den Herren schau'n (Cantata 93 : Oboe).
12. Seufzer, Thränen, Kummer, Noth (Cantata 21 : Oboe).

V (3). 1905. Bach-Jahrbuch 1904. Herausgegeben von der Neuen Bachgesellschaft.

In addition to sermons and addresses on the occasion of the second Bach Festival at Leipzig in 1904, the volume contains the following articles :

1. Bach und der evangelische Gottesdienst. By Karl Greulich.
2. Praktische Bearbeitungen Bachscher Kompositionen. By Max Seiffert.
3. Bachs Rezitativbehandlung mit besonderer Berücksichtigung der Passionen. By Alfred Heuss.
4. Verschwundene Traditionen des Bachzeitalters. By Arnold Schering.

VI (1). 1906. Ausgewählte Arien und Duette mit einem obligaten Instrument und Klavier- oder Orgelbegleitung. II Abteilung : Arien für Alt. Ed. Eusebius Mandyczewski.

1. Ach, bleibe doch, mein liebstes Leben (Cantata 11 : Violin).
2. Ach, es bleibt in meiner Liebe (Cantata 77 : Tromba).
3. Ach Herr ! was ist ein Menschenkind (Cantata 110 : Oboe d'amore).
4. Ach, unaussprechlich ist die Noth (Cantata 116 : Oboe d'amore).
5. Christen müssen auf der Erden (Cantata 44 : Oboe).
6. Christi Glieder, ach, bedenket (Cantata 132 : Violin).
7. Es kommt ein Tag (Cantata 136 : Oboe d'amore).
8. Gelobet sei der Herr, mein Gott (Cantata 129 : Oboe d'amore).
9. Ich will doch wohl Rosen brechen (Cantata 86 : Violin).
10. Jesus macht mich geistlich reich (Cantata 75 : Violin).
11. Kein Arzt ist ausser dir zu finden (Cantata 103 : Flauto)
12. Was Gott thut, das ist wohlgethan (Cantata 100 : Oboe d'amore).

VI (2). 1906. Ausgewählte Arien und Duette mit einem obligaten Instrument und Klavier- oder Orgelbegleitung. III Abteilung : Duette für Sopran und Alt. Ed. Eusebius Mandyczewski.

1. Die Armuth, so Gott auf sich nimmt (Cantata 91 : Violin).
2. Wenn Sorgen auf mich dringen (Cantata 3 : Violin or Oboe d'amore).
3. Er kennt die rechten Freudenstunden (Cantata 93 : Violin).

VI (3). 1906. Bach-Jahrbuch 1905. Herausgegeben von der Neuen Bachgesellschaft.

Contains the following articles :
1. Johann Sebastian Bachs Kapelle zu Cöthen und deren nachgelassene Instrumente. By Rudolf Bunge.
2. Geleitwort. By Arnold Schering.
3. Die Wahl Joh. Seb. Bachs zum Kantor der Thomasschule i. J. 1723. By Bernhard Fr. Richter.
4. Ein' feste Burg ist unser Gott. Kantata von Joh. Seb. Bach. By Fritz Volbach.
5. Verzeichnis der bisher erschienenen Literatur über Johann Sebastian Bach. By Max Schneider.
6. Reviews of books.

VII (1). 1907. Kantate No. 88 : ' Siehe, ich will viel Fischer aussenden.' Partitur. Ed. Max Seiffert.

VII (2). 1907. Kantate No. 88 : ' Siehe, ich will viel Fischer aussenden.' Klavierauszug mit Text. Ed. Max Seiffert und Otto Taubmann.

VII (3). 1907. Bach-Jahrbuch 1906. Herausgegeben von der Neuen Bachgesellschaft.

Contains the following articles :
1. Erfahrungen und Ratschläger bezüglich der Aufführung Bachscher Kirchenkantaten. By Wilhelm Voigt.

2. Über die Schicksale der der Thomasschule zu Leipzig angehörenden Kantaten Joh. Seb. Bachs. By Bernhard Fr. Richter.
3. Die grosse A-moll Fuge für Orgel [Novello bk. 7 p. 42] und ihre Vorlage. By Reinhardt Oppel.
4. Zur Kritik der Gesamtausgabe von Bachs Werken. By Max Seiffert.
5. Verzeichnis der bis zum Jahre 1851 gedruckten (und der geschrieben im Handel gewesenen) Werke von Johann Sebastian Bach. By Max Schneider.
6. Übersicht der Aufführungen J. S. Bachscher Werke von Ende 1904 bis Anfang 1907.
8. Notes.

VII (4). 1907. **Drittes deutsches Bach-Fest zur Einweihung von Johann Sebastian Bachs Geburtshaus als Bach-Museum [at Eisenach]. Fest- und Programmbuch [26-28 May 1907].**

The frontispiece is Carl Seffner's bust of Bach.

VIII (1). 1908. **Violinkonzert No. 2 in E dur. Partitur. Ed. Max Seiffert.**

See B.G. xxi (1) no. 2.

VIII (2). 1908. **Violinkonzert No. 2 in E dur für Violine und Klavier. Ed. Max Seiffert and A. Saran.**

VIII (3). 1908. **Bach-Jahrbuch. 4 Jahrgang 1907 : Im Auftrage der Neuen Bachgesellschaft herausgegeben von Arnold Schering.**

In addition to a sermon by Professor Georg Rietschel and an obituary notice of Joseph Joachim, the volume contains the following articles :

1. Sebastian Bach und Paul Gerhardt. By Wilhelm Nelle.
2. Stadtpfeifer und Alumnen der Thomasschule in Leipzig zu Bachs Zeit. By Bernhard Fr. Richter.

3. Angeblich von J. S. Bach komponierte Oden von Chr. H. Hoffmannswaldau. By —. Landmann.

4. Die neuen deutschen Ausgaben der zwei- und dreistimmigen Inventionen [Peters bk. 2792]. By Reinhardt Oppel.

5. Thematisches Verzeichnis der musikalischen Werke der Familie Bach. I. Theil. By Max Schneider.

6. Notes and Reviews of books.

IX (1). 1909. **Kantate No. 85 : ' Ich bin ein guter Hirt.' Partitur. Ed. Max Seiffert.**

IX (2). 1909. **Kantate No. 85 : ' Ich bin ein guter Hirt.' Klavierauszug mit Text. Ed. Max Seiffert and Max Schneider.**

IX (3). 1909. **Brandenburgisches Konzert No. 3. Partitur. Ed. Max Seiffert.**

See B.G. XIX. no. 3.

IX (4). 1909. **Brandenburgisches Konzert No. 3 für Klavier zu vier Händen. Ed. Max Seiffert and Max Schneider.**

IX (5). 1909. **Viertes deutsches Bach-Fest in Chemnitz 3-5 Oktober 1908. Fest- und Programmbuch.**

The frontispiece is a photograph of Carl Seffner's statue of Bach, unveiled at Leipzig May 17, 1908.

IX (6). 1909. **Bach-Jahrbuch. 5 Jahrgang 1908 : Im Auftrage der Neuen Bachgesellschaft herausgegeben von Arnold Schering.**

Contains the following articles :

1. Zu Bachs Weihnachtsoratorium, Theil 1 bis 3. By Woldemar Voigt.

2. Über Seb. Bachs Kantaten mit obligater Pedal. By Bernhard Fr. Richter.

3. Cembalo oder Pianoforte ? By Richard Buchmayer.

4. Bearbeitung Bachscher Kantaten. By Max Schneider.

5. Nachrichten über das Leben Georg Böhms mit spezieller Berücksichtigung seiner Beziehungen zur Bachschen Familie. By Richard Buchmayer.
6. Ein interessantes Beispiel Bachscher Textauffassung. By Alfred Heuss.
7. Edgar Tinel über Seb. Bach.
8. Notes.

X (1). 1910. Ausgewählte Arien und Duette mit einem obligaten Instrument und Klavier- oder Orgelbegleitung. IV Abteilung : Arien für Tenor. Ed. Eusebius Mandyczewski.

1. Dein Blut, so meine Schuld durchstreit (Cantata 78 : Flauto).
2. Die Liebe zieht mit sanften Schritten (Cantata 36 : Oboe d'amore).
3. Ergiesse dich reichlich, du göttliche Quelle (Cantata 5 : Viola).
4. Handle nicht nach deinen Rechten mit uns (Cantata 101 : Violin).
5. Ich will an den Himmel denken (Cantata 166 : Oboe).
6. Ja, tausendmal Tausend (Cantata 43 : Violin).
7. Mich kann kein Zweifel stören (Cantata 108 : Violin).
8. Seht, was die Liebe thut! (Cantata 85 : Violin or Viola).
9. Tausendfaches Unglück, Schrecken, Trübsal (Cantata 143 : Violin).
10. Wir waren schon zu tief gesunken (Cantata 9 : Violin).
11. Woferne du den edlen Frieden (Cantata 41 : Violoncello).
12. Wo wird in diesem Jammerthale (Cantata 114 : Flauto).

X (2). 1910. Brandenburgisches Konzert No. 1. Partitur. Ed. Max Seiffert.

See B.G. xix. no. 1.

X (3). 1910. Brandenburgisches Konzert No. 1 für Klavier zu vier Händen. Ed. Max Seiffert and Max Schneider.

X (4). 1910. Bach-Jahrbuch. 6 Jahrgang 1909 : Im Auftrage der Neuen Bachgesellschaft herausgegeben von Arnold Schering.

The volume contains the following articles :
1. Zum Linearprinzip J. S. Bachs. By Robert Handke.
2. Bachs Verhältnis zur Klaviermusik. By Karl Nes.
3. Zur Tenorarie [' Ich will an den Himmel denken ' : See x (1) no. 5, *supra*] der Kantate 166. By Reinhard Oppel.
4. Die Verzierungen in den Werken von J. S. Bach. By E. Dannreuther.
5. Konnte Bachs Gemeinde bei seinen einfachen Choralsätzen mitsingen ? By Rudolf Wustmann.
6. Buxtehudes musikalischer Nachruf beim Tode seines Vaters (mit einer Notenbeilage). By Reinhard Oppel.
7. ' Matthäuspassion,' erster Theil. By Rudolf Wustmann.
8. Zu den Beschlüssen des Dessauer Kirchengesangvereinstages. By Arnold Schering.
9. Notes.

X (5). 1910. Fünftes deutsches Bach-Fest in Duisburg 4 bis 7 Juni 1910. Fest- und Programmbuch.

Frontispiece, St. Thomas' Church and School, Leipzig, in 1723. Reproduced at p. 28 of the present volume.

XI (1). 1911. Ausgewählte Arien und Duette mit einem obligaten Instrument und Klavier- oder Orgelbegleitung. V Abteilung : Arien für Bass. Ed. Eusebius Mandyczewski.

1. Achzen und erbärmlich Weinen (Cantata 13 : Violin or Flute).

2. Die Welt mit allen Königreichen (Cantata 59 : Violin).
3. Endlich, endlich wird mein Joch (Cantata 56 : Oboe).
4. Erleucht' auch meine finstre Sinnen ('Christmas Oratorio,' Part V. no. 5 : Oboe d'amore).
5. Gleichwie die wilden Meeres-Wellen (Cantata 178 : Violin or Viola).
6. Greifet zu, fasst das Heil (Cantata 174 : Violin or Viola).
7. Herr, nun lässest du deinen Diener (Cantata 83 : Violin or Viola).
8. Hier, in meines Vaters Stätte (Cantata 32 : Violin).
9. Komm, süsses Kreuz ('St. Matthew Passion,' no. 57 : Violoncello).
10. Lass', O Welt, mich aus Verachtung (Cantata 123 : Flauto).
11. Tritt auf die Glaubensbahn (Cantata 152 : Oboe d'amore).
12. Wenn Trost und Hülf' ermangeln muss (Cantata 117 : Violin).

XI (2). 1911. **Bach-Jahrbuch.** 7 Jahrgang 1910 : Im Auftrage der Neuen Bachgesellschaft herausgegeben von Arnold Schering.

The volume contains the following articles :
1. Die Diatonik in ihrem Einfluss auf die thematische Gestaltung des Fugenbaues. By Robert Handke.
2. Bach und die französische Klaviermusik. By Wanda Landowska.
3. Sebastian Bachs Kirchenkantatentexte. By Rudolf Wustmann.
4. Über Joh. Kasp. Fred. Fischers Einfluss auf Joh. Seb. Bach. By Reinhard Oppel.
5. Hans Bach, der Spielmann. By Werner Wolffheim.
6. Vom Rhythmus des evangelischen Chorals. By Rudolf Wustmann.
7. W. Friedemann Bach und seine hallische Wirksamkeit. By C. Zehler.

8. Neues Material zum Verzeichnis der bisher erschienenen Literatur über Johann Sebastian Bach. By Max Schneider.
9. Reviews of books.

XII (1). 1912. **Ausgewählte Arien und Duette mit einem obligaten Instrument und Klavier- oder Orgelbegleitung. VI Abteilung : Arien für Sopran. 2 Heft. Ed. Eusebius Mandyczewski.**

1. Bereite dir, Jesu, noch itzo die Bahn (Cantata 147 : Violin).
2. Eilt, ihr Stunden, kommt herbei (Cantata 30 : Violin).
3. Erfüllet, ihr himmlischen, göttlichen Flammen (Cantata 1 : Oboe da caccia).
4. Genügsamkeit ist ein Schatz in diesem Leben (Cantata 144 : Oboe d'amore).
5. Hört, ihr Völker, Gottes Stimme (Cantata 76 : Violin).
6. Ich folge dir gleichfalls (' St. John Passion,' no. 9 : Flauto).
7. Jesus soll mein erstes Wort (Cantata 171 : Violin).
8. Liebster Jesu, mein Verlangen (Cantata 32 : Oboe).
9. Meinem Hirten bleib' ich treu (Cantata 92 : Oboe d'amore).
10. Seele, deine Spezereien sollen nicht (' Easter Oratorio,' no. 4 : Flauto or Violin).
11. Was Gott thut, das ist wohlgethan (Cantata 100 : Flauto).
12. Wie zittern und wanken der Sünder Gedanken (Cantata 105 : Oboe).

XII (2). 1912. **Bach-Jahrbuch. 8 Jahrgang 1911 : Im Auftrage der Neuen Bachgesellschaft herausgegeben von Arnold Schering. Mit 2 Bildnissen und 8 Faksimiles.**

The volume contains the following articles :
1. ' Mein Herze schwimmt im Blut ' [see *infra* XIII (2)]. By Werner Wolffheim.

2. Das sogenannte Orgelkonzert D-moll, von Wilhelm Friedemann Bach [Peters bk. 3002]. By Max Schneider.
3. Bachiana. By Werner Wolffheim.
4. Zur Geschichte der Passionsaufführungen in Leipzig. By Bernhard Fr. Richter.
5. Tonartensymbolik zu Bachs Zeit. By Rudolf Wustmann.
6. Über die Viola da Gamba und ihre Verwendung bei Joh. Seb. Bach. By Christian Döbereiner.
7. Carl Philipp Emanuel Bach und Joh. Gottl. Im. Breitkopf. By Hermann von Hase.
8. Zur 'Lukaspassion.' By Max Schneider.
9. Verzeichnis der Sammlung alter Musikinstrumente im Bachhaus zu Eisenach. By G. Bornemann.

The illustrations are, portraits of W. Friedemann Bach (aet. 72) and Johann Sebastian Bach (son of Carl P. E. Bach); facsimiles of Bach's arrangement of the D minor Vivaldi Organ Concerto (attributed to W. F. Bach) and 'Lukaspassion,' and of a letter written to J. G. I. Breitkopf by C. P. E. Bach, dated 28th February 1786.

XII (3). 1912. Sechstes Deutsches Bach-Fest in Breslau 15 bis 17 Juni 1912. Fest- und Programmbuch.

Frontispiece, J. S. Bach after the oil-painting by G. Haussmann in possession of St. Thomas' School, Leipzig (see Spitta, vol. i. frontispiece and XVI (1) *infra*).

XIII (1). 1913. Ausgewählte Arien mit obligaten Instrumenten und Klavierbegleitung. VII Abteilung : Arien für Sopran. 3 Heft. Weltliche Arien. Ed. Eusebius Mandyczewski.

1. Wenn die Frühlingslüfte streichen ('Weichet nur betrübte Schatten' : Violin).
2. Sich üben im Lieben ('Weichet nur betrübte Schatten': Oboe).

3. Des Reichtums Glanz ('Ich bin in mir vergnügt':
    Violin).[1]
4. Meine Seele, sei vergnügt ('Ich bin in mir vergnügt':
    Flauto).
5. Angenehmer   Zephryus   ('Der   zufriedengestellte
    Aeolus': Violin).
6. Schweigt, ihr Flöten ('O holder Tag': Flauto).
7. Ei! wie schmeckt der Coffee süsse ('Schweigt stille,
    plaudert nicht': Flauto).
8. Ruhig und in sich zufrieden ('Ich bin in mir vergnügt':
    2 Oboi).
9. Schafe können sicher weiden ('Was mir behagt':
    2 Flauti).
10. Ruhet hie, matte Töne ('O holder Tag': Violin and
    Oboe d'amore).
11. Jagen ist die Lust der Götter ('Was mir behagt':
    2 Horns).
12. Hört doch! der sanften Flöten Chor ('Schleicht, spiel-
    ende Wellen': 3 Flauti).

XIII (2). 1913. Solo-Kantate für Sopran, 'Mein Herze
    schwimmt im Blut,' ausgefunden und herausgegeben
    von C. A. Martiensen. Partitur.

XIII (3). 1913. Solo-Kantate für Sopran, 'Mein Herze
    schwimmt im Blut.' Klavierauszug mit Text von Max
    Schneider.

XIII (4). 1913. Bach-Jahrbuch. 9 Jahrgang 1912 : Im
    Auftrage der Neuen Bachgesellschaft herausgegeben von
    Arnold Schering. Mit 2 Noten-Anhängen.

The volume contains the following articles :
    1. Über die Motetten Seb. Bachs. By Bernhard Fr.
       Richter.
    2. Über die F-dur Toccata [N. bk. 9 p. 176] von J. S.
       Bach. By Woldemar Voigt.

---

[1] The original words are 'Die Schätzbarkeit der weiten Erden.'

3. Die Möllersche Handschrift. Ein unbekanntes Gegen-
   stück zum Andreas-Bach-Buche (mit einem Notenanhange). By Werner Wolffheim.
4. Bachs Bearbeitungen und Umarbeitungen eigener und
   fremder Werke. By Karl Grunsky.
5. Über die Kirchenkantaten vorbachischer Thomas-
   kantoren (mit einem Notenanhange). By Arnold
   Schering.
6. Beiträge zur Bachkritik. By Arnold Schering.
7. Aufführungen von Joh. Seb. Bachs Kompositionen.
   By Th. Biebrich.
8. Notes.

**XIV (1). 1914.[1] Joh. Seb. Bachs Kantatentexte. Im Auftrage
der Neuen Bachgesellschaft herausgegeben von Rudolf
Wustmann.**

Contains the literary texts of the Church Cantatas, with
critical notes.

**XIV (2). 1914. Bach-Jahrbuch. 10 Jahrgang 1913. Im
Auftrage der Neuen Bachgesellschaft herausgegeben von
Arnold Schering. Mit einem Titelbilde und einer
Beilage.**

The volume contains the following articles :
1. Studien zu J. S. Bachs Klavierkonzerten. By Adolf
   Aber.
2. Über Joh. Seb. Bachs Konzerte für drei Klaviere. By
   Hans Boas.
3. Die Kantata Nr. 150, ' Nach dir, Herr, verlanget mich.'
   By Arnold Schering.
4. Über die C-dur-Fuge aus dem i. Theil des ' Wohltem-
   perierten Klaviers.' By Wanda Landowska.
5. Die Varianten der grossen G-moll-Fuge für Orgel
   [Novello bk. 8 p. 127]. By Hermann Keller.
6. Ein Bachkonzert in Kamenz. By Hermann Kretzschmar.

---

[1] The title-page is dated 1913 and the Preface ' Im Advent auf
1914.'

7. Breitkopfsche Textdrucke zu Leipziger Musikauf-
führungen zu Bachs Zeiten.   By Hermann von Hase.
8. J. S. Bachs Aria, ' Erbauliche Gedanken eines Tabak-
rauchers.'   By Alfred Heuss.[1]
9. Johann Seb. Bachs und Christoph Graupners Kompositionen zur Bewerbung um das Thomaskantorat
in Leipzig 1722-23.   By Bernhard Fr. Richter.
10. Register zu den ersten 10 Jahrgängen des Bach-
Jahrbuchs 1904-13.   By Arnold Schering.

The frontispiece is a portrait of Bach, about thirty-five
years old, after the original in the Eisenach Museum by Joh.
Jak. Ihle.   See frontispiece of this volume.

XIV (3). 1914.   Fest- und Programmbuch zum 7 Deutschen
Bachfest der Neuen Bachgesellschaft.   Wien.   9 bis
11 May 1914.

The frontispiece is a picture of St. Thomas' Church and
School in 1723 (see p. 28 *supra*).

XV (1). 1914.   Ausgewählte Arien und Duette mit einem
obligaten Instrument und Klavier- oder Orgelbegleitung.
VIII Abteilung : Arien für Alt.   2 Heft.   Ed. Eusebius
Mandyczewski.

1. Bethörte Welt (Cantata 94 : Flauto).
2. Ein ungefärbt Gemüte (Cantata 24 : Violin or Viola).
3. Ermuntert euch (Cantata 176 : Oboe).
4. Gott ist unser Sonn' und Schild (Cantata 79 : Oboe
or Flauto).
5. In Jesu Demuth (Cantata 151 : Oboe d'amore or
Violin).
6. Jesus ist ein guter Hirt (Cantata 85 : Violin or Violoncello).
7. Kreuz und Krone (Cantata 12 : Oboe).
8. Schäme dich, O Seele, nicht (Cantata 147 : Oboe
d'amore).

---

[1] The Aria is no. 20 of A. M. Bach's ' Notenbuch ' for 1725. See
B.G. XLIII. (2) no. 20.

9. Von der Welt verlang' ich nichts (Cantata 64 : Oboe d'amore).
10. Weh der Seele (Cantata 102 : Oboe).
11. Willkommen ! will ich sagen (Cantata 27 : Cor Anglais).
12. Zum reinen Wasser (Cantata 112 : Oboe d'amore).

XV (2). 1915. Bach-Jahrbuch. 11 Jahrgang 1914 : Im Auftrage der Neuen Bachgesellschaft herausgegeben von Arnold Schering (Leipzig). Mit einem Titelbilde und einer Bilderbeilage.

The volume contains the following articles :
1. Neues über das Bachbildnis der Thomasschule und andere Bildnisse Johann Sebastian Bachs. By Albrecht Kurzwelly.
2. Zur Geschichte der Bachbewegung. Bericht über eine bisher unbekannte frühe Aufführung der Matthäus-passion. By Karl Anton.
3. Johann Christoph Friedrich Bach. By Georg Schüne-mann.
4. Die Wiederbelebung der Kurrende in Eisenach. By W. Nicolai.
5. Aufführungen von Joh. Seb. Bachs Kompositionen in der Zeit vom Oktober 1912 bis Juli 1914. By Th. Biebrich.
6. Bachaufführungen im ersten Jahre des deutschen Krieges. By Th. Biebrich.
7. Mitgliederversammlung der Neuen Bachgesellschaft. Montag, den 11 Mai 1914.
8. Reviews.
The frontispiece is a picture of Bach by Daniel Greiner.

XVI (1). 1916. Das Bachbildnis der Thomasschule zu Leipzig, nach seiner Wiederherstellung im Jahre 1913. Gemalt von E. G. Haussmann 1746.

A print of the renovated picture is at p. 48 of this volume.

XVI (2). 1916. Bach-Genealogie mit zwei Briefen von Carl
    Philipp Emanuel Bach. Herausgegeben von Professor
    Max Schneider in Breslau.[1]

XVI (3). 1916. Bach-Jahrbuch. 12 Jahrgang 1915. Im
    Auftrage der Neuen Bachgesellschaft herausgegeben von
    Arnold Schering (Leipzig). Mit dem Bildnisse J. S.
    Bachs nach der Gedenkbüste in der Walhalla.

The volume contains the following articles :
 1. Johann Sebastian Bach im Gottesdienst der Thomaner.
    By Bernhard Friedrich Richter.
 2. Karl Philipp Emanuel Bach und der Dresdner Kreuz-
    kantor Gottfried August Homilius im Musikleben
    ihrer Zeit. Ein Beitrag zur Geschichte der Stil-
    wandlung des 18 Jahrhunderts. By Rudolf Steglich.
 3. Eine Umdichtung des ' Zufriedengestellten Aeolus '
    (Mit einem Anhang über die Kantata ' Schleicht,
    spielende Wellen '). By Woldemar Voigt.
 4. Eine alte, unbekannte Skizze von Sebastian Bachs
    Leben. By Arthur Prüfer.
 5. Bachaufführungen im zweiten Jahre des deutschen
    Krieges. By Th. Biebrich.
 6. Reviews.
The frontispiece is a photograph of Professor F. Behn's
bust of Bach in the Walhalla.

XVII (1). 1916. Motette ' O Jesu Christ, mein's Lebens
    Licht.' Nach Bachs Handschrift zum ersten Male
    herausgegeben von Max Schneider. Partitur.

    [See B.G. XXIV.]

XVII (2). 1916. Motette ' O Jesu Christ, mein's Lebens
    Licht.' Klavierauszug mit Text von Max Schneider.

    [See B.G. XXIV.]

---

[1] This publication, announced for 1916, appears under a different
title as the third issue for 1917. See *infra*, XVII. (3).

XVII (3). 1917. Bach-Urkunden. Ursprung der musikal-isch-Bachischen Familie. Nachrichten über Johann Sebastian Bach von Carl Philipp Emanuel Bach. Herausgegeben von Max Schneider.

The volume contains a facsimile of the Bach Genealogy compiled by Joh. Seb. Bach and formerly in Carl Philipp Emanuel's possession, and two letters from the latter to J. N. Forkel.

XVII (4). 1917. Bach-Jahrbuch. 13 Jahrgang 1916. Im Auftrage der Neuen Bachgesellschaft herausgegeben von Arnold Schering (Leipzig).

The volume contains the following articles :

1. Die F.-Trompete im 2 Brandenburgischen Konzert von Joh. Seb. Bach. By Richard Hofmann.
2. Zur Frage der Ausführung der Ornamente bei Bach. Zählzeit oder Notenwert ? By Hans Joachim Moser.
3. Friedrich Bachs Briefwechsel mit Gerstenberg und Breitkopf. By Georg Schünemann.
4. Bachaufführurgen im dritten Jahre des deutschen Krieges. By Th. Biebrich.
5. Literarische Beigabe : ' Der Thomaskantor.' Ein Gemüth-erfreuend Spiel von deme Herren Cantori Sebastian Bachen, vorgestellt in zween Auffzügen durch Bernhard Christoph Breitkopfen seel. Erben : Breitkopf und Härtel 1917. By Arnold Schering.

XVIII (1). 1917. Konzert in D moll nach der ursprünglichen Fassung für Violine wiederhergestellt von Robert Reitz. Partitur.

[See B.G. XVII.]

XVIII (2). 1917. Konzert in D moll nach der ursprünglichen Fassung für Violine wiederhergestellt von Robert Reitz. Ausgabe für Violine und Klavier.

[See B.G. XVII.]

XVIII (3). 1918. Bach-Jahrbuch. 14 Jahrgang 1917 : Im
Auftrage der Neuen Bachgesellschaft herausgegeben von
Arnold Schering (Leipzig). Mit einem Bildnis.

The volume contains the following articles :

1. Gustav Schreck [d. 22 Jan. 1918].
2. Das dritte kleine Bachfest zu Eisenach :
   I. Der Festgottesdienst in der St. Georgenkirche zu
      Eisenach am 30 September 1917.
   II. Vorträge und Verhandlungen der Mitgliederver-
       sammlung des dritten kleinen Bachfestes in
       Eisenach am 29 September 1917.
3. Seb. Bachs Stellung zur Choralrhythmik der Luther-
   zeit. By Hans Joachim Moser.
4. Zur Motivbildung Bachs. Ein Beitrag zur Stilpsycho-
   logie. By Ernst Kurth.
5. Ein Programmtrio Karl Philipp Emanuel Bachs.
   By Hans Mersmann.
6. Hermann Kretzschmar [b. 19 Jan. 1848].
7. Review.

The frontispiece is a copy of the oil portrait of Bach after
Haussmann, copied by J. M. David in 1746.

APPENDIX IV

BIBLIOGRAPHY OF BACH LITERATURE

THE following list does not include magazine articles or technical works. A comprehensive bibliography, compiled by Max Schneider, will be found in the Bach-Jahrbuch for 1905 and 1910. Shorter lists are in C. F. Abdy Williams' 'Bach' (1900) and André Pirro's 'J.-S. Bach' (1906). Titles within square brackets in the following list are inserted upon the authority of the 'Bach-Jahrbuch,' but are not discoverable in the annual Book Catalogues. Since the absence of an Italian section may be remarked, it should be said that the 'Catalogo generale della Libreria Italiana, 1847-1899' (published in 1910) contains no reference to Bach. Nor does the Supplement of 1912.

I. GERMANY

Johann Christoph W. Kühnau, 'Die blinden Tonkünstler.' Berlin. 1810.
J. E. Grosser, 'Lebensbeschreibung des Kapellmeisters Johann Sebastian Bach.' Breslau. 1834.
Albert Schiffner, 'Sebastian Bachs geistige Nachkommenschaft.' Leipzig. 1840.
Johann T. Mosewius, 'Johann Sebastian Bach in seinen Kirch-Kantaten und Choralgesängen.' Berlin. 1845.
Johann Carl Schauer, 'Johann Sebastian Bachs Lebensbild : Eine Denkschrift auf seinen 100jähringen Todestag.' Jena. 1850.

C. L. Hilgenfeldt, 'Johann Sebastian Bachs Leben, Wirken und Werke.' Leipzig. 1850.

[W. Naumann, 'Johann Sebastian Bach. Eine Biographie.' Cassell. 1855.]

[Anon., 'Biographien und Charakteristiken der grossen Meister: Bach, Händel, Gluck, Haydn, Mozart, Beethoven, mit Porträts.' 2nd ed. Leipzig. 1860.]

C. H. Bitter, 'Johann Sebastian Bach.' 2 vols. Berlin. 1865. 2nd ed. 1880.

C. Albert Ludwig, 'Johann Sebastian Bach in seiner Bedeutung für Cantoren, Organisten, und Schullehrer.' Bleichroder. 1865.

Alfred Dörffel, 'Thematisches Verzeichniss der Instrumentalwerke von Joh. Seb. Bach. Auf Grund der Gesammtausgabe von C. F. Peters. Leipzig. 1867. 2nd ed. 1882.

Carl Tamme, 'Thematisches Verzeichniss der Vocalwerke von Joh. Seb. Bach. Auf Grund der Gesammtausgaben von C. F. Peters und der Bach-Gesellschaft.' Leipzig. n.d.

C. H. Bitter, 'C. P. E. und W. F. Bach und deren Brüder.' 2 vols. Berlin. 1868. New ed. 1880.

[Anon., 'J. S. Bach. Biographie.' Leipzig. 1869.]

L. Ramann, 'Bach und Händel.' Leipzig. 1869.

W. Junghans, 'Johann Sebastian Bach als Schuler der Partikularschule zu St. Michaelis in Lüneburg.' Lüneburg. 1870.

Emil Naumann, 'Deutsche Tondichter von Sebastian Bach bis auf die Gegenwart.' Berlin. 1871. 5th ed. 1882.

M. Schick, 'J. S. Bach: ein musikalisches Lebensbild.' Reutlingen. 1873.

Philipp Spitta, 'Johann Sebastian Bach.' 2 vols. Leipzig. 1873-1880.

E. Frommel, 'Händel und Bach.' Berlin. 1878.

Elise Polko, 'Unsere Musikklassiker. Sechs biographische Lebensbilder' [Bach, etc.]. Leipzig. 1880.

[Anon., 'J. S. Bach. Biographie.' [In 'Meister der Tonkunst,' no. 2.] Leipzig. 1880.]

August Reissmann, 'Johann Sebastian Bach. Sein Leben und seine Werke.' Berlin and Leipzig. 1881.

Otto Gumprecht, ' Warum treiben wir Musik ? ' [Bach and others.] Leipzig. 1883.

C. H. Bitter, ' Die Söhne Seb. Bachs.' Leipzig. 1883.

Jul. Schümann, ' Joh. Seb. Bach, der Kantor der Thomasschule zu Leipzig.' Leipzig. 1884.

A. L. Gräbner, ' Johann Sebastian Bach.' Dresden. 1885.

Fr. Spitta, ' Haendel und Bach. Zwei Festreden.' Bonn. 1884.

E. Heinrich, ' Johann Sebastian Bach. Ein kurzes Lebensbild.' Berlin. 1885.

E. Naumann, ' Deutsche Tondichter von J. S. Bach bis Richard Wagner.' Leipzig. 1886. 6th ed. 1896.

Paul Meyer, ' Joh. Seb. Bach. Vortrag.' Basel. 1887.

Ludwig Ziemssen, ' Johann Sebastian Bach. Lebensbild.' Glogau. 1889.

Richard Batka, ' J. S. Bach.' Leipzig. 1893.

Wilhelm His, ' Johann Sebastian Bach. Forschungen über dessen Grabstätte, Gebeine und Antlitz.' Leipzig. 1895.

Wilhelm His, ' Anatomisches Forschungen über J. S. Bach's Gebeine und Antlitz, nebst Bemerkungen über dessen Bilder.' Leipzig. 1895.

Armin Stein, ' J. S. Bach. Ein Küntstlerleben.' Halle. 1896.

Hans von Wolzogen, ' Bach ' [In ' Grossmeister deutscher Musik ']. Berlin. 1897.

[W. Kleefeld, ' Bach und Graupner.' Leipzig. 1898.]

[Fr. Thomas, ' Der Stammbaum des Ohrdruffer Zweigs der Familie von J. S. Bach.' Ohrdruf. 1899.]

[Fr. Thomas, ' Einige Ergebnisse über J. S. Bachs Ohrdruffer Schulzeit.' Ohrdruf. 1900.]

B. Stein, ' Johann Sebastian Bach und die Familie der " Bache." ' Bielefeld. 1900.

Fr. von Hausegger, ' Unsere deutschen Meister ' [Bach and others]. Munich. 1901.

Arnold Schering, ' Bachs Textbehandlung.' Leipzig. 1901.

[W. Tappert, ' Sebastian Bachs Kompositionen für die Laute.' Berlin. 1901.]

K. Söhle, ' Sebastian Bach in Arnstadt.' Berlin. 1902. 2nd ed. 1904.

Arthur Prüfer, ' Sebastian Bach und die Tonkunst des xix. Jahrhunderts.' Leipzig. 1902.

H. Barth, ' Joh. Sebastian Bach : Lebensbild.' Berlin. 1902.

Gustav Höcker, ' Johann Sebastian Bach.' Gotha. 1903.

Paul von Bojanowski, ' Das Weimar Johann Sebastian Bachs.' Weimar. 1903.

Jul. Schumann, ' Bach, Händel, Mendelssohn. Die protestantische Kirchenmusik in Lebensbildern.' Calw and Stuttgart. 1903.

[—. Weissgerber, ' J. S. Bach in Arnstadt.' Arnstadt. 1904.]

[K. Storck, ' J. S. Bach : Charakter und Lebensgang.' Berlin. 1905.]

[A. Pischinger, ' J. S. Bach.' Munich. 1905.]

Philipp Wolfrum, ' Joh. Seb. Bach.' Berlin. 1906.

Albert Schweitzer, ' J. S. Bach.' Berlin. 1908.

Friedrich Hashagen, ' Joh. Sebastian Bach als Sänger und Musiker des Evangeliums.' Wismar. 1909.

Max Trümpelmann, ' Joh. Sebastian Bach und seine Bedeutung für die Choralkomposition unserer Zeit.' Magdeburg. 1909.

August Wildenhahn, ' Joh. Sebastian Bach.' Eisenach. 1909.

Philipp Wolfrum, ' Johann Sebastian Bach.' 2 vols. Leipzig. 1910.

André Pirro, ' Johann Sebastian Bach. Sein Leben und seine Werke.' [Translated from the French by Bernhard Engelke.] Berlin. 1910.

Johannes Schreyer, ' Beiträge zur Bach-Kritik.' Leipzig. 1911.

Martin Falck, ' Wilhelm Friedemann Bach. Sein Leben und seine Werke, mit thematischem Verzeichnis seiner Kompositionen und zwei Bildern.' Leipzig. c. 1911-14.

K. Glebe, ' Johann Sebastian Bach.' Halle. 1912.

La Mara, ' Johann Sebastian Bach.' 5th edition. Leipzig. 1912.

H. Reimann, ' Johann Sebastian Bach.' 1912.

Armin Stein, ' Johann Sebastian Bach.' Halle. 1912.

Rudolf Wustmann, ' Joh. Seb. Bachs Kantatentexte.' Leipzig. 1914.

Max Ritter, ' Der Stil Joh. Seb. Bachs in seinem Choralsatze.'
 Bremen. 1913.
Ernst Kurth, ' Grundlagen des linearen Kontrapunkts.
 Einführung in Stil und Technik von Bachs melodischer
 Polyphonie.' Bern. 1917.

II. FRANCE

Johann Nikolaus Forkel, ' Vie, talents et travaux de Jean-
 Sébastien Bach.' [Translated from the German by Félix
 Grenier.] Paris. 1876.
Ernest David, ' La vie et les œuvres de J.-S. Bach, sa famille,
 ses élèves, ses contemporains.' [An abridged translation
 of Spitta.] Paris. 1882.
William Cart, ' Un maître deux fois centenaire : étude sur
 J.-S. Bach, 1685-1750.' Paris. 1884. New ed. 1898.
André Pirro, ' L'Orgue de Jean-Sébastien Bach.' Paris.
 1895.
[G. Fink, ' Étude biographique sur Jean-Sébastien Bach.'
 Angoulême. 1899.]
 [—. Daubresse, ' Haendel et Bach.' Paris. 1901.]
Albert Schweitzer, ' J. S. Bach, le musicien-poète.' Leipzig.
 1905.
André Pirro, ' J.-S. Bach.' Paris. 1906. 4th edition. 1913.
André Pirro, ' L'Esthétique de Jean-Sébastien Bach.' Paris.
 1907.

III. GREAT BRITAIN

Johann Nikolaus Forkel, ' Life of John Sebastian Bach.
 Translated from the German ' [by — Stephenson].
 London. 1820.
C. H. Bitter, ' The Life of J. Sebastian Bach. An abridged
 translation from the German.' [By Janet Elizabeth Kay
 Shuttleworth.] London. 1873.
R. Lane Poole, ' Sebastian Bach.' London. 1881.
Sedley Taylor, ' The Life of J. S. Bach in relation to his
 work as a Church musician and composer.' Cambridge.
 1897.
Philipp Spitta, ' Johann Sebastian Bach : His work and

influence on the music of Germany, 1685-1750.' Translated from the German by Clara Bell and J. A. Fuller Maitland. 3 vols. London. 1899.

C. F. Abdy Williams, ' Bach.' London. 1900.

A. Maczewski and F. G. Edwards, art. ' Bach ' in ' Grove's Dictionary,' vol. i. 1904.

E. H. Thorne, ' Bach.' London. 1904.

C. H. H. Parry, ' Johann Sebastian Bach.' London and New York. 1909.

Donald F. Tovey, art. ' J. S. Bach,' in ' Encyclopædia Britannica.' Vol. iii. 1910.

Albert Schweitzer, ' J. S. Bach. With a Preface by C. M. Widor. English translation by Ernest Newman.' 2 vols. London. 1911.

C. Sanford Terry, ' Bach's Chorals.' 3 vols. Cambridge. 1915, 1917, 1920.

W. G. Whittaker, ' Fugitive Notes on certain Cantatas and Motets by J. S. Bach.' London. 1920.

IV. UNITED STATES OF AMERICA

André Pirro, ' Johann Sebastian Bach, the Organist, and his works.' [Translated from the French by Wallace Goodrich.] New York. 1902.

Elbert Hubbard, ' Little voyages to the homes of great musicians.' New York. 1902.

Ludwig Ziemssen, ' Johann Sebastian Bach.' [Translated from the German by G. Putnam Upton.] Chicago. 1905.

Rutland Boughton, ' Bach.' New York. 1907.

V. HOLLAND

A. M. Oordt, ' Een koort woord over Bach.' Leiden. 1873.

VI. BELGIUM

Charles Martens, ' Un livre nouveau sur J.-S. Bach.' Brussels. 1905.

Victor Hallut, ' Les Maîtres classiques du dix-huitième siècle.' [Bach and others.] Brussels. 1909.

VII. Russia

[Kuschenaw Dmitrevsky, ' Das lyrische Museum ' (no. 25).
  [The oldest Russian biography of Bach.] Petrograd.
  1831].
[W. Th. Odoewsky, ' Sebastian Bach.' Petrograd. 1890.]
[G. M. Bazunow, ' J. S. Bach.' Petrograd. 1894.]
[S. M. Haljutin, ' J. S. Bach.' Minsk. 1894.]
[Adolf Chybinski, ' J. S. Bach.' Warsaw. 1910.]

APPENDIX V

A COLLATION OF THE NOVELLO AND PETERS EDITIONS OF THE ORGAN WORKS

Novello : Book I. EIGHT SHORT PRELUDES AND FUGUES.

Page   2. Prelude and Fugue in C major (P. bk. 247 p. 48).

5.	Do.	do.	D minor (*ib.* 51).
8.	Do.	do.	E minor (*ib.* 54).
11.	Do.	do.	F major (*ib.* 57).
14.	Do.	do.	G major (*ib.* 60).
17.	Do.	do.	G minor (*ib.* 63).
20.	Do.	do.	A minor (*ib.* 66).
23.	Do.	do.	B flat major (*ib.* 69).

Novello : Book II. PRELUDES, FUGUES, AND TRIO.

Page 26. Allabreve in D major (P. bk. 247 p. 72).

     30. Prelude in G major (*ib.* 82).

     34. Canzona in D minor (P. bk. 243 p. 54).

     38. Fugue (The Giant) in D minor (P. bk. 246 p. 78).

     41. Fugue in G minor (P. bk. 247 p. 85).

     44. Prelude and Fugue (the Short) in E minor (P. bk. 242 p. 88).

     48. Prelude and Fugue in C minor (P. bk. 243 p. 32).

     54. Trio in D minor (*ib.* 72).

Novello : Book III. FANTASIAS, PRELUDES, AND FUGUES.

Page 57. Fantasia in C minor (5 parts) (P. bk. 243 p. 66).

     60. Fugue in B minor (on a theme by Corelli) (*ib.* 46).

     64. Prelude and Fugue in A major (P. bk. 241 p. 14)

     70.   Do.   do.   C major (*ib.* p. 2).

76. Fantasia and Fugue in C minor (P. bk. 242 p. 55).
84. Fugue (the Short) in G minor (P. bk. 243 p. 42).

Novello : Book IV. Sonatas or Trios for Two Manuals
and Pedal.

Page 88. Sonata in E flat major (P. bk. 240 p. 2).
     97.   Do.   C minor (*ib.* 11).
   110.   Do.   D minor (*ib.* 24).

Novello : Book V. Sonatas or Trios for Two Manuals
and Pedal (IV.-VI.).

Page 124. Sonata in E minor (P. bk. 240 p. 36).
   134.   Do.   C major (*ib.* 46).
   151.   Do.   G major (*ib.* 63).

Novello : Book VI. Toccata, Preludes, and Fugues.

Page   2. Toccata and Fugue in D minor (P. bk. 243 p. 24).
    10. Prelude and Fugue in D major (*ib.* p. 14).
    21.   Do.   do.   F minor (P. bk. 241 p. 29).
    28.   Do.   do.   E flat major (P. bk. 242
                                          p. 2).

Novello : Book VII. Preludes and Fugues.

Page 42. Prelude and Fugue (the Great) in A minor (P. bk.
                                241 p. 54).
    52.   Do.   do.   B minor (*ib.* 78).
    64.   Do.   do.   C minor (*ib.* 36).
    74. Prelude and Fugue in C major (P. bk. 243 p. 2).
    80.   Do.   do.   G major (*ib.* 8).

Novello : Book VIII. Preludes and Fugues.

Page 88. Prelude and Fugue in C major (P. bk. 242 p. 62).
    98.   Do.   (the Great) in E minor (P. bk.
                                241 p. 64).
   112.   Do.   do.   G major (*ib.* p. 7).
   120.   Do.   in G minor (P. bk. 242 p. 48).
   127. Fantasia and Fugue (the Great) in G minor (P.
          bk. 241 p. 20).

Novello : Book IX. PRELUDES AND FUGUES.

Page 137. Toccata and Fugue (the Great) in C major
(P. bk. 242 p. 72).

150. Prelude and Fugue in D minor (*ib.* 42).

156.   Do.   (the Great) in C major (P. bk.
241 p. 46).

168. Fantasia in G major (P. bk. 243 p. 58).

176. Toccata and Fugue (the Great) in F major
(P. bk. 242 p. 16).

Novello : Book X. TOCCATA, PRELUDES, AND FUGUES.

Page 196. Toccata and Fugue (the Dorian) in D minor
(P. bk. 242 p. 30.)

208. Prelude and Fugue (the Short) in A minor (*ib.* 84).

214. Passacaglia in C minor (P. bk. 240 p. 75).

230. Fugue in C minor (P. bk. 243 p. 36).

238. Prelude in A minor (*ib.* 68).

Novello :   Book XI. FOUR CONCERTOS [after Antonio
Vivaldi].

Page   1. Concerto in G major (P. bk. 247 p. 2).

10.   Do.   A minor (*ib.* 10).

24.   Do.   C major (*ib.* 22).

49.   Do.   C major (*ib.* 44).

Novello : Book XII. PRELUDES, FANTASIAS, FUGUES,
TRIOS, ETC.

Page 55. Fugue in G major (P. bk. 2067 p. 18).

60. Fantasia and Fugue in A minor (*ib.* 3).

71. Fantasia with Imitation in B minor (P. bk. 215
p. 41).

75. Fantasia in G major (P. bk. 2067 p. 25).

83. Fugue in D major (P. bk. 2067 p. 22).

86.   Do.   G major (*ib.* 12).

91. Prelude in C major (P. bk. 247 p. 77).

92. Fantasia in C major (*ib.* 78).

94. Prelude in C major (*ib.* 76).

95. Fugue in C minor (P. bk. 243 p. 50).

89. Erstanden ist der heil'ge Christ (P. bk. 244 p. 16).
91. Erschienen ist der herrliche Tag (*ib.* 17).
94. Heut' triumphiret Gottes Sohn (*ib.* 30).
97. Komm, Gott, Schöpfer, heiliger Geist (P. bk. 246 p. 86).
99. Herr Jesu Christ, dich zu uns wend' (P. bk. 244 p. 28).
101. Liebster Jesu, wir sind hier (*ib.* 40).
103. Dies sind die heil'gen zehn Gebot' (*ib.* 14).
105. Vater unser im Himmelreich (*ib.* 52).
107. Durch Adams Fall ist ganz verderbt (*ib.* 15).
109. Es ist das Heil uns kommen her (*ib.* 18).
111. Ich ruf' zu dir, Herr Jesu Christ (*ib.* 33).
113. In dich hab' ich gehoffet, Herr (*ib.* 35).
115. Wenn wir in höchsten Nöthen sein (*ib.* 55).
117. Wer nur den lieben Gott lässt walten (*ib.* 57).
119. Alle Menschen müssen sterben (*ib.* 2).
121. Ach wie nichtig, ach wie flüchtig (*ib.* 2).

Novello : Book XVI. THE SIX 'SCHÜBLER' CHORALE
PRELUDES AND THE 'CLAVIERÜBUNG,' PART III.

(*a*) The Schübler Preludes.

Page 1. Wachet auf, ruft uns die Stimme (P. bk. 246 p. 72).
4. Wo soll ich fliehen hin, *or*, Auf meinen lieben Gott (*ib.* 84).
6. Wer nur den lieben Gott lässt walten (*ib.* 76).
8. Meine Seele erhebt den Herren (*ib.* 33).
10. Ach bleib bei uns, Herr Jesu Christ (P. bk. 245 p. 4).
14. Kommst du nun, Jesu, vom Himmel herunter (P. bk. 246 p. 16).

(*b*) The 'Clavierübung,' Part III.

19. Prelude in E flat major (P. bk. 242 p. 2).
28. Kyrie, Gott Vater in Ewigkeit (P. 246 p. 18)
30. Christe, aller Welt Trost (*ib.* 20).
33. Kyrie, Gott heiliger Geist (*ib.* 23).
36. Kyrie, Gott Vater in Ewigkeit (*ib.* 26).
37. Christe, aller Welt Trost (*ib.* 27).

38. Kyrie, Gott heiliger Geist (P. 246 p. 28).
39. Allein Gott in der Höh' sei Ehr' (Pk. b. 245 p. 10).
40.* Do.   do.   do   (*ib.* 12).
41. Do.   do.   do.   (*ib.* 29).
42. Dies sind die heil'gen zehn Gebot' (*ib.* 50).
47. Do.   do.   do   (*ib.* 54).
49. Wir glauben all' an einen Gott, Schöpfer (P. bk.
                                                246 p. 78).
52. Do.   do.   do.   (*ib.* 81).
53. Vater unser im Himmelreich (*ib.* 60).
61. Do.   do.   (P. bk. 244 p. 51).
62. Christ, unser Herr, zum Jordan kam (P. bk. 245
                                                p. 46).
67. Do.   do.   do.   (*ib.* 49).
68. Aus tiefer Noth schrei' ich zu dir (*ib.* 36).
72. Do.   do.   do.   (*ib.* 38).
74. Jesus Christus unser Heiland (*ib.* 82).
80. Do.   do.   (*ib.* 92).
83. Fugue in E flat major (P. bk. 242 p. 10).

Novello : Book XVII. The Eighteen Chorale Preludes.

Page   1. Komm, heiliger Geist, Herre Gott (P. bk. 246 p. 4).
       10. Do.   do.   do.   (*ib.* 10).
       18. An Wasserflüssen Babylon (P. bk. 245 p. 34).
       22. Schmücke dich, O liebe Seele (P. bk. 246 p. 50).
       26. Herr Jesu Christ, dich zu uns wend' (P. bk. 245
                                                p. 70).
       32. O Lamm Gottes unschuldig (P. bk. 246 p. 45).
       40. Nun danket alle Gott (*ib.* 34).
       43. Von Gott will ich nicht lassen (*ib.* 70).
       46. Nun komm, der Heiden Heiland (*ib.* 38).
       49. Do.   do.   do.   (*ib.* 40).
       52. Do.   do.   do.   (*ib.* 42).
       56. Allein Gott in der Höh' sei Ehr' (P. bk. 245 p. 26).
       60. Do.   do.   do   (*ib.* 22).
       66. Do.   do.   do.   (*ib.* 17).
       74. Jesus Christus, unser Heiland, der von uns (*ib.* 87).
       79. Do.   do.   do.   (*ib.* 90).

82. Komm, Gott, Schöpfer, heiliger Geist (P. bk. 246 p. 2).

85. Wenn wir in höchsten Nöthen sein, *or*, Vor deinen Thron tret' ich allhier (*ib.* 74).

Novello: Book XVIII. MISCELLANEOUS CHORALE PRELUDES (Part I.).

Page 1. Ach Gott und Herr (P. bk. 2067 p. 38).
      2.   Do.   do. (P. bk. 245 p. 3).
      3.   Do.   do. (P. bk. 2067 p. 39).
      4. Allein Gott in der Höh' sei Ehr' (not in P.).
      5.   Do.   do.   do. (P. bk. 245 p. 6).
      7.   Do.   do.   do. (*ib.* 30).
    11.   Do.   do.   do. (*ib.* 8).
    13. An Wasserflüssen Babylon (*ib.* 32).
    16. Christ lag in Todesbanden (*ib.* 43).
    19.   Do.   do. (*ib.* 40).
    23. Christum wir sollen loben schon, *or*, Was fürcht'st du, Feind Herodes, sehr (P. bk. 244 p. 9).
    24. Das Jesulein soll doch mein Trost (P. bk. 2067 p. 47).
    26. Der Tag der ist so freudenreich (not in P.).
    28. Durch Adams Fall ist ganz verderbt (P. bk. 245 p. 56).
    30. Ein' feste Burg ist unser Gott (*ib.* 58).
    35. Erbarm' dich mein, O Herre Gott (not in P.).
    37. Gelobet seist du, Jesu Christ (P. bk. 244 p. 102).
    38.   Do.   do.   do. (*ib.* 20).
    39.   Do.   do.   do. (P. bk. 245 p. 61).
    41. Gottes Sohn ist kommen (P. bk. 244 p. 22).
    42.   Do.   do. (P. bk. 245 p. 64).
    43. Herr Christ, der ein'ge Gottes-Sohn (P. bk. 244 p. 25).
    44. Herr Gott, dich loben wir (Te Deum Laudamus) (P. bk. 245 p. 65).
    50. Herr Jesu Christ, dich zu uns wend' (P. bk. 244 p. 28).
    52.   Do.   do.   do. (not in P.).
    53. Herzlich thut mich verlangen (P. bk. 244 p. 30).

54. Ich hab' mein' Sach Gott heimgestellt (P. bk. 245
            p. 74).
58.   Do.   do.   do.   (not in P.).
59. In dich hab' ich gehoffet, Herr (P. bk. 245 p. 94).
61. In dulci jubilo (P. bk. 244 p. 103).
64. Jesu, meine Freude (P. bk. 245 p. 78).
69. Jesus, meine Zuversicht (P. bk. 244 p. 103).
70. Liebster Jesu, wir sind hier (*ib.* 105).
71.   Do.   do.   (*ib.* 105).
72.   Do.   do.   (*ib.* 39).
73. Lob sei dem allmächtigen Gott (*ib.* 41).
74. Lobt Gott, ihr Christen, allzugleich (*ib.* 106).
75. Meine Seele erhebt den Herren (Magnificat)
    (P. bk. 246 p. 29).
80. Nun freut euch, lieben Christen g'mein, *or*, Es
    ist gewisslich an der Zeit (*ib.* 36).
83. Nun komm, der Heiden Heiland (P. bk. 244 p. 45).

Novello: Book XIX. MISCELLANEOUS CHORALE PRELUDES
(PART II.) AND VARIATIONS.

(*a*) Preludes.

Page   2. Valet will ich dir geben (P. bk. 246 p. 53).
     7.   Do.   do.   (*ib.* 56).
  12. Vater unser im Himmelreich (*ib.* 66).
  14. Vom Himmel hoch, da komm ich her (*ib.* 67).
  16.   Do.   do.   do.   (*ib* 68).
  19.   Do.   do.   do.   (P. bk. 244
                           p. 106).
  21. Wer nur den lieben Gott lässt walten (*ib.* 56).
  22.   Do.   do.   do.   (*ib.* 56).
  23. Wie schön leuchtet der Morgenstern (not in P.).
  28. Wir Christenleut' (P. bk. 2067 p. 52).
  30. Wir glauben all' an einen Gott, Vater (P. bk. 246
    p. 82).
  32. Wo soll ich fliehen hin (P. bk. 2067 p. 48).
           (*b*) Variations.
  36. Christ, der du bist der helle Tag (P. bk. 244 p. 60).

44. O Gott, du frommer Gott (P. bk. 244 p. 68).
55. Sei gegrüsset, Jesu gütig (*ib*. 76).
73. Vom Himmel hoch, da komm ich her (*ib*. 92).

The Peters volumes 244, 245, 246, 2067 contain movements
excluded from the Novello edition, *viz.* :—

Book 244 : the figured Choral (Herr Christ, der ein'ge
Gottes-Sohn) on p. 107, and the Variant
texts on pp. 108-112.

Book 245 : the Variant texts on pp. 96-113.

Book 246 : the Variant texts on pp. 86-103 (excepting the
B version of ' Komm, Gott, Schöpfer,
heiliger Geist ').

Book 2067 : the Choral Preludes on pp. 39 (Auf meinen
lieben Gott), 40 (Wir glauben all' an
einen Gott), 42 (Jesu Leiden, Pein und
Tod), 44 (Ach Gott, vom Himmel sieh
darein), 54 (Aus der Tiefe ruf' ich),
56 (Christ lag in Todesbanden), and the
' Kleines harmonisches Labyrinth ' on
p. 16.

APPENDIX VI

GENEALOGY OF THE FAMILY OF BACH[1]

TABLE I.

HANS BACH, b. c. 1520; 'Gemeindevormundschaft' in Wechmar, near Gotha, in 1561 (i. 4).

1. VEIT, b. c. 1550-60. Baker or miller in Wechmar; migrated to Hungary; returned to Wechmar on the eve of the Thirty Years' War; d. March 8, 1619 (i. 4).

2. JOHANNES, b. c. 1580; 'Spielmann' and carpet-maker in Wechmar; married Anna Schmied, dtr. of the Wechmar innkeeper (d. Sept. 18, 1635); d. Dec. 26, 1626 (i. 6). (See notice in 'Bach-Jahrbuch,' 1910.)

3. LIPS, d. Oct. 10, 1620 (i. 9).

See Table II.

4. JOHANNES, b. Nov. 26, 1604; Director of the Town Musicians and Org. of the Prediger-Kirche, Erfurt; m. in 1635, Barbara Hoffman, dtr. of the Town Musician of Suhl (no issue), and (2) Hedwig Lämmerhirt; d. May 13, 1673 (i. 14-20).

5. CHRISTOPH, b. Ap. 19, 1613; Court and Town Musician at Arnstadt; m. Maria Magdalena Grabler, of Prettin, Saxony (d. Oct. 6, 1661); d. Sept. 12,[2] 1661 (i. 142).

6. HEINRICH, b. Dec. 16,[3] 1615; Org. in Arnstadt; m. Eva Hoffmann, dtr. of the Town Musician of Suhl; d. July 10, 1692 (i. 27).

HANS (?), d. young, Nov. 6, 1636; m. Dorothea (d. May 30, 1678) (i. 8).

HANS, the younger; m. Martha (1634), (i. 8).

ABRAHAM, b. March 29, 1645 (i. 8).
CASPAR, b. March 9, 1648; Shepherd in Wechmar (i. 8).
Son, b. March 27, 1656 (i. 8).

See Table III.

See Table IV.

See Table VI.

[1] The Tables are compiled from Spitta's text, to which references are given in the brackets. Occasional details found in Schweitzer are marked 'Sch.' See also art. 'Bach' in Grove's 'Dictionary.' The numerals preceding the names refer to the number of the corresponding entry in the Bach Genealogy, which was once in Carl Philipp Emmanuel Bach's possession, a facsimile of which is published by the New Bachgesellschaft under the title 'Bach-Urkunden,' ed. Dr. Max Schneider. See supra, p. 285. Names that are not preceded by a numeral are not in the Genealogy.
[2] Spitta gives the dates of Christoph and his wife's deaths incorrectly. I have corrected them from the Genealogy.
[3] Spitta has September.

TABLE II.

(See Table I.)   3. LIPS BACH, probably son of Veit Bach [1] (d. 1619); d. Oct. 10, 1620 (i. 9.)

LIPS, d. Sept. 21, 1620 (i. 9)).

WENDEL, b. 1619; farmer (?) at Wolfsbehringen, near Gotha; d. Dec. 18, 1682 (i. 10).

JAKOB, b. 1655; Cantor at Steinbach and (1694) Ruhla; d. 1718 (i. 10).

JONAS, sent to Italy (with two unnamed brothers) for his musical advancement by the Count of Schwarzburg-Arnstadt; blind (i. 9).

GEORG MICHAEL (1703-71), teacher in the Halle Lutheran Town College (i. 12).

NIKOLAUS EPHRAIM, Organist to the Abbess Elizabeth of Gandersheim; d. Aug. 12, 1760 (i. 11).

JOHANN LUDWIG, b. 1677; Court Cantor and Kapell-Direktor at Meiningen; d. 1741 (i. 10).

GOTTLIEB FRIEDRICH (1714-85); Court Organist at Meiningen (i. 10).

JOHANN CHRISTIAN (1743-1814); music teacher at Ruhla; called 'der Clavier Bach' (i. 12).

SAMUEL ANTON (1713-81); pupil of J. S. B.; Court Organist at Meiningen (i. 10).

JOHANN PHILIPP, b. 1751; Court Organist at Meiningen; d. 1846 (i. 10).

1 Veit Bach certainly had another son than Hans: whether Lips Bach was he cannot be stated positively. On the other hand, Wendel Bach (1619-82) certainly was the son of Hans Bach's brother. Hence the relationship of his descendants to Johann Sebastian is established.

TABLE III.

4. JOHANNES BACH (See Table I). (1604-73).

7. JOHANN CHRISTIAN, b. Aug. 2, 1640; settled at Eisenach; m. (Aug. 28, 1665) Anna Margaretha Schmidt, dtr. of the Town Musician, and (June 11, 1679) Anna Dorothea Peter; Director of the Town Musicians, Erfurt; d. 1682 (i. 21).

8. JOHANN ÆGIDIUS, b. Feb. 9, 1645; Town Musician and Organist of St. Michael's Church, Erfurt; m. (June 9, 1674) Susanna Schmidt, dtr. of the Town Musician, Eisenach, and (Aug. 24, 1684) Julitha Katharina Syring; d. 1717 (i. 23).

9. JOHANN NIKOLAUS, b. 1653; Town Musician (? Erfurt); m. (Nov. 29, 1681) Sabina Katharina Burgolt; d. of the plague, 1682 (i. 27).

JOHANN JAKOB, b. Ap. 26, 1650, not a musician; surviving 1686 (i. 27).

20. JOHANN NIKOLAUS (Posthumous), b. Aug. 31, 1682; surgeon in East Prussia (i. 27n.).

JOHANN CHRISTOPH, b. Ap. 2, 1675, **JOHANN CASPAR,** b. June 7, 1678. **JOHANN GEORG,** b. Jan. 6, 1680. All three died young (i. 23n.).

Four daughters (i. 23).

18. JOHANN BERNHARD, b. Nov. 23, 1676; Organist of the Kaufmanns-Kirche, Erfurt, and at Magdeburg later; and (1703) Eisenach; Kammermusikus at Eisenach; d. June 11, 1749 (i. 23).

19. JOHANN CHRISTOPH, b. Aug. 15, 1685; Director of the Town Music, Erfurt; surviving in 1735 (i. 27).

36. JOHANN ÆGIDIUS, Schoolmaster (i. 27n.).

37. WILHELM HYERONIMUS (i. 27n.).

35. JOHANN FRIEDRICH, b. 1703(?) Schoolmaster (i. 27n.).

34. JOHANN ERNST, b. Sep. 1, 1722; Kapellmeister of Saxe-Weimar, 1756; d. Jan. 28, 1777 (iii. 297).

17. JOHANN CHRISTOPH, b. 1673; Cantor and Org. at Unter-Zimmern, near Erfurt; m. (1693) Anna Margaretha König, of Erfurt; Cantor at Gehren (1698), near Arnstadt; d. 1727 (i. 22).

(2) **ANNA SOPHIA** (i. 22).

(2) **JOHANN CHRISTIAN,** b. 1682 (i. 22).

33. JOHANN GÜNTHER, b. 1703; Teacher in Kaufmanns-Kirche, Erfurt, 1785 (i. 22n.).

32. JOHANN CHRISTIAN, b. 1696; d. young (i. 22n.).

16. JOHANN JAKOB, b. 1668; Musicians' Assistant at Eisenach; d. 1692 (i. 21).

(1) **31. JOHANN SAMUEL,** b. 1694; d. 1720; Schoolmaster at Gundersleben (i. 22n.).

U

TABLE IV.

5. CHRISTOPH BACH (See Table I.)
(1613-61).

10. GEORG CHRISTOPH, b. Sept. 6, 1642; Cantor at Themar (1668) and Schweinfurt; founder of the Franconian Bachs; d. Apr. 24, 1697 (i. 155).

11. JOHANN AMBROSIUS (twin), b. Feb. 22, 1645; settled at Erfurt, 1667, as Town Musician; m. (Apr. 8, 1668) Elisabeth Lämmerhirt (d. May 1694), dtr. of Valentin L., furrier at Erfurt; settled in Eisenach, 1671, as Town Musician; m. (Nov. 27, 1694) Barbara Margaretha Bartholomäi, of Arnstadt; d. Jan. 1695 (i. 156, 173, 181).

12. JOHANN CHRISTOPH (twin), b. Feb. 22, 1645; Hofmusikus at Arnstadt, 1671; m. Martha Elizabeth Eisentraut, 1679; d. Aug. 25, 1693 (i. 156, 157, 162, 171).

BARBARA MARIA, b. Apr. 30, 1651 (i. 175 n.).

DOROTHEA MARIA, b. Apr. 10, 1653; d. 1679 (i. 175 n.).

See Table v.

21. JOHANN VALENTIN, b. Jan. 6, 1669; Town Musician in Schweinfurt; m. (Sept. 25, 1694) Anna Margaretha Brandt; d. Aug. 12, 1720 (i. 156).

JOHANN CHRISTIAN, b. Mar. 15, 1679; d. June 16, 1707 (i. 156).

JOHANN GEORG, b. Nov. 11, 1683; d. Mar. 13, 1713 (i. 156).

38. JOHANN LORENZ, b. Sept. 10, 1695; Organist at Lahm, Franconia; d. Dec. 14, 1773 (i. 156).

39. JOHANN ELIAS, b. Feb. 12, 1705; Cantor at Schweinfurt; d. Nov. 30, 1755 (i. 156).

JOHANN HEINRICH, b. Jan. 27, 1711; d. young (i. 156).

BARBARA KATHARINA, b. May 14, 1680 (i. 173 n.).

25. JOHANN ERNST, b. Aug. 5, 1683; succeeded J. S. B. as Organist at Arnstadt, 1707; m. (2) Magdalena Christiane Schober (1725) of Gotha (i. 171).

JOHANN HEINRICH, b. Dec. 3, 1686 (i. 172).

26. JOHANN CHRISTOPH, b. Sept. 12,[2] 1689; Organist at Kenla (?) and dealer at Blankenhain (?); d. 1736 (i. 172).

JOHANN ANDREAS, b. 1691, d. 1694 (i. 172).

3 infant sons (i. 172).

[1] So the Genealogy.   Spitta has Aug. 8.
[2] So the Genealogy.   Spitta has Sept. 13.

TABLE V.

(See Table IV.) 11. JOHANN AMBROSIUS BACH (1645-95);
m. (1668) Elisabeth Lämmerhirt (d. 1694).

SON,
b. c. 1670;
d. young
(i. 174).

22. JOHANN CHRISTOPH,
b. June 16, 1671;
Organist at Ohrdruf
(1690); m. Dorothea
von Hof (1694);
pupil of Pachelbel
and teacher of Joh.
Seb. Bach; d. Feb. 22,
1721 (i. 174, 184).

JOHANN
BALTHASAR,
b. Mar. 4, 1673;
d. April 1691
(i. 175).

JOHANN
JONAS,
b. Jan. 3, 1675;
d. young
(i. 175).

MARIA
SALOME,
b. May 27, 1677;
m. —— Wie-
gand (i. 175).

JOHANNA
JUDITHA,
b. Jan. 26, 1680;
d. by 1707
(i. 175).

23. JOHANN JAKOB,
b. Feb. 9, 1682;
Town Musician
at Eisenach; oboe
player in the
Swedish Guard
(1704); Hof-Musi-
kus at Stockholm
(i. 140, 175, 235);
d. 1722 (?) [1]

24. JOHANN
SEBASTIAN,
b. Mar. 21 (?),
1685; d. July
28, 1750.
-->
See Tables VII.
and VIII.

40. TOBIAS FRIEDRICH,
b. 1695; Cantor at
Uttstädt from 1721
(i. 185 n.). [2]

41. JOHANN BERNHARD,
b. Nov. 24, 1700;
Organist at Ohr-
druf; d. 1743 (i.
524; Pirro, p. 79).

42. JOHANN CHRISTOPH,
b. 1702; Cantor at
Ohrdruf, where his
descendants were
surviving in 1873
(i. 185 n.).

43. JOHANN HEINRICH,
b. 1707 (Cantor at
Oehringen (i. 185
n.).

44. JOHANN ANDREAS,
b. 1713; Organist
at Ohrdruf after
1744 (i. 185 n.); d.
1779 (?) [1]

1 So in the Genealogy.

2 The Genealogy names a son as his successor.

TABLE VI.

6. HEINRICH BACH. (See Table I.) (1615-92).

15. JOHANN GÜNTHER, b. July 17, 1653; deputy Organist at Arnstadt (1682); m. (1682) Anna Margaretha, dtr. of Bürgermeister Kril, of Arnstadt; d. April 8, 1683 (i. 33, 34).

MARIA KATHARINA, b. Mar 17, 1651; m. (1668) Christoph Herthum, Organist at Ebeleben, near Sondershausen, and later at Arnstadt (1692); (i. 33, 34).

14. JOHANN MICHAEL, b. Aug. 9, 1648; Town Clerk and Organist at Gehren, near Arnstadt (1673); m. (1675) Katharina Wiedemann[1] (d. Oct. 19, 1704), dtr. of the Town Clerk of Arnstadt; d. May 1694 (i. 33, 39, 328).

JOHANNES MATTHÄUS, b. Jan. 3, 1645; d. 1646-7 (i. 33).

13. JOHANN CHRISTOPH, b. Dec. 8, 1642; Organist at Eisenach (1666); m. (1667) Maria Elisabeth Wiedemann,[1] dtr. of the Town Clerk of Arnstadt; d. March 31, 1703 (i. 29, 33, 38).

MARIA BARBARA, b. Oct. 20, 1684; m. (Oct. 17, 1707) Johann Seb. Bach; d. July 1720 (i. 328, 339; ii. 11).

See Table VII.

4 dtrs. (i. 40).

GOTTFRIED, b. Mar. 20, 1690; d. 1691 (i. 40).

MARIE SOPHIE, b. March 24, 1671 or 1674.

CHRISTINE DOROTHEA, b. Sept. 20, 1678.

ANNA ELISABETH, b. June 4, 1689 (i. 38 n.).

30. JOHANN MICHAEL, b. 1680-90; learnt art of organ-building; possibly settled in Stockholm (i. 140).

29. JOHANN FRIEDRICH, b. 1674-78; succeeded J. Seb. Bach as Organist at Mühlhausen (1708); m. but had no children; d. 1730 (i. 141).

28. JOHANN CHRISTOPH, b. Aug. 27, 1674; taught the clavier in Erfurt, Rotterdam, England (until 1730), (i. 38, 140).

53. JOHANN HEINRICH,[3] Clavier player; d. unmarried (i. 141 n.), c. 1730.

27. JOHANN NIKOLAUS, b. Oct. 10, 1669; Org. to the Town and University of Jena (1695); travelled in Italy (1696); m. (1697) Anna Amalia Baurath, of Jena (d. 1713); m. (1718) Anna Sibylla Lange, dtr. of Isserstedt; sometime pastor of Isserstedt; d. Nov. 4, 1753 (i. 38. 131).

52. son,[2] d. young (i. 132).

8 dtrs. (i. 132).

51. JOHANN CHRISTOPH,[2] b. 1717; d. 1788 (i. 132).

1 So the Genealogy. Spitta has Wedemann.
2 Spitta has Johann Christian.
3 So the Genealogy.

TABLE VII.

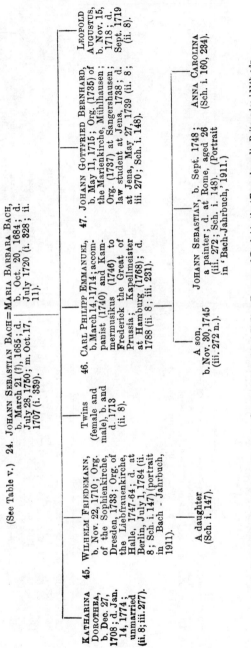

(See Table v.) **24. JOHANN SEBASTIAN BACH**=**MARIA BARBARA BACH,**
b. March 21 (?), 1685 ; d.   b. Oct. 20, 1684 ; d.
July 28, 1750 ; m. Oct. 17,   July 1720 (i. 328 ; ii.
1707 (i. 339).   11).

KATHARINA
DOROTHEA,
b. Dec. 27,
1708 ; d. Jan.
14, 1774 ;
unmarried
(ii. 8; iii. 277).

45. WILHELM FRIEDEMANN,
b. Nov. 22, 1710 ; Org.
of the Sophienkirche,
Dresden, 1733 ; Org. of
the Liebfrauenkirche,
Halle, 1747-64 ; d. at
Berlin, July 1, 1784 (ii.
8; Sch. i. 147) (portrait
in Bach - Jahrbuch,
1911).

Twins
(female and
male), b. and
d. 1713
(ii. 8).

46. CARL PHILIPP EMMANUEL,
b. March 14, 1714 ; accom-
panist (1740) and Kam-
mermusikus (1746) to
Frederick the Great of
Prussia ; Kapellmeister
at Hamburg (1768) ; d.
1788 (ii. 8 ; iii. 231).

47. JOHANN GOTTFRIED BERNHARD,
b. May 11, 1715 ; Org. (1735) of
the Marienkirche, Mühlhausen ;
Org. (1737) at Sangershausen ;
law student at Jena, 1738 ; d.
at Jena, May 27, 1739 (ii. 8 ;
iii. 270 ; Sch. i. 148).

LEOPOLD
AUGUSTUS,
b. Nov. 15,
1718 ; d.
Sept. 1719
(ii. 8).

A daughter
(Sch. i. 147).

A son,
b. Nov. 30, 1745
(iii. 272 n.).

JOHANN SEBASTIAN, b. Sept. 1748 ;
a painter ; d. at Rome, aged 26
(iii. 272 ; Sch. i. 148). (Portrait
in 'Bach-Jahrbuch,' 1911.)

ANNA CAROLINA
(Sch. i. 160, 284).

1 So the Genealogy. Spitta has March 8. See also article 'Carl Philipp Emmanuel Bach,' in the 'Encyclopedia Britannica,' 11th edn.

TABLE VIII.

(See Table v.) 24. JOHANN SEBASTIAN BACH = ANNA MAGDALENA WÜLKEN, youngest daughter of Johann Caspar Wülken, Court Trumpeter at Weissenfels; b. 1700; Court singer at Cöthen; b. Mar. 21 (?) 1685; d. July 28, 1750; m. Dec. 3, 1721 (ii. 147). d. Feb. 27, 1760; (ii. 147; iii. 277).

CHRISTIANE SOPHIE HENRIETTE, b. 1723; d. June 29, 1726 (iii. 350).

CHRISTIANE BENEDICTA, b. Dec. 30 (?), 1729; d. Jan. 4, 1730 (iii. 351).

48. GOTTFRIED HEINRICH, b. Feb.[1] 26, 1724; d. Feb. 1761[2]; imbecile (iii. 350, 268).

CHRISTIAN GOTTLIEB, b. Ap. 12 (?), 1725; d. Sept. 21, 1728 (iii. 350).

CHRISTIANE DOROTHEA, b. March 16 (?), 1731; d. Aug. 30 or 31, 1732 (iii. 351).

49. JOHANN CHRISTOPH FRIEDRICH, b. June 21,[1] 1732; Kammermusikus (1750) to Count von Lippe at Bückeburg; d. Jan. 26, 1795 (iii. 270, 351).

ELISABETH JULIANE FRIEDERIKE, b. Ap. 3 (?), 1726; m. (Jan. 20, 1749) Johann Christoph Altnikol, Organist of St. Wenceslas', Naumburg; date of death unknown (iii. 271, 350).

JOHANN SEBASTIAN, b. Oct. 4, 1749 (iii. 271).

JOHANN AUGUST ABRAHAM, b. Nov. 3 (?) 1733; d. Nov. 6, 1733 (iii. 351).

ERNESTUS ANDREAS, b. Oct. 28 (?), 1727; d. Nov. 1, 1727 (iii. 351).

REGINE JOHANNA, b. Oct. 8 (?), 1728; d. Ap. 25, 1733 (iii. 351).

50. JOHANN CHRISTIAN, b. Sept. 5,[1] 1735; Organist of Milan Cathedral, 1760-62; musicmaster to Queen Caroline of Great Britain; m. (1767) Cecilia Grassi; d. Jan. 1, 1782 (iii. 351; Sch. i. 149).

JOHANNA CAROLINE, b. Oct. 28 (?), 1737; d. Aug. 18, 1781 unmarried (iii. 271, 351).

REGINE SUSANNA, b. Feb. 20 (?), 1742; d. Dec. 14, 1809 unmarried (iii. 271, 351).

WILHELM FRIEDRICH ERNST, b. May 27, 1759; Cembalist to Queen Louisa of Prussia; sole direct representative of Johann Sebastian present at the unveiling of the Leipzig statue in 1843; d. Dec. 22, 1845 (i. 10; Sch. i. 148). His death extinguished his grandfather's line.

1 So in the Genealogy.
2 Spitta has 1768.

INDEX

780.924
B1184F

45066

3 4711 00096 1740